Invention is 1% inspiration and 99% perspiration.
—Thomas Edison

The same can be said for the development of new products. The challenge in developing new products is making the most of the 99%. The road from the patent office is strewn with good ideas that never made the leap from concept to market.

The light turning on is just the beginning. High performance teams learn to break beyond the boundaries of the bulb to see things in new and fresh ways.

Breakthrough products not only make the most of the 99%; they shatter the limitations of existing perceptions of what products can be.

Creating Breakthrough Products
Innovation from Product Planning to Program Approval

ISBN 0-13-969694-6

90000

9 790139 696946

FINANCIAL TIMES
Prentice Hall

In an increasingly competitive world, it is quality
of thinking that gives an edge—an idea that opens new
doors, a technique that solves a problem, or an insight
that simply helps make sense of it all.

We work with leading authors in the various arenas
of business and finance to bring cutting-edge thinking
and best learning practice to a global market.

It is our goal to create world-class print publications
and electronic products that give readers
knowledge and understanding which can then be
applied, whether studying or at work.

To find out more about our business
products, you can visit us at www.ft-ph.com

Pearson
Education

Creating Breakthrough Products

Innovation from Product Planning
to Program Approval

Jonathan Cagan   I   Craig M. Vogel

Foreword by Bruce Nussbaum

FINANCIAL TIMES
Prentice Hall

Prentice Hall PTR
Upper Saddle River, NJ 07458
www.ft-ph.com

Library of Congress Cataloging-in-Publication Data

A CIP catalog record for this book can be
obtained from the Library of Congress.

Editorial/Production Supervision: *Patti Guerrieri*
Acquisitions Editor: *Jim Boyd*
Editorial Assistant: *Allyson Kloss*
Marketing Manager: TC *Leszczynski*
Buyer: *Maura Zaldivar*
Cover Design: *Nina Scuderi*
Cover Design Director: *Jerry Votta*
Art Director: *Gail Cocker-Bogusz*
Interior Design: *Meg Van Arsdale*
Cover Photography: *Larry Rippel*

© 2002 Prentice Hall PTR
Prentice-Hall, Inc.
Upper Saddle River, NJ 07458

The publisher offers discounts on this book when ordered in bulk quantities.
For more information, contact
Corporate Sales Department
Prentice Hall PTR
One Lake Street
Upper Saddle River, NJ 07458
Phone: 800-382-3419; FAX: 201-236-7141
E-mail (Internet): corpsales@prenhall.com

Printed in the United States of America

10 9 8 7 6 5 4 3 2 1

ISBN 0-13-969694-6

Pearson Education LTD.
Pearson Education Australia PTY, Limited
Pearson Education Singapore, Pte. Ltd.
Pearson Education North Asia Ltd.
Pearson Education Canada, Ltd.
Pearson Educación de Mexico, S.A. de C.V.
Pearson Education—Japan
Pearson Education Malaysia, Pte. Ltd.

FINANCIAL TIMES PRENTICE HALL BOOKS

For more information, please go to www.ft-ph.com

Deirdre Breakenridge
Cyberbranding: Brand Building in the Digital Economy

Jonathan Cagan and Craig M. Vogel
Creating Breakthrough Products: Innovation from Product Planning to Program Approval

Subir Chowdhury
The Talent Era: Strategies for Achieving a High Return on Talent

Sherry Cooper
Ride the Wave: Taking Control in a Turbulent Financial Age

James W. Cortada
21st Century Business: Managing and Working in the New Digital Economy

James W. Cortada
Making the Information Society: Experience, Consequences, and Possibilities

Aswath Damodaran
The Dark Side of Valuation: Valuing Old Tech, New Tech, and New Economy Companies

Nicholas Evans
Business Agility: Strategies for Gaining Competitive Advantage through Mobile Business Solutions

David Gladstone and Laura Gladstone
Venture Capital Handbook: An Entrepreneur's Guide to Raising Venture Capital, Revised and Updated

David R. Henderson
Joy of Freedom: An Economist's Odyssey

Dale Neef
E-procurement: From Strategy to Implementation

John R. Nofsinger
Investment Madness: How Psychology Affects Your Investing... And What to Do About It

Jonathan Wight
Saving Adam Smith: A Tale of Wealth, Transformation, and Virtue

Yoram J. Wind and Vijay Mahajan, with Robert Gunther
Convergence Marketing: Strategies for Reaching the New Hybrid Consumer

To DéDé Greenberg and Leslie Frank Cagan

for their support and perseverance

Contents

Foreword   xvii

Preface   xxi

Acknowledgments   xxvii

Glossary of Acronymns and Terms   xxxi

Part One   The Argument   1

Chapter One   What Drives New Product Development   2

Redefining the Bottom Line   3
   Positioning Breakthrough Products   5
   Products and Services   7
Identifying Product Opportunities: The SET Factors   9
POG and SET Factor Case Studies   12
   The OXO GoodGrips Peeler   14
   The Motorola Talkabout   18
   The Crown Wave   22
   Starbucks   26
Summary Points   31
References   31

Chapter Two　　　Moving to the Upper Right　　　**32**

Integrating Style and Technology　　33
Style vs. Technology: A Brief History of the Evolution
　　of Style and Technology in the 19th and 20th Centuries　　36
In the Beginning　　36
The Growth of Consumer Culture　　36
The Introduction of Style to Mass Production　　38
Post World War II Growth of the
　　Middle Class and the Height of Mass Marketing　　40
The Rise of Consumer Awareness and the End of Mass Marketing　　41
The Era of Customer Value, Mass
　　Customization, and the Global Economy　　42
Positioning Map: Style vs. Technology　　43
Lower Left: Low Use of Style and Technology　　43
Lower Right: Low Use of Style, High Use of Technology　　44
Upper Left: High Use of Style, Low Use of Technology　　45
Upper Right: High Use of Style and Technology　　45
Positioning Map of OXO GoodGrips　　46
Positioning Map of Motorola Talkabout　　48
Positioning Map of Crown Wave　　48
Positioning Map of Starbucks　　49
Knockoffs and Rip-offs　　50
Revolutionary vs. Evolutionary Product Development　　51
Summary Points　　53
References　　53

Chapter Three　　　The Upper Right: The Value Quadrant　　　**54**

The Sheer Cliff of Value—The Third Dimension　　55
The Shift in the Concept of Value in Products and Services　　56
Qualities and a Customer's Value System: Cost vs. Value　　59
Value Opportunities　　62
Emotion　　63
Aesthetics　　64
Product Identity　　64
Impact　　65
Ergonomics　　65
Core Technology　　68
Quality　　68
Value Opportunity Charts and Analysis　　69
VOA of OXO GoodGrips　　71
VOA of Motorola Talkabout　　73

VOA of Crown Wave   75
VOA of Starbucks   77
The Time and Place for Value Opportunities   78
VOs and Product Goals   79
The Upper Right for Industrial Products   79
Summary Points   82
References   83

Chapter Four

The Core of a Successful Brand Strategy: Breakthrough Products and Services   **84**

Brand Strategy and Product Strategy   85
Corporate Commitment to Product and Brand   88
Corporate Values and Customer Values   91
Managing Product Brand   92
Building an Identity   92
Company Identity vs. Product Identity   93
Building Brand vs. Maintaining Brand   95
Starting from Scratch: Iomega   96
Maintaining an Established Identity: Harley   99
Brand and the Value Opportunities   101
Summary Points   103
References   103

Part Two   The Process   **105**

Chapter Five

A Comprehensive Approach to User-Centered, Integrated New Product Development   **106**

Clarifying the Fuzzy Front End of New Product Development   107
A New Way of Thinking   108
iNPD Is Only Part of the Process   109
User-Centered iNPD Process   110
Resource Allocation   132
Allocating the Time Resource: Scheduling   134
Allocating the Cost Resource: Financing   134
Allocating the Human Resource: Team Selection   135
Summary Points   136
References   136

Chapter Six   Integrating Disciplines and Managing Diverse Teams   **138**

User-Centered iNPD Facilitates Customer Value   139
Understanding Perceptual Gaps   142
Team Functionality   146
   Team Collaboration   146
   Negotiation in the Design Process   148
   Team Performance   150
Part Differentiation Matrix   153
   Team Conflict and the PDM   160
   PDM and the Role of Core Disciplines   162
Issues in Team Management: Team Empowerment   163
   Understand the Corporate Mission   164
   Serve as a Catalyst and Filter   164
   Be Unbiased   165
   Empower and Support the Team   166
   Let the Team Become the Experts   167
   Recognize the Personality and Needs of the Team   167
   Use of an Interests-Based Management Approach   168
   Visionaries and Champions   169
   Summary: The Empowered Team   170
iNPD Team Integration Effectiveness   171
Summary Points   172
References   172

Chapter Seven   Understanding the User's Needs, Wants, and Desires   **174**

Overview: Usability and Desirability   175
An Integrated Approach to a User-Driven Process   180
Scenario Development (Part I)   181
New Product Ethnography   183
   Using Ethnography to Understand Customers at Polaroid   188
Lifestyle Reference   190
Ergonomics: Interaction, Task Analysis, and Anthropometrics   192
   Interaction   192
   Task Analysis   194
   Anthropometrics   197
Scenario Development (Part II)   201
Broadening the Focus   203
   Other Stakeholders   203
   Identifying Users in Non-Consumer
      Products: Designing Parts Within Products   204
Product Definition   205
Visualizing Ideas and Concepts Early and Often   206

Summary Points   210
References   211
Research Acknowledgements   211

Part Three   Further Evidence   **213**

Chapter Eight   Case Studies: The Power of the Upper Right   **214**

Overview of Case Studies   215
Baseball Moving to the Upper Right   216
Black & Decker SnakeLight™   218
Marathon Carpet Cleaner Designed by Herbst Lazar Bell (HLB)   228
DynaMyte Augmentative Communicator by
   DynaVox Systems and Daedalus Excel Product Development   231
Service Industry: UPS Moves Beyond the Package Delivery Industry   238
Herman Miller Aeron Chair   242
Apple iMac   248
Freeplay Radio   251
Summary Points   253
References   253

Chapter Nine   Automotive Design: Product
Differentiation through User-Centered iNPD   **254**

The Dynamic SET Factors of the Auto Industry   255
The Design Process and Complexities   257
Breaking Down the Process   260
Door System   263
Rear Wiper System for Lincoln Navigator/Ford Expedition   263
Positioning: Move to the Upper Right   266
The Move of the SUVs   266
The Retro Craze   268
Positioning: Segmentation through
Ethnography for Compact Truck Segmentation   275
Positioning: After-Market Products for Trucks —
A Case Study of iNPD at Carnegie Mellon University   277
SideWinder: Side Worktable   279
MasterRack: Reconfigurable Rail Storage   280
NoFuss: Camping Storage System with Rail Guide Technology   282
Implications of User-Centered iNPD on the Auto Industry   283
Summary Points   286
References   286
Research Acknowledgments   287

Epilogue   289

Future Trends   289
Have Faith in the Leap   292
References   294

Index   295

Foreword

Bruce Nussbaum, Editorial Page Editor and Design Editor, *BusinessWeek*

Design has come to play a critical role in our economic lives. For many decades Corporate America neglected design, treating style as superficial, fashion as transitory. Design was felt to be last-minute gloss to be applied after the real product development was done. No longer. Design is fast becoming a key corporate asset, essential to establishing and extending brands, transforming new technologies into usable products, and bridging company identities and customer loyalties. CEOs and managers are scrambling to learn how to use it to maximize their sales and profits. Most believe that design is a business tool, a way of gaining advantage in the marketplace for products and services. That's true but a few chief executives understand that design is much more — it's a strategy, a business behavior, a way to bring together the very best a corporation has to offer and focus it directly on the consumer. Design increases the odds of winning in the global marketplace.

For the past decade, I have been fortunate in having *BusinessWeek* embrace this point of view. Its coverage is distinct from other "design" magazines in that it focuses on design as a powerful core competency for Corporate America. The dozens and dozens of articles that I've written as the design editor of *BusinessWeek* are all basically stories about how companies use design as part of their overall business strategies or how design firms develop products that bust open new markets or extend brands. I've tried to demystify the process of design by describing how some of the best product designers actually work. Jonathan Cagan and Craig M. Vogel have the same goals in their book, *Creating Breakthrough Products*. They show readers how to peel back the mystery of design to reveal how it actually works. They describe how companies can harness design to buttress their bottom line. And they provide simple methods for achieving the best design.

This is especially important in a period of fast technological change such as the one we are in now. When new technologies throw up a multitude of options and possibilities, design can filter them, fitting them appropriately to what people actually want and need. Really good design operations integrate the engineering of functions and features as well as the marketing goals of brand identity and brand extension. Teaming product industrial designers with engineers and marketing people is often the key to quick success.

When companies rely on the new technologies themselves to attract consumers, they often stumble. They make the mistake of thinking that more functions translate into better products, when often the very opposite is true. We all remember the first personal digital assistant, the Apple Newton, which had the ability to do all kinds of things, none of them, it turned out, all that well. People wanted simplicity in their PDAs and had to wait years for Palm to offer it to them.

Indeed, there is no better example of the bottom-line power of design than the creation of the breakthrough Palm. Three programmers developed handwriting software that organized data. They were smart enough to learn from the Newton fiasco and kept their product very simple — datebook, address book, memo pad, and to-do list, plus a very simple hot-synch with the PC. They then brought in a savvy West Coast design firm, Palo Alto Design Group, which designed an amazingly easy-to-use form. But Palo Alto Design Group went even further. It arranged for the tooling and manufacturing to take place in Asia. The whole development cycle took less than a year. From the writing of the software to the actual Palm being sold in electronics stores took a mere 12 months. That's the power of design. So powerful, in fact, that Palo Alto Design Group was recently bought by Flextronics, one of the largest manufacturers in the world.

And that is precisely the message from *Creating Breakthrough Products: Innovation from Product Planning to Program Approval*. Jonathan Cagan and Craig M. Vogel at Carnegie Mellon University show the way to designing such breakthrough products and services as the OXO GoodGrips, the Motorola Talkabout, the Crown Wave, and the Starbucks coffee experience. In fact, there are a whole slew of case studies in the book, including the Black & Decker SnakeLight, the Herman Miller Aeron Chair, and the Apple iMac. These are products we love, products we lust after.

But Cagan and Vogel go beyond just presenting detailed examinations of the best products. They offer up a best practices approach to design, a systematic approach to creating innovative, brand-enhancing products. It is a guidebook that corporations, large and small, can follow. It's a methodology that everyone involved in product development can use, be they engineers, marketeers, manufacturing people, sales people, or industrial designers. And it's step by step, focusing on user-driven, not just technology-driven, development, integrating and balancing teams and disciplines, shaping the process and raising the odds of success in the marketplace. And their advice is right on: "If a product does not connect with the values of a customer, it will fail." It's not just the utility of a product that's important. It's the emotional component — the experience people have with it and the values they want expressed by it — that's key.

To guide the way, Cagan and Vogel have developed a number of valuable models and useful methodologies. They are very helpful. Take the SET Factors. To really understand consumer trends and catch the moment when opportunities present themselves, product developers need a systematic approach. Hence SET — Social trends, Economic forces, and Technological advances. Follow them and companies can get to the edge of the new in society. And once they understand the SET Factors of their marketplace, they can picture the Product Opportunity Gap (POG) that makes itself available. With the OXO potato peeler, determining the SET Factors involved a growing number of aging Boomers with arthritic hands, an unwillingness to be stigmatized, a willingness to spend more on kitchen utensils than their parents, and an openness to new materials and shapes. Enter Sam Farber and Smart Design and you have the building of one of the most successful new brands in recent history. Ergonomically sound tools for the kitchen were extended to the garden, the car, and on and on. Brilliant. The book shows how they did it, why they did it, and how others can follow.

There is tremendous detail in *Creating Breakthrough Products* for the product development specialists. On one level, the entire book is aimed at them. It provides a path down which companies can enter to increase their chances of success in launching new products. But anyone interested in the design of everyday things in our lives would appreciate this book. It shows how good design can be made and why there is no longer any excuse for not having it in all the things we love to use.

—Bruce Nussbaum

Preface

For nearly a decade, we have worked as a team in teaching, research, and consulting. As a result, we have developed a unique understanding of the product development process. We constantly identify and analyze examples of successful products, many illustrated in this book, and look for new techniques for user-centered research and integrated New Product Development (iNPD). We have come to believe that breakthrough products should provide an optimum experience for the people who buy and use them. They should also provide an equally rewarding and gratifying experience for the product development teams who create them.

We have been consultants to and conducted research with small and large companies. We have also conducted professional development seminars in iNPD. During this time we have also co-taught an annual course in integrated New Product Development at Carnegie Mellon University, which has resulted in patented products. Through our consulting, research, and teaching we have identified a number of factors that contribute to successful products. We are not just talking about products that are competitive but products that redefine their markets and often transcend their original program goals to create new markets. This book summarizes our findings in a form that will aid practitioners and managers in the product development process.

This book is a proof of our process. We began by identifying the opportunity for a book by recognizing the difficulty that companies have in working through the early stages of product development. We did extensive research, building on our existing base, to understand what managers and practitioners who create new products (our target market) required in their process that they did not already have. The focus on breakthrough products, the integration of disciplines, the merging of style and technology, and the creation of true consumer value, all at the Fuzzy Front End, became the themes that drove the development of this book. We identified expert users who had the vision and insight to help us identify critical issues and weed through many ideas. We created prototypes that these expert users read and used to provide feedback. After several iterations, we moved into the design refinement stage to finally deliver what we hope is a useful, usable, and desirable book to help you create breakthrough products.

What to Expect from This Book

In this book you will find some new ideas in product development. You will also find seasoned best practices used by large or small companies. We have integrated these different approaches into a logical framework that takes you from product planning to program approval. You can expect to gain an understanding of the following six aspects of the new product development process:

1. methods to obtain insights into emerging trends in consumer and industrial markets;

2. a means to navigate and control what is often called the "Fuzzy Front End" of the product development process, that portion of the design process when the product and market are not yet defined and qualitative tools are needed to complement quantitative research;

3. the use of qualitative research to understand who the customer is;

4. techniques to assist in the integration of diverse team players, especially engineers, industrial and interaction designers, and market researchers and planners;

5. a complete product development process that brings the product from its opportunity identification stage through to program approval and product patenting;

6. an approach that connects strategic planning and brand management to product development.

We then provide case studies that demonstrate the successful use of the methods introduced in this book. We show that these methods apply to both products and services.

The book's logical flow is designed to provide a useful guide for anyone involved in the product development process. Readers can also use the book by first scanning and then focusing on the areas initially perceived as most relevant. In either case, we have tried to make sure that the book is interconnected and cross referenced so that issues addressed in one part are referred to again in other parts.

The book is divided into three main sections. The first section (Chapters 1–4) establishes our main argument that the best new products are designed by merging style and technology in a way that connects with the lifestyle and values of intended customers. The second section (Chapters 5–7) presents a process for creating such products by integrating different disciplines with a focus on the needs, wants, and desires of the customers. The final section (Chapters 8 and 9) provides additional case studies as further support of our argument and its application to several product categories.

Chapter 1 explains the forces that generate opportunities for new product development. This chapter introduces the process of scanning Social, Economic, and Technology (SET) Factors that leads to Product Opportunity Gaps (POGs) and new market segments. Four case studies of successful companies and the products or services they deliver are used to illustrate this process: the OXO GoodGrips, the Motorola Talkabout, the Crown Wave, and the services provided by Starbucks coffeehouses.

Chapter 2 outlines our major premise. In order to produce new products, a company needs to commit to "Moving to the Upper Right." This phrase represents an integration of style and technology through added product value based on insight into the SET trends that respond to customers' emerging needs for new products and services. Our Positioning Map is introduced to model and map Upper Right products.

Chapter 3 focuses on consumer-based value and further refines product opportunities into what we call "Value Opportunities" (VOs). We have identified seven Value Opportunity classes — emotion, aesthetics, identity, ergonomics, impact, core technology, and quality — that each contribute to the overall experience of the product. The challenge is to interpret the VOs and their attributes and translate them into the right combination of features and style that match with current trends.

Chapter 4 discusses, through corporate and product branding, how to make Moving to the Upper Right a core part of a company's culture. Products and services are the core of a company's strategic planning and brand strategy and they should be driven by the theme of user-centered interdisciplinary product development. The establishment of a clear brand identity necessitates the integration of customer values with company values in a way that differentiates a company and its products in the marketplace.

Chapter 5 is devoted to the planning of product development programs through the presentation of an integrated New Product Development — iNPD — process for the early stages of product development (i.e., the Fuzzy Front End). Most product programs go through a stage where the product opportunity is researched, prototyped, and evaluated. Many companies, however, do not have clear methodologies for this frequently underdeveloped stage of the product development program costing them significant resources. The process we have developed helps companies navigate and control this process by keeping focus on the user. The process is broken into four phases that brings the development team from the stage of identifying opportunities to the program approval stage where intellectual property is protected.

Chapter 6 focuses on team integration and management. Effective interaction of disciplines is integral to the product development process. We describe how team members, and in particular designers and engineers, can work in a context of positive tension where they use their different perspectives to a competitive advantage for the whole team. We also lay out a strategy for breaking down actual parts and components of the product and, by understanding their impact on customer lifestyle and complexity, determining where integration is required to effectively design them. The chapter concludes with insights on how to manage interdisciplinary teams.

Chapter 7 focuses on developing a comprehensive approach to understanding the user's behavior. We discuss the use of existing and emerging methods for understanding how consumers use products and translating that understanding into what we refer to as "actionable insights," which become the basis for developing appropriate product characteristics. These approaches empower the product development team to translate customer preferences into appropriate style, ergonomics, and features.

Chapter 8 highlights nine additional case studies of successful new product development representing a range of product and service categories and types of product development teams.

Chapter 9 highlights the user-centered iNPD process for automobiles, a particularly complex and exciting consumer product market.

The Epilogue concludes with a look at future trends for new product development and final thoughts on why companies should commit to use of the iNPD process.

User's Guide

Through our many interactions with industry, people have asked us questions that relate to their product development problems. We have answered many of them in this book. In this section, we list these questions together with pointers to the chapters where they are answered. Readers with a specific issue may want to begin the book here. They are divided into five areas: 1) how to get started; 2) how to become user-driven instead of technology driven; 3) how to balance team, people, and discipline interactions; 4) how to commit the time, money, and people for an integrated New Product Development (iNPD) process; and 5) how to succeed in the marketplace.

I. How to Get Started

How do you learn a successful user-centered iNPD process?	The whole book
What is the Upper Right?	Chapter 1
What does it mean to design for fantasy?	Chapter 1
How do you jumpstart the process?	Chapters 1 and 5
What is the Fuzzy Front End?	Chapter 5
How do you develop a core competency that separates you from your competitors?	Chapters 5 and 7
Why is quality for manufacture no longer enough?	Chapters 1, 2, 3, and 4
How do you balance up-front research and development with downstream refinement in the product development process?	Chapter 5

II. How to Become User-Driven Instead of Technology-Driven

How do you know when you have a true product opportunity?	Chapters 1, 2, 3, and 5
How do you get beyond being tech driven?	Chapters 5 and 7
What is ethnography and how do you use it?	Chapter 7
How do you determine the user value in different parts of a product?	Chapter 6
How do you design for a full sensory experience?	Chapters 3 and 5
How do you successfully use qualitative research to understand the needs of a user?	Chapters 5 and 7
How do you use psycheconometrics to determine what users want and what they will pay for it?	Chapters 3 and 7

III. How to Balance Team, People, and Discipline Interactions

How do you plan and manage an effective product development process?	Chapter 5
How do you prevent turf battles from having a negative effect on the product development process?	Chapters 5 and 6
How do you maintain an interdisciplinary approach that keeps different disciplines communicating effectively?	Chapter 6
How do you get team members to respect each other's capabilities?	Chapter 6
How does team integration affect career development for individuals?	Chapter 6
How do you effectively partner with suppliers?	Chapters 6 and 9

IV. How to Commit Resources to an iNPD Process

How do you determine how much time, money, and personnel to commit to the iNPD process?	Chapter 5
How do you know how long it will take to address the Fuzzy-Front End?	Chapter 5
How do you meet deadlines within the product development process?	Chapter 5
How do you integrate industrial, interface, and communication design into your company's product development process?	Chapters 1, 5, 6, 8, and 9

V. How to Succeed in the Marketplace

How do you create a product that reaches the majority of customers in the marketplace?	Chapter 5
How do you gain confidence that the product warrants the capital investment?	Chapters 1, 5, 8, and 9
How do you balance being cost-driven and being profit-driven?	Chapters 3 and 6
Have there been any successes from this approach?	Case studies throughout book, especially Chapters 1, 2, 4, 8, and 9
How does the development of services differ from that of products?	Chapter 1
How can you develop a brand strategy that integrates your products and services with your corporate structure?	Chapter 4

Acknowledgments

There are many people and organizations to whom we are indebted in developing this book.

To begin, we are honored to have Bruce Nussbaum, Editorial Page Editor and Design Editor at *BusinessWeek*, write the Foreword to this book. Bruce has been a major influence in the recognition of breakthrough products as editor for the annual IDEA Awards sponsored by IDSA and *BusinessWeek*.

The following individuals became our expert advisors, taking significant time from their incredibly busy lives to read prototypes of our book and discuss many of the issues presented throughout these pages: Susan Ambrose, Jeff Calhoun, Bruce Claxton, Terry Duncan, Lorraine Justice, Dee Kapur, Craig Metros, Bruce Hanington, Chris Magee, Ron Mayercheck and the group at SPIRC, Pattie Moore, Nancy Phillipart, Pat Schiavone, Bob Schwartz, Dave Smith, Beth Tauke, and John Wesner. The insight and enthusiasm of these individuals helped us differentiate our product and Move it to the Upper Right.

Special thanks go to Laurie Weingart, our colleague and collaborator in our research on perceptual gaps and team integration presented in Chapter 6. In our work toward making high-performing teams, Prof. Weingart's insights into team conflict and negotiation have brought a new outlook and level of formality.

We also acknowledge our colleague John Mather for his many years of collaboration in teaching the integrated New Product Development course at CMU. Prof. Mather's enthusiasm toward teaching and students, and years of marketing experience, have helped to give the iNPD course its strong international and local reputation.

We dedicate this book to our wives, Leslie Frank Cagan and DéDé Greenberg. Not only have they both supported us through this and many other projects throughout our careers, but each has served as a sounding board for many of our ideas as they have developed. Their insights and love are always welcomed and enjoyed.

We are grateful to Adnan Akay, Richard Buchanan, John Anderson, Indira Nair, and Martin Prekop at CMU who have provided the environment and resources to enable us to teach the iNPD course and develop the methodology within this book. We would also like to recognize the late Paul Christiano who, as Provost, supported an academic environment that fosters interdisciplinary teaching and research. Thanks as well to Peggy Martin who supported and, when we weren't available, ran the in-house production facility to create this book.

We are grateful to Stacy Mitchell for her design of the illustrations that appear throughout this work.

We feel fortunate to have been able to work with our editor, Jim Boyd, of Financial Times Prentice Hall, as we added details to this manuscript and brought it to press. If there is an ideal editor, Jim is it. His energy, enthusiasm, and support for this project, along with his staff, helped to move this manuscript further to the Upper Right, and quickly to production.

We thank Anne Akay for her publishing advice, Hillary Carey for her discussions, Kat Cohen and Erika Persson for their visualizations and early renderings in the formation of this book, and Chriss Swaney for helping to resolve issues surrounding the publication of this book.

We owe thanks to John Cain and Jason Nims from Sapient (at the time E-Lab) for their contribution to the development of our ethnography methods.

Many individuals at various companies spent a great deal of time working with us to develop the case studies. In addition to several listed above, we thank: Matt Beale, Penni Bonaldi, Bob Bruce, Don Carter, Mark Dziersk, Sam Farber, James Gallagher, Francine Gemperle, Martin Gierke, Sanja Gould, Allison Howitt, David Laturi, Fran McMichael, Gary Natsume, Truman Pollard, James Raskin, Ann Smith, Scott Smith, Bill Stumpf, Ken Sternard, and Rob Veksler.

The following companies are acknowledged for providing images and facts to support our case studies: Apple Computer, Black & Decker, Crown Equipment Corp., Daedelus Excel, DaimlerChrysler Corp., DynaVox Systems, Eastman Kodak Company, Ford

Motor Company, Freeplay Group, Frogdesign, General Motors, The Headblade Company, Henry Dreyfuss Associates, Herbst Lazar Bell, Herman Miller, Iomega Corp., Lowey Design, Mazda, Motorola, OXO/Smart Design, Pittsburgh Post-Gazette, Polaroid, Sapient, Starbucks Coffee Company, Stumpf Weber Associates, TBWA Chiat Day, UPS, VistaLab Technologies, and Volkswagen.

We owe a great deal of debt to all of the students who have taken our iNPD class throughout the last decade.

Beyond all of the research and consulting projects behind this work, there is still a great deal of finances required to pull it all together into a book. We wish to thank Phil Dowd and the Dowd Fellowship at the Carnegie Institute of Technology at CMU and the University Education Committee at CMU for providing funds to support the development of this book.

Glossary of Acronyms and Terms

iNPD: integrated New Product Development, an approach to product development that supports team integration based on fulfilling the needs, wants, and desires of customers and interests of other significant stakeholders.

iNPD Phases: Four phases in the iNPD process from product planning to program approval:

  Phase I: Identifying the Opportunity
  Phase II: Understanding the Opportunity
  Phase III: Conceptualizing the Opportunity
  Phase IV: Realizing the Opportunity

Perceptual Gaps: The differences in perspectives that team members have that stem from discipline-specific thinking and prevent teams from developing an integrated interests-based conflict resolution process.

POG: *Product Opportunity Gap*, the gap between what is currently on the market and the possibility for new or significantly improved products that result from emerging trends.

Positioning Map: Style versus Technology; the Upper Right quadrant has the third dimension of Value and is where you want to be.

SET Factors: The changes in Social, Economic, and Technological Factors that produce new trends and create Product Opportunity Gaps (POGs).

Style: The sensory aspects that represent the aesthetic and human factors of a product or service.

Technology: The core function that drives the product, the resulting interaction components that are required to use the product, and the methods and materials used to produce the product.

Value: The level of effect that people personally expect from products and services represented through lifestyle effect, enabling features, and meaningful ergonomics, which together result in a useful, useable, and desirable product.

VO: *Value Opportunity*, the attributes of value (emotion, aesthetics, identity, ergonomics, impact, core technology, and quality) that make up the elements people assess in products.

VOA: *Value Opportunity Analysis*, the qualitative comparison of two product concepts or opportunities based on the VO attributes.

Part One

The Argument

Chapter 1   What Drives New Product Development

Chapter 2   Moving to the Upper Right

Chapter 3   The Upper Right: The Value Quadrant

Chapter 4   The Core of a Successful Brand Strategy:
Breakthrough Products and Services

Chapter One

What Drives
New Product Development

Breakthrough products result from the appropriate combination of style and technology and help to create experiences that people find both rewarding and valuable. In this chapter, we focus on the first step in developing a breakthrough product: learning to interpret the interconnected factors of Social change, Economic trends, and Technological innovation. Interpreting these SET Factors leads to the identification of Product Opportunity Gaps in the marketplace. Converting product opportunities into breakthrough products requires a combination of vision and sound methodology. As highlighted in the case studies in this chapter, the comprehensive approach introduced in this book applies equally to the development of products and services.

Redefining the Bottom Line

This book introduces ideas and methods for companies that want to be market leaders through the development of breakthrough products. Breakthrough products create new or redefine existing markets, support the customer's experience in using the product and create a lifestyle fantasy about who that customer is, and generate higher profit for the company that produces them

We have found the process of product development to be analogous to rock climbing, a challenging, invigorating, and empowering experience. To succeed at rock climbing, you need to have a set of appropriate tools, a good plan for the climb, and an interdependent team that works together to use the tools when appropriate. The climb is constant and well thought out, but the team has the training to adapt to issues that emerge along the way. Successful product development also requires a well-planned process using tools to help you negotiate difficult terrain. Teams of engineers, designers, and market researchers must work in unison to recognize promising product directions and work through the Fuzzy Front End of the product development process to create a product that meets the needs, wants, and desires of the customer. Managing the Fuzzy Front End is an underlying theme that permeates this book. The Fuzzy Front End is the part of the product development process that starts with the general goals of the program and covers the early stages of new product development. Making the most of the Fuzzy Front End is essential in creating breakthrough products. Companies that see the process as a climb see every part as essential and understand that the preparation and the climb have equal importance. The process requires the skill and patience necessary to use the tools successfully to develop products that you are confident will succeed in the marketplace.

There are many companies that approach product development as if it were parachuting instead of rock climbing. They have a core technology (their plane) and capital (the parachute) and then they free fall through the Fuzzy Front End to quality programs for manufacturing, expecting a smooth landing. These companies think the free fall will take care of itself, or in product terms they quickly jump to a focus on one product concept that they think will become a marketable product if it meets manufacturing quality standards. Product development in this way succeeds only by chance. By failing to maximize the Fuzzy Front End, these well-manufactured products fail in the market because they do not respond to customer's needs, wants, and desires. The result is a loss of brand equity, profit, time, and investor confidence.

New product development is a climb, not a free fall. The more prepared you are for the challenges of the terrain, the better the climb will be. This book will help you climb through the Fuzzy Front End of the product development process and will give you the tools that make your product more likely to succeed in the marketplace.

■ The goal is to increase profits while simultaneously maintaining a healthy internal structure that balances innovation and continuity.

There are a number of challenges that make it difficult for companies to maintain a leading position in a particular product category. These challenges are forcing companies to redefine the bottom line and the path to get there. The goal is to increase profits while simultaneously maintaining a healthy internal structure that balances innovation and continuity. So, while companies are trying to realize their stated goals in sales and profit projections, they are also trying to resolve the following issues:

- ■ Finding the right opportunities for new products and appropriate innovation to improve existing products;

- ■ Designing products and services that customers perceive as truly valuable by appropriate integration of style and technology;

- ■ Maximizing front-end decisions to minimize downstream corrections;

- ■ Reducing cycle times without reducing innovation and quality;

- ■ Building and maintaining brand equity through a strong product;

- ■ Integrating design, marketing, and engineering by reducing "perceptual gaps" and producing products that are considered useful, usable, and desirable by the customer;

- ■ Appropriately positioning the role of technology in product development;

- Recognizing the significance of industrial and interaction design in the product development process;

- Attracting, preparing, and retaining the best people.

To be successful in meeting these challenges, a shared vision must flow from top management through middle and lower management down to individual members of product development teams. While an opportunity for new products can be identified at any level, the vision of the product potential must be shared and championed at all levels. Not only do successful products help customers create maximum experiences in their everyday lives, but the process of developing the products themselves must be an equally powerful and rewarding experience for the product team. Developing products should be a form of serious fun. If everyone on the team is enjoying the process, it usually means that everyone in the company profits from the experience.

Positioning Breakthrough Products

Consumer demand for better products has been continually increasing during the last three decades. During the 1980s and early '90s, quality development programs, reengineering, and concurrent design were the initiatives that drove companies worldwide to constantly improve their products. At the beginning of a new century, the emphasis has shifted from the back end to the front of the product development process. It is increasingly harder to find the right product concept and the time and processes needed to bring that concept to market. Technological innovation and maintenance of manufacturing standards are still intrinsic parts of developing successful products. But if, however, a product does not connect with the values of consumers, it will fail.

■ Form and function must fulfill fantasy.

People use products to improve their experience while doing tasks. They relate these experiences to their fantasies and dreams. Successful products fulfill a higher emotional value state, whether it is the excitement and security of driving in an SUV, the comfort and effectiveness of cooking in the kitchen, the relaxation and escapism of sipping coffee in a coffeehouse, or the independence and adventure of using a two-way communication device. The mantra that form follows function is no longer relevant; we are now in a period where *form and function must fulfill fantasy*.

What is it that makes some product programs fail and others succeed? How did Black & Decker corner the flashlight market from 1994 to 1997 with a product called the SnakeLight? How could OXO evolve from a single product, GoodGrips, to a full line of products, a significant market penetration, the most prominently displayed product line in stores that carry the OXO line, and reinvent the profit margins in the industry?

How could Motorola develop a major presence in the consumer product category with the hit of one new product, the Talkabout? How could Starbucks, initially a small coffee house in Seattle, reinvent how Americans drink coffee and turn a 50 cent cup o' Joe into a $3.00 Café Latte Grande (make that skim milk)? How could car companies look to the past for ideas that would sell so effectively in the present, as they did starting with the Mazda Miata, following with the Volkswagen Beetle, and continuing with the Chrysler PT Cruiser?

In evaluating the value impact of all these products, we found that they were all highly successful in communicating value in the key categories that connected them to their customers and moved them ahead of their competition. If you look at most positioning maps, the optimum quadrant is usually the upper right, where each positioning attribute is maximized. In this book we introduce a Positioning Map (Figure 1.1) that charts style against technology through added value. The Upper Right, with integrated style and technology and the only place with *significant* value, is the place to which a company must move and be positioned in order to best differentiate itself from the competition and to succeed. All of the breakthrough products mentioned above are positioned in that quadrant. Getting there is not easy because of the third dimension, which acts as a cliff that needs to be climbed. As mentioned previously, product development is akin to rock climbing. This "Sheer Cliff of Value" is the rock that the product development team must climb to succeed. Every progressive company sets its strategy to move there, but it often fails to find the methods to achieve the goal. This book will help you get there. We call this approach *Moving to the Upper Right*.

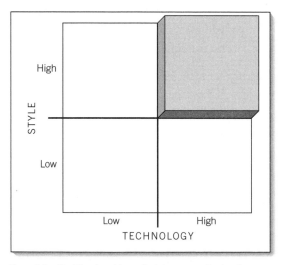

Figure 1.1 Positioning Map of style versus technology; great products are value-driven and found in the Upper Right.

Products and Services

This book primarily focuses on physical products. Products succeed when they play a major role in creating optimal experiences for customers. Service companies need to provide support that optimizes experiences as well. We recognize that the development and realization of products and services require similar approaches. In order to be successful, it is necessary that both approaches utilize the integration of a number of areas of expertise, and a solid understanding of the customer and their desired experience.

A *product* is a device that provides a service that enhances human experience. It is always part of a company that provides a service to its customers. That is why Xerox became "the document company" (now "the digital document company"). The service they provide is the production of documents, which they do by producing printing and copying equipment. A *service* is an activity that enhances experience; it requires an array of products to deliver its core activity. If your company is a web service provider, you use and produce products to provide that service. If your company produces automobiles, the service you provide is transporting people and things. The auto industry produces automobiles; one of the highest profit areas for GM is, however, financing automobile purchases, which is a service. Where would UPS, a delivery service, be without their brown trucks, jets, and information management products? We will discuss both products and services in this book, for the issues that make a product or service successful are the same. Both products and services are connected to understanding the experience that the end customer wants and then translating that understanding into a product or service that enhances a particular interaction with objects, environments, and/or other people.

It sounds simple but understanding customers and then translating customer understanding into products and services is extremely difficult. The number of people and resources that must be brought together to produce a successful product is enormous. The complexity of this task explains why so many product attempts fail. In larger companies, by the time a customer buys a product, hundreds or thousands of people and thousands of man-hours went into the identification, planning, development, production, distribution, and sales. Understanding of the customer can easily be lost in the product development programs in large companies as secondary factors come to dominate decisions about cost, features, and form. While small companies have a better chance of keeping the customer in the loop throughout the process, they often lack the balance of disciplines necessary to generate the research and development of product characteristics for the market. No matter what the size of the company, all of the people involved are *stakeholders* in the product process, and the success of the product depends on the coordinated involvement of all of them.

We also see products and services as the core element of a company's brand (discussed in detail in Chapter 4). If all elements of a brand are effective, they all play a roughly equal role. The interaction of a customer with the product or service is the heart of the brand delivery. While corporate mission, strategic planning, advertising, and identity programs are all essential, they cannot offset weak, non-competitive products or services.

We have found that there are three key factors that must be present to guarantee the highest potential of success.

■ First is the ability to identify product opportunities. As cultures continue to change, opportunities emerge for new products. These products do not just solve existing problems, they also create possibilities for new experiences.

■ The second is a heightened understanding of customer needs translated into actionable insights that define attributes. These attributes serve as a guide in developing the product's form and features. In order for products to be successful, they must have features and forms that consumers quickly recognize as *useful, usable*, and *desirable.*

■ Third is a true integration of engineering, industrial design, and marketing. Merely putting teams together in a multidisciplinary context is not sufficient. They must be supported and managed effectively in an atmosphere where each discipline respects and appreciates the perspective of the others.

■ In order for products to be successful, they must have features and forms that consumers quickly recognize as useful, usable, and desirable.

Failure to achieve success in any one of these areas can significantly jeopardize the success of a product, yet most companies are fortunate to be good in even one area. The successful companies have found ways to incorporate the product development trends of the '80s and early '90s into new ways of developing products by including deeper consumer insight and better integration of teams. These companies have strategically "Moved to the Upper Right."

While a number of companies claim they use a customer-centered interdisciplinary approach, they have failed to make a total company commitment to this approach. Their management structure encourages a turf mentality through a vertical, or "silo," reporting structure. Customer characteristics are often generated by mass-marketing methods that provide limited insight because they are based solely on highly quantitative surveys. These companies are often hammers looking for nails as they seek new ways to package or repackage impressive but inaccessible technologies. For companies to succeed, they can no longer afford to be either marketing, technology, *or* design driven. In order to stay competitive, they must integrate the way designers, engineers, market researchers, and market strategists work. Corporations can no longer just rely on large statistical surveys or just search for applications for promising technologies. Instead, qualitative research tools have proven to be an excellent source for deep understanding of the potential customer and product opportunities. This new trend means that companies should plan technological innovation around an insightful understanding of consumer trends and the constant changes in the needs, wants, and desires of the customer. Companies must learn to *identify opportunities* for the potential of products before they think in terms of concrete product concepts.

Identifying Product Opportunities: The SET Factors

The identification of product opportunities should be the core force that drives companies that manufacture products, supply services, and process information. A product opportunity exists when there is a gap between what is currently on the market and the possibility for new or significantly improved products that result from emerging trends. A product that successfully fills a Product Opportunity Gap (POG) does so when it meets the conscious and unconscious expectations of consumers and is perceived as useful, useable, and desirable. No one asked for a SnakeLight before it came out and no one in the auto industry expected the success of the Mazda Miata. Successfully identifying a POG is a combination of art and science. It requires a constant sweep of a number of factors in three major areas: Social trends (S), Economic forces (E), and Technological advances (T) (see Figure 1.2).

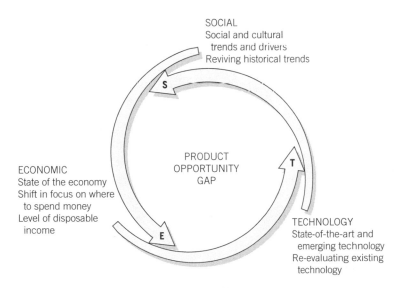

SOCIAL
Social and cultural
trends and drivers
Reviving historical trends

S

ECONOMIC
State of the economy
Shift in focus on where
to spend money
Level of disposable
income

PRODUCT
OPPORTUNITY
GAP

T

E

TECHNOLOGY
State-of-the-art and
emerging technology
Re-evaluating existing
technology

Figure 1.2 Scanning SET Factors leads to POGs.

The Social factors focus on culture and social interaction. The Social factors include

- family and work patterns (e.g., the number of single parents with two jobs or double income households with flexible hours),

- health issues (e.g., people living longer with more active lives),

- the use of computers and the Internet,

- political environments,

- successful products in other fields,

- sports and recreation (e.g., X-generation snow boarders creating a new "loose fitting grunge wear" fashion aesthetic and lifestyle),

- sporting events (e.g., the emergence of new, retro state-of-the-art facilities and the athletes who perform in them),

- the entertainment industries including film and television,

- vacation environments (e.g., the fantasy fulfillment provided by Disney World, Las Vegas, and Club Med),

- books (e.g., the Oprah Book Club),

- magazines, and

- music (e.g., from hip-hop to new classic-chic).

The second major SET Factor is Economics. The economic factors focus on excess income that people perceive they have, or that they expect to have, to give them purchasing power. We call this *psycheconometrics*, namely the spending power people believe they have to buy the products and services they believe will enhance their lifestyle. These factors are influenced by the overall strength of and forecast for the economy, fuel costs, raw material costs, loan rates, availability of venture capital, the stock market and its forecasts, and real disposable income. Other economic issues that influence product development come from understanding who has the income, who is doing the purchasing, and for whom the purchasers are buying. As social factors change, where people spend their money changes.

The Technology factors focus on direct and imagined results from new scientific discoveries in corporate, military, and university research and the implied capabilities stemming from that research. These factors include the amazing growth in computing power predicted by Moore's Law (Intel co-founder Gordon Moore's prediction in 1965 that the number of transistors per square inch on integrated circuits would double every year) and the analogous reduction in physical size of peripherals and supporting functions, new material and manufacturing advances, electrical and mechanical inno-vations, aerospace and military technologies, film and sports entertainment technologies, and micro- and bio-technologies.

This SET of factors generates opportunities for producing new products that can have an effect on the way people live their lives at any given moment. The goal is to create products and services by identifying an emerging trend and to match that trend with the right technology and understanding of the pur-

■ The goal is to create products and services by identifying an emerging trend and to match that trend with the right tech-nology and understanding of the purchas-ing dynamics.

chasing dynamics. The window of opportunity is often small and a product that comes out either too early or too late can fail even if the opportunity was there initially. For exam-ple, in the 1970s AMC introduced the Pacer, a shorter, wider car with a larger window area to maximize the internal sense of space. Many of the attributes the Pacer incorpo-rated became the goal of all car manufacturers in the two decades that followed. The Apple Newton was an early PDA with many of the attributes of PDAs today, but cost and size compromised its appeal beyond the lead users and early adopters. Perhaps the most salient example of introducing products too late is the US automotive industry's failure to understand the potential growth in small, well-made, fuel-efficient cars, which allowed Japanese car manufacturers to dominate the 4- and 6-cylinder engine car market for decades. Even today, American car manufacturers generate their profits from small trucks and SUVs, rather than the smaller fuel-efficient vehicles.

Successful new products become necessary once they hit the market. Most consumers are not even aware they need the product because they are immersed in the trend. If the company hits the trend at the point it is just catching on, the product will become instantly desirable. The length of a trend combined with the attributes of use and usability will determine the lifetime of the product. Las Vegas has continued to be successful by complementing the fantasy and dreams of gambling with the quality of a family amusement park; Disney World extended its market by creating vacation programs and packages for adults as well as kids. Coca-Cola has been able to main-tain its position as the leading soft drink for an entire century while Tang (the drink of astronauts) was a hit when NASA was a major cultural influence and has now been replaced by Michael Jordan and Gatorade. Barbie has lasted decades; the Cabbage Patch Dolls frenzy lasted for only a few years.

Changes in the SET Factors produce Product Opportunity Gaps (POGs). Once a POG is identified, the challenge becomes translating the POG into the development of a new product or the significant modification of an existing product. In both cases, these products are a hybrid combination of a new aesthetic and a set of features stemming from the possibilities of new technology that match emerging shifts in consumer preference. An example of a product hybrid that successfully filled a gap is the Apple iMac. By integrating the monitor and CPU, and by using translucent plastic combined with a variety of bright candy colors, the iMac has become easier and more fun to use than other computer. Offices and homes look sharp with an iMac on the desk, setup is a breeze, and cable management issues have all but disappeared.

You may not find that all of the products and services included in this book are ones that you would buy. This is an important point to make. The products that we include are highly successful within their *intended* markets. Understanding how your views differ from the user's views is critical to the development of successful products. The SET Factors identify POGs for a targeted user group; that target may not be you.

POG and SET Factor Case Studies

The remainder of this chapter examines four case studies that illustrate how the SET Factors and resulting POGs have led to successful products in the marketplace. The studies also give a brief introduction to the issues laid out in the rest of the book and we will refer to them often. These examples from the Upper Right represent simple and complex products and services. These four products join a comprehensive collection of case studies appearing throughout the book. While all products in this book are on the market at the time of this writing, some have recently been introduced while others have established an impressive run of market success.

Figure 1.3 1957 Chevy and 1959 pink Cadillac. (Reprinted with permission of General Motors.)

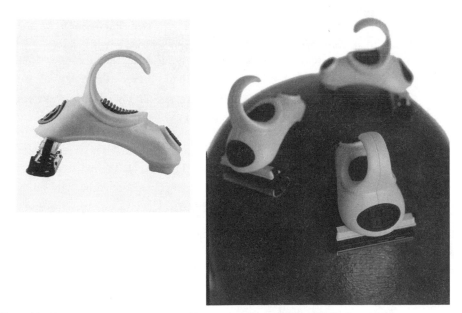

Figure 1.4 The HeadBlade. (Reprinted with permission of The HeadBlade Company.)

The OXO GoodGrips Peeler

The kitchen tools designed by OXO GoodGrips were recently awarded a "Design of the Decade" Award by the Industrial Designers Society of America (IDSA) and *BusinessWeek* magazine. These products have won numerous awards in recognition of their usability, aesthetics, and innovative use of materials. Even after designing 350 products, the company continues to win new awards every year. It is important to revisit the basis of the initial success to understand how this company has continued to maintain its competitive edge in the marketplace.

Sam Farber is a successful entrepreneur who has owned several companies. He sensed there was a product opportunity in the housewares industry. The insight for this opportunity came from his wife, who had developed arthritis in her hands. She liked to cook but found that most cooking and food preparation utensils were painful to use. She also found that most of the solutions, because they were ugly, stigmatized the person with disabilities while using them. In addition, these solutions often supplied only minimal relief or support. The opportunity (POG) was not just to design cooking utensils that were comfortable to hold in your hand; the products also had to set a new aesthetic trend that would not stigmatize the user as "handicapped." The product that had the most opportunity for improvement was the vegetable peeler. The generic peeler (Figure 1.5) was the technological evolutionary equivalent of the alligator; it had existed since the beginning of the industrial revolution without change. Comfort and dignity were two attributes (aspects of *Value Opportunities* which will be introduced in Chapter 3) that Sam Farber recognized were key to making a better cooking utensil.

In retrospect, the executives in the housewares industry have had to ask why no one else saw this opportunity earlier. It is surprising that it took so long to replace the original design. If, however, someone had observed the potential need twenty years ago, the public may not have been ready for the idea. There were several SET Factors at work here that made OXO the right product at the right time (Figure 1.6). The four primary ones were:

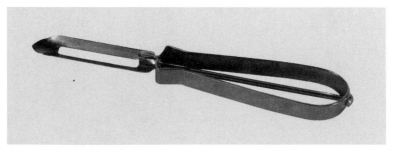

Figure 1.5 Generic potato peeler.

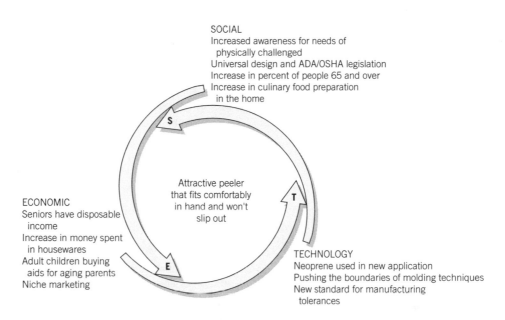

Figure 1.6 SET Factors that led to the GoodGrips peeler.

■ The American public became sensitive to the needs of people with physical challenges.

■ Those with challenges demanded that products be made to accommodate their needs.

■ Another factor was the change in the nature of business: mass marketing gave way to niche markets—the one-size-fits-all mentality that allowed the original potato peeler to last for over a century gave way to a new market segmentation approach.

■ The fourth factor was an increase in interest in the best products for use in the home, particularly in food preparation. The economic boom of the '90s fueled this trend. Consequently, spending up to $7 for a peeler was acceptable.

In essence, trends had changed and people were able to recognize and were willing to pay for the *value* embedded in this product.

The product opportunity was translated into several opportunities to add value. The product function was already established as useful: a peeler is a necessity for any kitchen. The two major areas for improvement were the limited usability and the ugly form-follows-function 19th-century aesthetic of the generic peeler. The product had to be usable by a broad range of people. The handle had to be comfortable to grip for short and long periods of use and it had to be able to be held securely when wet. The latter feature, in particular, was responsible for the higher costs and so it needed to be perceived as being of much higher quality and innovative. The product had to be desirable. If the product ended up looking clumsy and awkward the core market would have rejected it. The optimum result would be a new aesthetic that would establish a new trend in products for the home and would be seen as usable and desirable by all potential customers.

The next move was equally insightful. Instead of paying design consultants a large up-front fee, Sam Farber offered to make them partners with a share of the profits. Smart Design, true to its name, jumped at the opportunity to create the GoodGrips peeler (Figure 1.7). After extensive human factors tests, an ideal overall shape was developed for the handle. The overall handle shape included fins carved perpendicular to the surface of the handle that allowed the index finger and thumb to fit comfortably around it and added greater control. A suitable material was sought for the handle that would make a comfortable interface between the hand and the peeler and would also provide sufficient friction that would prevent the handle from slipping in your hand when wet. The result was the use of Santoprene, a neoprene synthetic elastomer with a slight surface friction, soft enough to squeeze, firm enough to keep its overall shape, and capable of being cleaned in the dishwasher.

A number of manufacturers decided that molding the fins was not possible to do in Santoprene. The product development team found manufacturers in Japan who felt the product specs were achievable. Their willingness to work within the high standards that OXO was looking for helped to create the product quality that became such a successful attribute of the product. Subsequently, the standards developed by the Japanese manufacturers were successfully transferred to a less expensive manufacturing company in

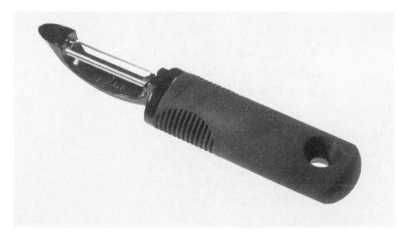

Figure 1.7 OXO GoodGrips. (Reprinted with permission of Smart Design.)

Taiwan. This became necessary when the strength of the dollar against the Yen made it too costly to use the original manufacturer.

Figure 1.8 shows that the peeler has attributes that combine aesthetics, ergonomics, ease of manufacture, and optimum use of materials. Taking full advantage of the surface friction of Santoprene, the handle was press-fit around a plastic core. The core extended out of the handle to form a protective curve over the blade and ended in a sharp point that can be used to remove potato eyes. The plastic guard also serves as the holder for the metal blade (the only metal part left) and the blade is made out of high-grade metal that is sharper and lasts longer than the blade on the original all-metal version. A final detail was a large counter-sunk hole carved into the end of the handle to allow owners to hang the peeler on a hook if they preferred. This hole also added an aesthetic detail that offset the large mass of the handle and, along with the

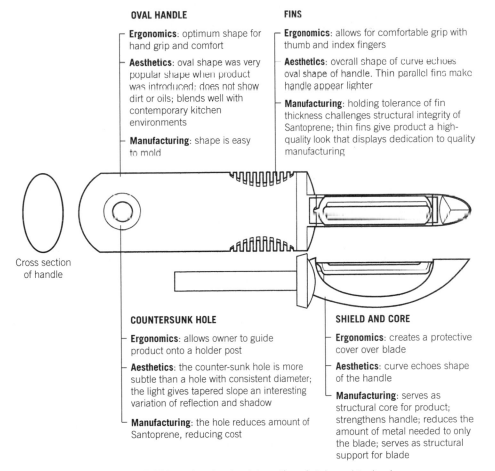

OVAL HANDLE

Ergonomics: optimum shape for hand grip and comfort

Aesthetics: oval shape was very popular shape when product was introduced; does not show dirt or oils; blends well with contemporary kitchen environments

Manufacturing: shape is easy to mold

FINS

Ergonomics: allows for comfortable grip with thumb and index fingers

Aesthetics: overall shape of curve echoes oval shape of handle. Thin parallel fins make handle appear lighter

Manufacturing: holding tolerance of fin thickness challenges structural integrity of Santoprene; thin fins give product a high-quality look that displays dedication to quality manufacturing

Cross section of handle

COUNTERSUNK HOLE

Ergonomics: allows owner to guide product onto a holder post

Aesthetics: the counter-sunk hole is more subtle than a hole with consistent diameter; the light gives tapered slope an interesting variation of reflection and shadow

Manufacturing: the hole reduces amount of Santoprene, reducing cost

SHIELD AND CORE

Ergonomics: creates a protective cover over blade

Aesthetics: curve echoes shape of the handle

Manufacturing: serves as structural core for product; strengthens handle; reduces the amount of metal needed to only the blade; serves as structural support for blade

Figure 1.8 Product details of OXO peeler showing integration of style and technology.

fins, gave the product a contemporary look that made it appealing to a much broader audience than originally targeted.

The overall effect is that of a very sophisticated product with a contemporary look that is superior in every way to its predecessor except for one aspect, the cost. As will be shown in Chapters 2 and 3, a comparison of the original peeler with the OXO clearly represents where the opportunities for added value were met and exceeded by OXO. Sam Farber felt that the public would recognize the value designed into the product and would be willing to pay the difference. He had the insight to predict that the public would pay several times the price of the original peeler. He went against the advice of most of his peers. He was right. The SET Factors were in place and consumers were ready to show their appreciation for a useful, usable, and desirable product and were more than willing to pay the difference. This product won numerous awards and, as a result of the positive praise generated by word of mouth, the product has never been aggressively advertised. As adult children bought the product for their older parents, they found that they liked the product as well. Younger children found it more fun to use and more comfortable to hold. The market swelled and the momentum grew.

The OXO peeler is also a good example of how one successful product can become a brand strategy that can be extended to other products. The success of the handle of the OXO peeler established the core competency of the company and became the secondary phase in the brand identity and labeling of the company (OXO GoodGrips). The company decided to build its brand strategy by extending the value designed into the peeler to the grip of every future product that they produce. The core concept has now extended beyond kitchen tools and has been applied to all subsequent products that are held by the hand, which includes teakettles, salad spinners, cleaning devices, tools, and gardening equipment. OXO has introduced a new material into the housewares industry. Santoprene was not perceived as a material suitable for use in the kitchen prior to OXO's success. Since OXO's debut, many other housewares manufacturers have used neoprene, the generic name for Santoprene, in their products to catch up with the success of the OXO brand. The use of new manufacturing techniques for thin features and tighter mold tolerances has also become commonplace. Combining insight, design, material choice, and manufacturing processes led to the creation of a new product that has redefined kitchen utensils.

The Motorola Talkabout

The Talkabout (Figure 1.9) is another excellent example of a manufacturer understanding the change in SET dynamics. Motorola is well known for its communication products. Its reputation was built on high-quality wearable and portable communication,

Figure 1.9 Motorola Talkabout two-way radio. (Reprinted with permission of Motorola.)

primarily for professional applications. With the advent of small portable phones in the '90s, Motorola moved from the business sector to the private sector seamlessly as "business phones" became useful in everyday life. The growth of wireless portable communication became an inexorable trend. Cellular phones generated a new trend that allowed families to "stay in touch," no matter where they were, throughout the day. But the cost of multiple phones and constant calls made this format impractical for constant communication during family activities. The wireless and portable phone was complemented by the use of wireless transmitters and receivers as devices that allowed parents to keep tabs on their infants. These various trends in combination created a new trend: parents wanting to constantly monitor their children. Sensational cases in the media of child kidnapping and murders created an atmosphere of fear that led parents to believe that they needed to monitor their child throughout childhood. At the same time, parents in active families were attempting to include their children in activities both as a way to have more fun and concern for the need to stay in touch as part of the parent-child relationship. These SET Factors created the POG for a new communication product that stood to be a big growth area in an entirely new market for Motorola: hand-held two-way radios, or what used to be called walkie-talkies (Figure 1.10). The advantage of this type of device was that it allowed for communication without having to pay for each call.

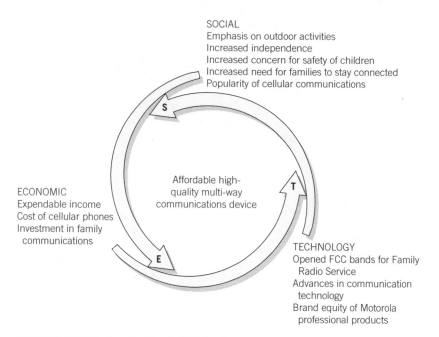

SOCIAL
Emphasis on outdoor activities
Increased independence
Increased concern for safety of children
Increased need for families to stay connected
Popularity of cellular communications

S

ECONOMIC
Expendable income
Cost of cellular phones
Investment in family
communications

Affordable high-
quality multi-way
communications device

T

E

TECHNOLOGY
Opened FCC bands for Family
Radio Service
Advances in communication
technology
Brand equity of Motorola
professional products

Figure 1.10 SET Factors that led to Talkabout.

However, at that time walkie-talkies had limited range and a low number of frequencies available. These were some of the obstacles Motorola had to overcome.

The challenges were finding the right value opportunities and then combining the right features, look, and cost that would allow Motorola to gain a fast penetration into the consumer market, as consumers had come to expect high-performance, compact wireless communication. The product opportunity was the gap between high-cost, professional two-way radio systems used by police, fire departments, and the military, and the low-cost, poor performing walkie-talkies serving a small market niche. The existing consumer products did not have the range, nor were they rugged enough or contemporary enough to fit into the current market opportunity. There were several challenges to finding the right level of value and quality that would allow Motorola to extend its established professional brand identity into a consumer market. The cost of Motorola's professional products was much higher than the products purchased by consumers. While the perceived value for these products had increased, the gap between the cost of professional products and consumer products was significant. There were two questions the development team had to answer. The first was how much would consumers pay. The second was how much could Motorola afford to redefine its technology, i.e., from supporting "mission critical," namely use in extreme situations where people's lives are at stake, to augmenting lifestyle. They also had to be sure not to damage their brand equity in the professional sector at the same time. Motorola also had the legislative challenge of obtaining new frequencies for two-way public communication from the FCC.

Because consumer walkie-talkies were considered to be of poor quality, the team decided to benchmark against other product categories that were comparable in feel and level of expression, rather than in application. So they looked at expensive athletic shoes, inline skates, the Walkman, and the Discman. For aesthetic benchmarking, they drew from outdoor products that were rugged and dependable. They also looked at icons of American culture: the Jeep, Levis, Coke. The team successfully lobbied for and received permission from company management to develop a new way of looking at commercial products for integration into the consumer world. Motorola anticipated that the increase in the number of public radio service frequencies would come in time for product introduction, and also worked with the government to make this happen. This example demonstrates both a scanning of the SET Factors and an ability to influence change in those factors by a large company. The program could only start with the confidence that Motorola could get the approval in time for the proposed product launch.

As illustrated in Figure 1.11, the Talkabout nicely integrates state-of-the-art technology into a carefully designed form. The rounded bottom presents a palm-friendly shape and the large display and push-to-talk button communicate to the user that it is an easy-to-use device. The push-to-talk button is located on the front center of the product; the location made the function obvious and the oversized button makes it easy to locate visually and by feel. The visual and tactile aesthetics were designed to fit into an active, outdoor, wireless consumer lifestyle, while the textured black details capture the look of contemporary X-generation products. This is a product that fulfills the motto "high tech, high touch."

■ Finding the right level of core technology and visual interaction in the product produced the right fit for the evolving market.

Through the appropriate reduction of cost and performance features from professional products, designing the right look and feel, and the approval of their Family Radio Service band, Motorola was able to fill the POG perfectly. The shift in social dynamics created the opportunity for a new communication device. The successful economy created the purchasing opportunity allowing consumers to buy an array of communication products for every phase of life. Finding the right level of core technology and visual interaction in the product produced the right fit for the evolving market. As you will see later, the Motorola product development team improved the value of the product significantly over the competition and successfully differentiated the product from its own line of professional products, creating a new family-targeted communications category.

CORE TECHNOLOGY

Manufacturing: internal components designed in-house; developed in conjunction with external aesthetics and ergonomics

COVER

Manufacturing: high impact materials molded into an accessible form

GRAPHICS DISPLAY

Ergonomics: large and easy to read

Aesthetics: matches contemporary displays and digital sports watches

TEXTURE

Ergonomics: provides a large area to speak into and listen

Aesthetics: breaks up the large oval shape

BUTTON

Ergonomics: large and easy to find and push

Aesthetics: creates a friendly, sophisticated look

BASE TRIM

Ergonomics: helps to provide good grip particularly when wearing gloves

Aesthetics: rugged outdoor look

CURVE SHAPE

Ergonomics: comfortable to hold with or without gloves

Figure 1.11   Product details of Talkabout showing integration of style and technology.

The Crown Wave

The Wave, developed by Crown Equipment Corporation, is another success story that supports the SET theory. The Wave, which stands for <u>W</u>ork <u>A</u>ssist <u>Ve</u>hicle, is a new product for Crown and a new product in the lift truck market (Figure 1.12). In fact it is not really a lift truck in the traditional sense. Crown produces lift trucks and devices for use in industrial settings, particularly warehouses and retail environments. While a relatively small company by international standards, this privately owned company, based in New Bremen, Ohio, holds a significant market share in battery-powered lift equipment. Tom Bidwell, Executive Vice President, was the visionary who saw the POG for

(a)

(b)

(c)

Figure 1.12 Crown Wave: (a) product shot, (b) operator controls, (c) product in use. (Reprinted with permission of Crown Equipment Company.)

a new type of lift device. He had been at a warehouse and seen the difficulty the employees had in using rolling ladders to get parts. He then spoke to Dave Smith, a long-term design consultant for Crown, who worked with Bidwell to clarify the product opportunity emerging from a number of Social and Economic factors. Social factors included changes in employers' attitude toward workers in the warehouse industry, changes in policy by insurance companies and OSHA (Occupational Safety and Health Administration), while Technology factors included changes in the types of warehousing for parts and packages and the compression of technology (see Figure 1.13).

The incidence of repetitive stress and injury as a result of falling and lifting has become a major concern for employers, insurance companies, and OSHA. The result of these injuries has created a loss of work time, limitations in worker effectiveness upon returning to the workplace, significant lifelong injuries, and the need to constantly replace workers as they "burn out."

Crown is a company that creates products which allow people to move heavy objects. However, it has a core competency that is slightly broader. Crown moves people and/or objects with the goal of redistributing goods with the safest and most effective interaction between the operator and others in the work environment. The Wave concept was a new POG that fit in that slightly broader brand identity.

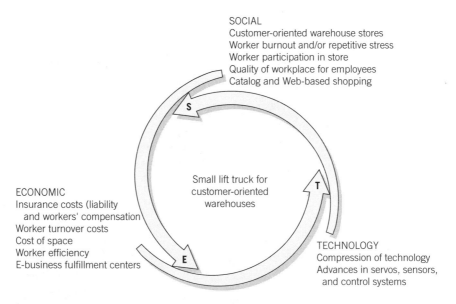

Figure 1.13 SET Factors that led to the Wave.

There have been numerous products developed to fill this POG including orthotics designed to give support and protect areas of the body most often affected. Ten years ago, companies would not have seen the economic value in having a product that could address the needs of a small parts picker or a restocking employee. Even with the orthotics, high turnover was a common trend in this type of occupation and employers accepted the economic consequences of that turnover. However, the cost of doing business and attitudes toward turnover have since changed.

Employees in warehouse stores are often experts in and are expected to perform multiple tasks. It is harder to find people to fill the jobs in stocking and picking, particularly when paying insurance and training new employees can have a significant impact on stores that are working on a small profit margin. Reducing injury and repetitive stress and creating more meaningful work environments are the new mission for store managers. In many ways, this trend began at Disney theme parks, where every employee is a performer and the environment is their stage. Every aspect of a store employee's performance and attitude should contribute to a positive atmosphere for consumers, who view shopping as a form of entertainment. Home Depot's employees are all trained to be expert advisors on their area of the store. Target has made the biggest move toward the Disney philosophy and has been a major investor and supporter of the new Wave. It makes good sense; employers realize that long-term employees are more invested in the success of a store and can develop better relationships with customers.

As a result of changes in products and methods for storing parts, a new type of warehouse has emerged. These new warehouses store small parts in smaller aisles that cannot be easily serviced by current lift equipment, which is designed for larger aisles and heavier parts and packages. The development of new warehouse store interiors with large shelves and storage typically located on top of those shelves created the need for new lift equipment that can work effectively while safely operating in areas with customers in retail environments. A "just in time" mentality has also put pressure on store managers to maintain an active relationship between storage and retail shelves, with restocking being a constant job not just for after-store hours. In addition, there is the need to constantly change merchandise on shelves to match seasonal changes and new product promotions. During this evolution, storeowners have used a variety of solutions. As noted by Dave Smith, this ranged from roller skates to rolling ladders. Sometimes companies have used palette trucks inside of stores, distracting and annoying customers with the constant watch for the beeping lift trucks moving down the aisles or backing away from a shelf.

In order to respond to this new POG, Crown needed to develop an entirely different product. It had to be an extension of Crown's core ability but at a scale and weight that Crown had not been used to. Dave Smith ran a "skunk works" offsite interdisciplinary team for 10 months to develop the initial product concept. The co-located team consisted of one engineer, two designers, plus a design intern, and a part-time marketing and manufacturing person. Once the product concept was acceptable to both the company and potential customers, the product development process was brought back into Crown for design-to-manufacture. Creating a light duty lift vehicle that can lift and move an operator with a minimal footprint proved to be a significant challenge for Crown. In addition to the design impact (the visual design, product graphics, and choice of material), the team took advantage of emerging technology in the industry to add safety, nimbleness, and control to the design. Innovation came from unusual places such as borrowing the simple two-finger control mechanism from electric wheelchairs.

Comparing the value of the Wave and previous attempts to accomplish the same task demonstrates how successful Crown has been. They have created a product that improves employee sense of security and makes a series of dull tasks enjoyable. The product is safe, easy to learn to use, and reduces time. It successfully blends a sense of ergonomics, aesthetics, and technical performance consistent with the performance of Crown's other products. The Wave product identity is distinct and the use of the word "Wave" in conjunction with a swish of color gives it a lighter contemporary look. Crown has strategically chosen to make its corporate identity secondary to the product for the first time in its history.

The result has surpassed the original projections for the product and created a new market for Crown. Employees in stores and warehouses that use the product are reporting more effective and less stressful completion of their tasks. The product has led to higher morale and job satisfaction and is fun and easy to operate. It has allowed one operator to do the job usually done by two people. The Wave has been used in a variety of new tasks. The product has spawned a new company line and other variations are in development to build on the success of the Wave.

Starbucks

Starbucks is an example of a service company that provides an optimal experience to the customer. Starbucks recognized the possibility of taking a core part of the American culture and integrating it with the style and attitude of an Italian café. The act of drinking coffee has been transformed from a quick, mindless experience into a major new form of cultural interaction and entertainment. Starbucks is an interesting hybrid between a product and service company. The core product that Starbucks provides is coffee. The service it provides is serving coffee using a range of options and complementary products in a comfortable environment that significantly enriches the experience of drinking coffee and enhances the beginning, middle, or end of your day.

Starbucks filled a POG that started in one city, Seattle, and then spread exponentially across the U.S. and then internationally. It has had the same effect at the end of 20th century that Coca-Cola had at the beginning and McDonalds had at mid-century. It is our latest global export. What were the factors that allowed Starbucks to become the last great food specialty retailer of the century? If you have ever traveled to Seattle, you will notice that it is a city with some unique attributes. The city not only started the new coffee culture, but it also helped to start the new beer culture with the development of microbreweries. Seattle has a gray, cloudy climate and stays fairly cool throughout the year. Many people commute using the ferry system and then drive or walk to work. Americans in general rarely have time to eat breakfast before they leave the house; breakfast on the run is a common experience. Early morning fatigue is also a common situation that most commuters have to deal with, especially in Seattle's climate. Drinking coffee is a custom that many Americans use to ramp up for the day, to maintain momentum during the day, and to relax at the end of the day. Seattle is also one of the primary new centers of the information age and, as home to Microsoft, is the land of expendable income. Howard Schultz, the visionary and CEO of Starbucks, saw the POG after experiencing the espresso bars in Milan. Given the Social (S) and Economic (E) factors that are both highlighted by Seattle inhabitants and more recently shared by the rest of the U.S. and the world, it is not surprising that Starbucks started in the Great Northwest and spread to the rest of the country and beyond (see Figure 1.14). It is now possible to get a café latte in local neighborhoods and on university campuses and on turnpikes and now in Taipei and London (see Figure 1.15). Now that is what we call a global brand!

In lower Manhattan, there is an area known as Little Italy, just north of Canal Street. Canal is the street that separates Little Italy from China Town. Both areas are favorite sites for New Yorkers and tourists. For a long time, there have been a number of little restaurants where you can order espresso and dessert, often after eating dinner in China Town. This concept never expanded outside of Little Italy, except in other Italian neighborhoods in other big cities.

Berkeley, California, home of UC Berkely and the '60s revolution, has for years had coffee houses in which students and faculty pontificated, studied, and hung out. Pete's Coffee

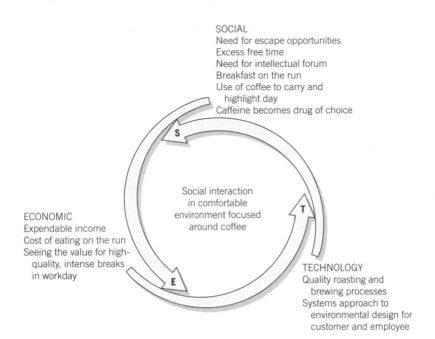

SOCIAL
Need for escape opportunities
Excess free time
Need for intellectual forum
Breakfast on the run
Use of coffee to carry and
    highlight day
Caffeine becomes drug of choice

ECONOMIC
Expendable income
Cost of eating on the run
Seeing the value for high-
    quality, intense breaks
    in workday

Social interaction
in comfortable
environment focused
around coffee

TECHNOLOGY
Quality roasting and
    brewing processes
Systems approach to
    environmental design for
    customer and employee

Figure 1.14 SET Factors that led to Starbucks' success.

Figure 1.15 Starbucks' global positioning shown through unique mug designs from international cities: London, New York, Taipei, Vancouver, and Boston.

began there in 1966 and preceded Starbucks. As a matter of fact, Alfred Pete trained the founders of Starbucks in the art of roasting arabica coffee beans. An addiction of locals, Pete's is well known to anyone who has lived in or visited Berkeley. Once a Berkeley resident rented a ski chalet in the Swiss Alps; it turned out the chalet owner had lived in Berkeley and regularly mail ordered Pete's coffee all the way to Switzerland.

Why didn't one of the restaurants in Little Italy become the original inspiration for Starbucks? Even though eventually Pete's would become the coffee of choice for the Au Bon Pain bakery chain, why wasn't Pete's Coffee the first to expand across the country? The SET Factors were not right in New York and no one in the Bay Area either saw or acted on the potential that Starbucks' visionary Schultz saw in Seattle. Not only do the SET Factors have to be right, they also have to be scanned, interpreted, and developed with a vision.

Part of the technology of Starbucks is in the machines used to prepare the coffee. The best machines for producing hot or cold coffee (and now tea) drinks are used and promoted along with the sounds they produce. Each Starbucks is a retro factory hissing and steaming away, producing espresso and lattes at a constant rate. Other aspects of technology include special water filtration systems in each store and sophisticated roasting facilities. Their investment and partnerships in R&D have led to innovations such as a process to extract the essence of their coffee for use in products such as Frappuccino® and ice cream.

The interiors of Starbucks stores have been designed to transcend the original concept of an Italian brasserie and to combine the global nature of coffee bean production with a comfortable old college coffee house including sophisticated contemporary colors, graphics, and furniture. It is inviting to walk into as an individual or with others. When you are in Starbucks, you are not just drinking coffee, you are having a mind-altering experience. Even if you order one to go, you can leave with a sense of the store experience while holding onto a cup with a protective corrugated holder that clearly states that it is made from recycled paper. It doesn't get any better than that. Starbucks has developed a flexible brand identity (discussed in Chapter 4), which uses a consistent color theme that allows for variation in secondary graphics for packaging, products, and store interiors (Figure 1.16). The response to Starbucks has been equally impressive, with the emergence of a number of national, regional, and local competitors fighting for their share of this new, lucrative market. As traditional coffee makers have responded to the trend, Starbucks has countered by extending their products into grocery chains by offering dark arabica coffee beans and even a range of ice cream flavors.

In his book *Pour Your Heart Into It*,[1] Schultz chronicles the evolution of Starbucks. Starbucks is a company that epitomizes the characteristics found in a company in the

Figure 1.16 Starbucks store interior and logo. (Reprinted with permission of Starbucks Coffee Company.)

Upper Right. They see their product as the coffee, the people who work for the company, and the experience of buying and drinking coffee in their stores. The company maintains a high standard of values, from the CEO to each employee, and connects to the values of their customers. These values are clearly articulated in a corporate mission statement. The company sees its people as core to its brand in parallel with its coffee and recognizes that the company's long-term success is dependent on high standards for both. Each employee of the company is called a "partner" and given stock options. Even part-time employees are given full health care benefits. Starbucks has relied on the power of its experiential brand, loyally conveyed by its customers, to promote the company, rather than falling back on advertising. As Schultz says, "Starbucks built up brand loyalty one customer at a time." Finally, the company is constantly looking for the next new product to "surprise and delight" the customer, from new coffee drinks, to Frappuccino, to ice cream, to jazz CDs.

Upper Right products, services, and companies merge style and technology in a way that creates strong customer value and promotes a positive user experience. Strong brand, corporate values, and connection to customer values lead to both short-term and long-term customer satisfaction. Many breakthrough products stay in the Upper Right through the constant injection of useful, usable, and desirable features for the customer. The end result is greater profits to shareholders.

Summary Points

❏ Social, Economic, and Technology (SET) Factors lead to Product Opportunity Gaps (POGs).

❏ Breakthrough products merge style, technology, and value.

❏ It takes a combination of vision and sound methodology to succeed in developing breakthrough products.

❏ These ideas and methods are applicable to both tangible products and services.

References

1. Schultz, H., and D. J. Yang, *Pour Your Heart Into It*, Hyperion, New York, 1997.

Chapter Two

Moving to the Upper Right

This chapter introduces a Positioning Map, which shows how break-through products are differentiated from the competition. The Upper Right quadrant of the Map integrates the attributes of Style and Technology and adds a third dimension: Value. Each remaining quadrant contains products that emphasize only style, technology, or low cost. Through the integration of the attributes represented in the Upper Right, breakthrough products meet the needs, wants, and desires of customers, resulting in increased sales, profit, and brand equity.

Integrating Style and Technology

■ We call the successful integration of style and technology "Moving to the Upper Right."

The last chapter presented four case studies as examples of how companies can develop products that are successful because they differentiate themselves from their competition through style, technology, and added value. OXO GoodGrips, Starbucks, the Crown Wave, and the Motorola Talkabout demonstrate a range of products and services from simple to highly complex. Additional case studies are presented throughout the book. We call the successful integration of style and technology *Moving to the Upper Right*. This integration results in the creation of breakthrough products that are perceived as having high value. While technology-driven or style-driven products do have some value, it is limited and so are their markets.

It is important at this point to establish the definition of style and technology. While we realize these terms mean many things and can be interpreted in a number of ways, we are using them in a specific way.

Style refers to the sensory elements that communicate the desired aesthetic and human factors of a product or service. The style of a product must respond to a consumer's expectations. It also produces the identity of the product. Style is the measure of how well a product responds to the lifestyle of the people who are the core of the intended market. The look, feel, and sound are all attributes that fit into style. Ergonomic issues must complement the aesthetics, including comfort, ease of use, and safety.

Technology refers to the core function that drives the product, the interaction of components that are required to use the product, and the methods and materials used to produce the product. The core functionality can be mechanical, electrical, electromechanical, chemical, digital, or any combination of these. Interaction with core technology can require as little as one button, or can be operated by a complex set of physical buttons and screen or voice commands. The choice of materials and manufacturing must be appropriate to the projected cost, fulfill the requirements of internal components, and complement the style requirements of the product.

We will define *value* in more detail in the next chapter. In essence, a product is deemed of value to a consumer if it offers a strong effect on lifestyle, enabling features, and meaningful ergonomics resulting in a useful, usable, and desirable product.

Marketing, engineering, and industrial and interaction design are required to blend style and technology in order to produce products that will be perceived to be of value. The challenge is getting these groups to work in a cohesive way.

The Positioning Map shows how different products in the same category can be located in a matrix with Style and Technology as the two axes (Figure 2.1). This Map has a third dimension, Value (Figure 2.2), which primarily exists in the Upper Right quadrant (and is only represented there) where companies make a concerted effort to integrate style and technology by responding to the needs of consumers. All of the companies that we highlight in this book realize that the playing field is three-dimensional. While this approach can lead to increased cost in production, that cost can often be easily returned

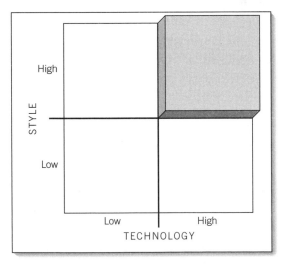

Figure 2.1 Positioning Map of Style versus Technology.

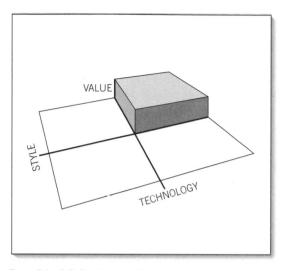

Figure 2.2 3-D Positioning Map—Value, the third axis found primarily in the Upper Right.

with interest by establishing a higher price for the product, increased sales, increased interest in the company's product lines, or establishing or reaffirming a company's brand recognition. People will pay more for quality and value if they feel they connect to their goals and aspirations. Further, products in the Upper Right have clearly recognized high levels of quality and value achieved through the appropriate articulation and integration of features and style.

▌ No one buys everything to match their lifestyle, but everyone buys something that does.

With the growing sophistication of consumer awareness, products that lack an integration of style and technology are not perceived as valuable by customers. For most of the 20th century, value was defined as the most features for the lowest price, namely value based on price, not value based on customers' insight into what they value. The generic vegetable peeler is perhaps the symbol of this phenomenon (see Chapter 1). This view of value is changing. While people are price sensitive in many of their purchases, everyone has certain purchases that are driven by lifestyle compatibility. The higher the lifestyle compatibility, the less important price plays a role in determining purchase. In the old era of mass marketing, purchasing tended to be consistent along taste and economic lines. In the new era of "de-massification," purchasing is highly variable. A person can live in low-rent housing but drive a Mercedes. Another person may own the most expensive climbing equipment and dress in only jeans and t-shirts. No one buys everything to match or project his or her lifestyle, however everyone buys something that does.

Style vs. Technology: A Brief History of the Evolution of Style and Technology in the 19th and 20th Centuries

In the Beginning

The historical integration of style and technology into products has been a slow and uneven process. The two primary factors that people valued were cost and emerging technology. During the late 19th and most of the 20th centuries, companies and inventors developed new products based primarily on technological innovations. For the period 1850–1950, hand made production methods (existing) were changed to mechanical and electromechanical (preferred) ways of doing things. The challenge became making things that worked and that could be produced in large quantities at low prices, not on making things that were beautiful to look at or even easy to use. Since these advances were new, the public had no way to compare products and many were eager to embrace the labor- and time-saving devices. The Arts and Crafts Movement attempted to offset this trend. The emphasis on craft versus mass manufacture did little to stem the inexorable trend of invention and change over aesthetics and refinement. Aesthetics and human factors were always secondary or non-existent in the development of products. The term "form follows function" was a term often used to an extreme to support the development of ugly, under-developed products that were only tech driven.

During the 19th century, the agrarian lifestyle and craft manufacture were replaced by mass produced products and an industrial/service economy. Major milestones in this period include the development of Morse's telegraph, the continental railroad system, Edison's creation of an electrical distribution system, Eastman's camera and celluloid film, Ford's assembly line and the Model T, and the Wright brothers' development of powered flight. Technology during the industrial revolution made products and services available to the emerging industrial urban middle class at an unprecedented rate. The camera, phonograph, refrigerator, VCR, computer, and microwave are all the results of product opportunities that stemmed from the major basic SET Factors that evolved in the late 19th and early 20th centuries. There are several factors that made this possible: time (both the speed of doing things and the concept of free time); disposable income (the ability to have income that allows ownership or the ability to establish the credit to purchase things on time); increased literacy and other social reforms; and, finally, rapid advances in science and technology, which created a plethora of new product opportunities.

The Growth of Consumer Culture

The technological advances of mass production met the growing appetite for mass consumption. As work hours decreased and wages increased, free time and excess income created the need for more products, services, and forms of entertainment. A variety of product opportunities emerged, as office workers and homemakers looked for more efficient ways to work at the evolving speed of business and save time for more enjoyable activities in the home. [1,2] Many early versions of products resulting from new technological advances were ugly, crude, and dangerous. As the telephone became standard business equipment, telephone wires filled the streets of most cities; early powered farm equipment was extremely dangerous; early home appliances caused burns and electrical fires; and children were often hurt by exposed mechanisms, burnt by toasters and ovens, or shocked by outlets.

The word "kluge" was invented to describe underdeveloped technology-based products. The advantages these products provided in speed, power, and communication far outweighed the danger and visual clutter at first. Products were difficult to use but, as Donald Norman has observed, humans often adapt to new products and blame themselves for their own ineptitude, instead of blaming the manufacturer.[3] This human trait of adaptation combined with a huge influx of cheap immigrant labor, the need for work at any cost in any condition, and the lack of unions and government standards to insure reasonable working conditions.

During the late 19th and early 20th centuries, progress and change were more important than refinement and human factors. The developers of new technological products often neglected craft finish as a waste of time or rejected any hint of sophistication in favor of an extreme "form follows function" approach that could more accurately be described as form resulting from the limitations of manufacturing and the non-human elements of function. For instance, the early Model T was designed to be produced inexpensively, in a series of steps on an assembly line; there was little attention paid to issues of ergonomics and style. An airplane propeller is designed strictly for the function of creating thrust, but does not interact with human beings at all. For much of the early 20th century, technology alone was enough to drive the development of products for consumer purchase. It took roughly a century for consumers to start to demand more of new products. As competition grew in consumer and certain industrial markets, companies started to use human factors and visual style as a way to differentiate their products from their competitors' and give them a more up-to-date look. In order to create a major impact in an industry today, the merging of style and technology is required from the beginning. Products must change to respond to an ongoing set of factors that determine what customers expect. The tide is turning. While Don Norman's observation was right for those raised in the depression era and WWII, Baby Boomers and their children expect products to conform to their needs, not the other way around.

The Introduction of Style to Mass Production

In the United States, the integration of style and technology did not occur until the mid to late 1920s. American industrialists were inspired by the Decorative Arts Exposition in Paris in 1925 and decided to try to bring that level of sophistication to American products. In 1926, Henry Ford was caught completely off guard by GM's introduction of market segmentation and styling under the direction of Harley Earl. The Model T had dominated auto sales for 20 years and Ford felt it could continue for another 20. He did not see the product opportunity that the roaring twenties provided, but GM did. Earl brought style and color to GM cars. During the 1930s, trains were redesigned in the emerging stream-lined style when railroad companies realized that the growing aviation industry posed a significant threat to their hold on public transportation (see Figure 2.3). Bus lines soon followed suit; the Greyhound bus company did a thorough overhaul of their vehicles in

Figure 2.3 NY Central Hudson Locomotive by Henry Dreyfuss, 1938. (Reprinted with permission of Henry Dreyfuss Associates.)

the 1940s. Large bent sheet metal was used to cover appliances to separate internal technology both visually and physically from consumers and their families. Companies put windows in washers and dryers to enable consumers to watch their machines do their work. Vacuum cleaners were made more efficient, lighter and easier to move.

The 1935 Sears Coldspot Refrigerator (see Figure 2.4), developed with the input of designer Raymond Loewy, dramatically improved the style and function of the refrigerator. The product was given a clean new look and the cooling unit was covered with sheet metal. The doors were easy to open even when a person's hands were full of groceries. The interior metal shelves were replaced with aluminum to prevent rusting. The

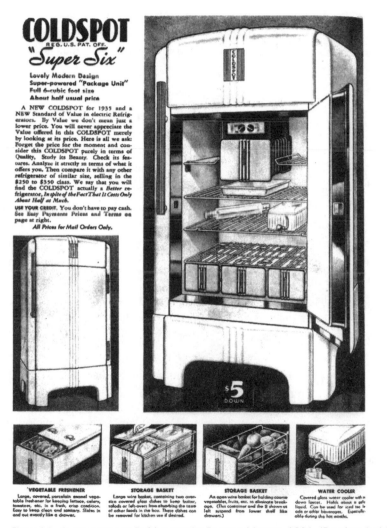

Figure 2.4 Sears Coldspot Refrigerator by Raymond Loewy, 1934. (Reprinted with permission of Loewy Design.)

resulting dramatic increase of sales was an early example of success through the integration of style and technology. When the 1934 Coldspot was introduced, sales went from 65,000 units per year to 275,000. [4] Even the advertisement for the Coldspot shown in Figure 2.4 had a view of "value" that would emerge again as relevant today: "By Value we don't mean just a lower price… Forget the price for the moment and consider this Coldspot purely in terms of Quality. Study its Beauty. Check its features. Analyze it strictly in terms of what it offers you…."

Other merges of style and technology at the time included the design of a new telephone for AT&T, aided by the design consultant Henry Dreyfuss, resulting in an integrated, elegant new look and increased ergonomic comfort of the headset and base. It quickly became the standard for both the workplace and home and will be discussed further in Chapter 7 (and shown in Figure 7.10). The 1939 World's Fair also celebrated the future of America as a land of prosperity with endless product options for the home and business.

Post World War II Growth of the Middle Class and the Height of Mass Marketing

Initially, high-end products for the upper class were well designed but products for the middle and lower classes were not. It was not until after WWII that the merging of style and technology started to appear in products available to all economic levels. The United States's involvement in the war resulted in American companies achieving maximum manufacturing capacity and fostered the development of new technologies, three major examples being the computer, the jet engine, and the nuclear bomb. The combination of manufacturing capacity, the return of career and family-oriented GIs, and the subsequent Baby Boom generated a tremendous market for new products. The design of cars in the 1950s reflected the exuberance of the era—cars sported fins of all types and sizes. This "supersonic" style combined with 8-cylinder engines, mass production capability created by the retooling after WWII, and low gas prices, epitomized the integration of style and technology of the era. The cost of low-end cars became affordable to many more people. Buyers could identify a brand that connected to their lifestyle and buy their way from Chevy to Cadillac or Ford Fairlane to Lincoln.

During the late 1950s and early '60s, IBM and Westinghouse developed comprehensive brand identity programs that merged their state-of-the-art products with the emerging International style. Graphic identity, products, work environments, and architecture were all subjected to rigorous guidelines under the direction of external consultants Elliot Noyes and Paul Rand.

This post-war boom era lasted until the oil embargo of the 1970s. It was a time when mass manufacturing potential was met by mass consumption. Consumers behaved in consistent patterns of purchasing and could be grouped into large mass markets.

The Rise of Consumer Awareness and the End of Mass Marketing

By the 1970s, consumer patterns started to change. The age of consumer awareness evolved as Ralph Nader attacked the lack of safety and quality of American products. This type of product evaluation gave rise to a variety of consumer protection groups (e.g., state public interest research groups), publications (e.g., a modified *Consumer Reports* and *Consumer's Digest*), and legislation (e.g., the Americans with Disabilities Act). Consumer groups started to split into smaller niches that were defined by age, geography, education, and income. This new consumer awareness led to the trend of demassification, namely the breakup of 50th percentile-based marketing into a smaller cluster of markets, which became known as *niche marketing*. There was a break between the generation that survived through the Depression and WWII, and the baby boomers who had only known prosperity and wanted peace at all costs. Civil rights, women's rights, and environmentalism created entirely new types of consumers. They expected more from the products they bought and had very particular demands and a new range of interests that exceeded their own personal needs, wants, and desires.

■ The technology alone did not sell the Mac to the masses. The added usability and style along with the technical capabilities are what sold the computer.

When IBM tried to transfer its business machine mainframe mentality and austere modern corporate identity to the design of personal home computers they had trouble "crossing the chasm" from lead users to the early majority.[5] Although their use of a Charlie Chaplin imitator was the right image in commercials for the ordinary guy, their computer was not for the average person. IBM could not escape the cold design and poor interface of their business machines. The first Macintosh computer had a new look and interface that consumers responded to. Apple beat IBM in the emerging home computing era of the 1980s. The Mac was user friendly and the product looked cute, not technological. The mouse was an easy-to-use peripheral product that added an additional friendly form to this new technology. While the overall idea was developed at Xerox PARC, Steve Jobs was the one that saw the POG and acted on it. The software was easy to learn to use, allowing people to start up quickly and become functional users. The technology alone did not sell successfully to the mass public; the added usability and style along with the technical capabilities are what sold the computer. This feat was recreated when Apple recently saved their company by introducing the iMac—it succeeded for exactly the same reason that the first Mac did. Technology alone was not enough.

The same was true in other industries as well. The U.S. auto industry was caught completely off guard by the oil embargo of the '70s, allowing Japan to take over the U.S. small car market with low cost, fuel-efficient, and eventually near zero-defect cars. People's needs, wants, and desires had changed. However, the U.S. auto industry hadn't recognized the need for change. Xerox lost their once-dominant control of the copier industry by failing to recognize that consumers wanted copiers that were more reliable. Xerox had been able to get incomplete technology into the market by backing it with excellent service. Japanese companies saw this gap and filled it with copiers that did not need service and looked better in the office environment.

The Era of Customer Value, Mass Customization, and the Global Economy

At the beginning of the 21st century, the concept of product development has changed in all markets at all economic levels. Companies are now competing globally in more diverse and demanding markets. In the current global market, a small, previously unknown Finnish company, Nokia, can effectively compete against a giant like Motorola in the design of cellular phones. Consumers today no longer behave in large, predictable groups. They do not follow simple, consistent patterns of purchasing. We are now in the era of information with segmented markets and consumers that can research and buy their products through a number of media channels. The access to cultural patterns of change is higher than it has ever been. Almost everyone in industrial nations can watch television, see movies, surf the Web, read magazines and newspapers, and listen to the radio. Many people do a number of these things simultaneously.

What every consumer is searching for is a sense of integrity and their own version of value and quality that can help them fulfill their lives. Today's consumers have a much clearer sense of their own identity and who they want to connect with (market segment) and they are also well aware of the range of products available. Customers are looking for products that are well made, safe, and match their lifestyle. Everyone has a number of product categories, where they expect a product to make a statement about who they are and how they want to live their lives.

■ Moving to the Upper Right means committing to style, technology, and value.

Products can no longer simply provide a service, nor will simply styling a product work. Integrating style and technology through features is the only way to be competitive and maintain a customer's loyalty. Moving to the Upper Right means committing to style, technology, and value.

Positioning Map: Style vs. Technology

We can compare how products differ in their use of style vs. technology by placing them on a Positioning Map as shown in Figure 2.1. The four quadrants represent differences in the amount of style and technology that is designed into the product. The Upper Right quadrant is the one to be in if your goal is to be a leader in the marketplace and you want to maximize your profit. The products in the Upper Right exhibit an integrated approach with a balance of both style and technology. In the Upper Right, balance is achieved through the use of the third axis: understanding the value systems of the intended market (Figure 2.2). These products maximize lifestyle impact, features, and ergonomics. The third axis, value, is not integrated into the products placed in the other three quadrants. Note that in the 2D Map, the Upper Right is separated from the rest of the map. We do this to emphasize the third dimension of value in that quadrant. We will now examine each of these quadrants in more detail.

Lower Left: Low Use of Style and Technology

Products in this quadrant are typically generic, designed with established technologies and minimal styling. As shown in Figure 2.5, they have minimal lifestyle impact, features, and ergonomics. These unrefined products sell to consumers who do not seek out

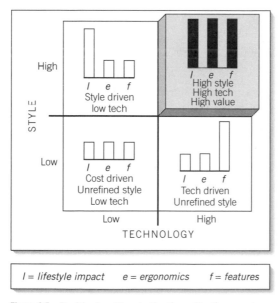

l = lifestyle impact   e = ergonomics   f = features

Figure 2.5 Positioning Map indicating effectiveness in lifestyle impact, features, and ergonomics.

value but instead are driven primarily by low price: functionalism at low cost. These products may have been innovative early in their existence, however they have failed to respond to change and have become obsolete on a number of levels. Products in this quadrant establish the baseline of the product category. They are usually manufacturing- and materially-driven, that is, they rely on minimal use of material, quick cycle time, and minimal assembly time and keep a low cost per unit to make a profit. These products have few if any distinguishing features to differentiate them from other similar products. This approach was the classic for mass production and mass marketing and is still an approach that can work for commodities that have little value potential. This concept still works if you understand the advantages and disadvantages. Their undistinguished, low-cost design demands a minimal price, resulting in low profit per item produced.

A generic potato peeler, paper clips, a stepladder, the standard first class business letter delivered by the U.S. Postal Service, or a cup of coffee in a coffee shop are all examples of generic products. In this quadrant, companies and customers seek value in the mass marketing sense. The product is made as cheaply as possible and distributed as widely as possible. Profit is made by high volume and low profit margin per item.

Lower Right: Low Use of Style, High Use of Technology

Products in this quadrant are driven by technology, with an expectation of sales based only on the added technological advantage or originality of the product. They maximize features but almost ignore lifestyle effects and, generally, ergonomics (see Figure 2.5). These products are often the first of their type and thus offer technological advance as their major competitive advantage. These products also work well in professional applications where style and ergonomics are not as important from a competitive standpoint. The same is true for military applications, even though attention to ergonomics may be more salient. In both cases, however, they require a skilled user that is willing to overlook ease of use for performance. Profit in this quadrant is based on technological innovation and the primary market is lead users and early adopters. They are willing to pay a premium to be the first with the new technology. However, this profit margin and early success does not continue past these aggressive segments. As Geoffrey Moore states in *Crossing the Chasm*,[5] the early success of lead users is a false positive that does not translate to more conservative consumers who are interested in ergonomics and style. While these products can achieve greater profit margins than those in the Lower Left, they usually have a limited market growth (the VCR is a notable exception) and must move to the Upper Right if they want to compete in consumer markets.

Manufacturing equipment, business-oriented computers and peripherals, and professional-quality service products all succeed in the Lower Right. Hewlett-Packard has been one of the most successful companies operating in the Lower Right. Their testing equipment, medical equipment, and plotters were standards in the professional markets. However, in order to compete in consumer markets they have had to Move to the Upper Right. As discussed in Chapter 4, the Iomega Zip Drive is a great example of a company that started in this quadrant and successfully Moved to the Upper Right. The Windows operating system is far less user friendly than Mac OS. However, Windows dominates through its position as the primary software for the Wintel PC and the one most used in business. As such, the PC, still in the Lower Right, is a product driven by more features for less money than the higher cost, more usable alternative. The VCR is the classic case of a tech-driven product with lots of capabilities yet with a horrendous interface that makes it nearly unusable. Its neutral look is also undesirable. People buy them to use the minimal number of features, with cost and brand loyalty the only deciding factors.

Upper Left: High Use of Style, Low Use of Technology

Products in this quadrant are driven only by style. Some companies that live in this quadrant explore the boundary of aesthetic experimentation (lifestyle impact) and usually fail in the application of human factors (ergonomics) and core technology (features)—see Figure 2.5. Examples include Alessi products from Italy, which lead new aesthetic trends for the home; Disney and Alessi designs, and lower cost versions for Target by Michael Graves; and products by French designer Philippe Stark. Other designers like Philippe Stark develop products that push the boundaries of form, material, and tactile experience. Designers often look to these progressive ideas as a point of departure for future designs that can flow back into other more complex and mainstream products. Profit in this quadrant is the result of either a market seeking out image and art, or by tricking consumers into believing that the highly styled look of these products is backed by competent ergonomic and technology design. This cosmetic approach usually fails for the opposite reasons that a high tech product fails. Consumers quickly realize that these products are a compromise and that they rarely perform as anticipated. These companies are often looking for niche markets willing to sacrifice usability for expression alone.

Upper Right: High Use of Style and Technology

The Upper Right quadrant contains products that integrate style and technology and add the final factor that makes them successful: value. Here lifestyle impact, features, and ergonomics come together to enable personal expression, cutting-edge capabilities, and usability (see Figure 2.5). This combination allows products to differentiate themselves from the competition and define the state of the art for their market. How to successfully "Move to The Upper Right" is the focus of this book. We have already discussed examples of breakthrough products in the Upper Right in Chapter 1, such as the Motorola Talkabout, the Crown Wave, the OXO GoodGrips, and Starbucks. Sometimes

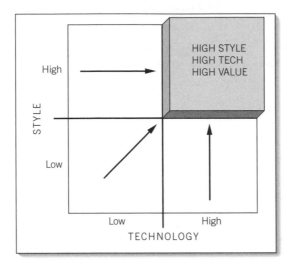

Figure 2.6 Moving to the Upper Right.

these products and services cost more to design and produce than those in the other quadrants, however consumers are willing to pay a premium for them. At other times, the resourceful and meticulous effort it takes to create an Upper Right product allows for a more efficient use of materials, technology, and manufacturing processes, resulting in a higher-profit product that costs no more to produce.

The goal is for new products to "Move to the Upper Right," i.e., end up with a product in the Upper Right quadrant, as shown in Figure 2.6. Mapping your products and your competitors on the Positioning Map allows you to understand the scope of your competition and also to understand how to differentiate yourselves from that field. You can then use that understanding to plan out a strategy to Move to the Upper Right. The process is not as simple as merely putting an industrial designer and engineer together. The process is deep and intricate. We will devote the remainder of this book to understanding the way products in the Upper Right differentiate themselves from the rest of the field.

Positioning Map of OXO GoodGrips

Re-examining the products discussed in Chapter 1 through the use of the Positioning Map highlights their success. Figure 2.7 shows the Positioning Map for the OXO GoodGrips. At the time the GoodGrips was created, the standard vegetable peeler was the generic peeler that had existed for over a century. The product was designed for manufacture at a minimum cost and sold for under a dollar. The generic design was manufacturing-driven,

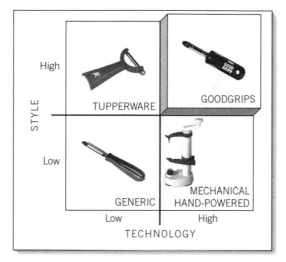

Figure 2.7 OXO Positioning Map.

■ The choice of materials and manufacturing process can play as significant a role as core technology.

with no sense of style or consideration of human factors. It is in the Lower Left quadrant. Also in existence were mechanical peelers that, while they showed the potential for speed, were difficult to use and tended to remove more than just the peel when used. These products are low in style and are either driven mechanically or electromechanically, and thus are placed in the Lower Right quadrant of the Positioning Map. The OXO peeler contains a balance of technology (material choice and its integration, and manufacturing), style, and value, especially through ergonomics, to position it in the Upper Right. We will describe how the OXO peeler moved there and how OXO was able to charge several times the cost of the generic peeler in the next chapter. After OXO's initial success, a number of other houseware companies tried to copy the successful design. Just about all of them compromised on one of the three aspects and tried to undersell the GoodGrips. As will be discussed shortly, most of these products end up off the map altogether. The few exceptions attempted to create an artistic expression in the Upper Left, significantly sacrificing the ergonomics and technology. The Tupperware peeler shown in the upper left of Figure 2.7 is an excellent example of these products. It is important to note that technology does not always need to include complex mechanical, electromechanical, or digital components. The choice of materials and manufacturing process can play as significant a role as core technology. In the case of the OXO peeler, the choice of Santoprene molded with tight tolerances and structure was as innovative as the ergonomic research and the styling. The successful integration of these factors was as powerful as the Talkabout's combination of high technology internal communication and the exterior interface.

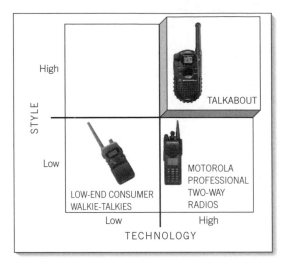

Figure 2.8 Motorola Talkabout Positioning Map. (Image of professional two-way radio and Talkabout two-way radio reprinted with permission of Motorola.)

Positioning Map of Motorola Talkabout

The Talkabout (Figure 2.8) is an example of a product that converted a core corporate technology into a successful Upper Right product. Prior to the Talkabout, there were generic short-range consumer walkie-talkies with minimal features, lifestyle impact, and attention to ergonomics in the Lower Left. Motorola's core wireless communications technology, which was used for professional applications, was in the Lower Right. Motorola had to change the performance standards from its professional line to meet projected price points in the consumer market. However consumers felt the resulting quality was still much higher than the competition's. As it turned out, Motorola had to increase the amount charged for the product over what they had originally targeted. However, through careful cost reduction they still maintained a high profit margin on this highly successful product, which still meets the needs of the market. At the time this book was written, Motorola had close to 80% of the shelf space in most electronics stores as compared to their Lower Left competition or off-the-Map rip-offs.

Positioning Map of Crown Wave

The Crown Wave (Upper Right, Figure 2.9) introduced an original solution to the problem of stocking and picking in small parts warehouses and super stores. Prior to the Wave, a variety of product options existed in the Lower Left. These products included the rolling ladder and a pair of running shoes. While inexpensive, they are an exhausting and potentially harmful experience for the stock employee. Higher tech, Lower Right

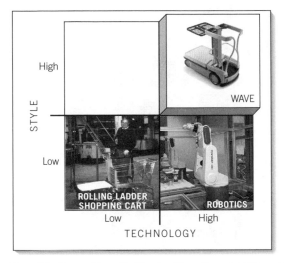

Figure 2.9 Crown Wave Positioning Map. (Image of Wave and lead designer Dave Smith with Lower Left solutions reprinted with permission of Crown Equipment Corporation.)

solutions included scissor lift trucks, which were large, cumbersome to operate, and expensive to purchase; hydraulic lifts, which were difficult to move; and robots, also expensive and difficult to fine tune. Crown identified a significant Product Opportunity Gap in the marketplace, and targeted it with a mid-priced, easy-to-use lift device. The Wave combines value with ergonomics and style with technological innovation, which thus results in a machine with a small footprint that can maneuver through store aisles and lift a person up to eight feet in height. The success of the Wave will likely inspire non-differentiating, cost-driven, Lower Left versions or off-the-Map rip-offs.

Positioning Map of Starbucks

Our arguments can also be applied to Starbucks, a service-based company (Figure 2.10). Prior to Starbucks, the most popular group meeting place was a coffee shop or diner (Lower Left). People would meet for business, discussion, and, of course, coffee. Minimal service and customer turnover meant profit (low profit per person but high volume); the idea of hanging out with a laptop and sipping a cup of Java was an opportunity that most people did not see. For people seeking out the quick and reliable cup of coffee, Lower Right fast food restaurants had the technology to deliver a consistent, though not necessarily enjoyable, brew in a (usually) stark atmosphere. Upper-end restaurants (in the Upper Left) provided an inviting atmosphere but without a guaranteed consistent brewing quality.

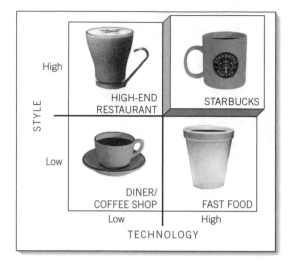

Figure 2.10 Starbucks Positioning Map.

Starbucks introduced and brought into the American mainstream the concept of a European café integrated with a West Coast contemporary look and feel. Starbucks, clearly in the Upper Right, combines technology through roasting and brewing, with style through the upscale retail environment. Starbucks' first store opened in 1971. It wasn't until 1984 that Starbucks opened its second store in Seattle. By 1999, the company had grown to 2,500 stores in over 13 countries. As discussed in Chapter 1, the Starbucks line has extended into supermarkets, other products such as ice cream, and peripherals for coffee and tea drinkers. The Starbucks chain gave rise to a host of national and local copies. Some are poor copies while others have attempted to Move to the Upper Right by offering a different but still high-quality product. Bookstores have installed coffee shops to heighten the book buying and browsing experience and make them more like libraries combined with coffee houses, most notably Barnes & Nobles who is partnering with Starbucks.

Knockoffs and Rip-offs

As already indicated, once a product succeeds in the Upper Right, it often inspires a multitude of companies looking to copy its success without the investment in the value represented through lifestyle impact, features, and ergonomics. There are three directions that companies take. Established value-oriented companies cannot just copy for fear of blurring their brand. These companies are forced to develop different Upper Right solutions that have equal perceived value. Many companies, however, have the goal of competing by charging less and skimming the profits of the original Upper Right product, thus appealing to customers who believe they can get the same value for less cost. These companies configure themselves to actually copy. They want to take advantage of the brand identity of the leading company. Unless a product can differentiate itself from one in the Upper Right, then it will end up back in the Lower Left or off the Map altogether. Those companies driven toward a lower price point but able to create a genuine product end up in the Lower Left. Most times, however, companies interested in ripping off success use a cosmetic approach but sacrifice on choice of material and manufacturing quality. The product is neither technology- nor style-driven and lacks the sincerity of a generic product. This pushes the product off the Map altogether. Consumers quickly realize that these products are a compromise and they rarely perform as anticipated. The companies who do this are usually positioned for sales in lower-end retail stores and are often looking for short profit cycles with no investment in brand loyalty.

There have been many companies trying to rip off the look of GoodGrips products; all of them are cheaper in price but none of them work as well. The Black & Decker SnakeLight, an Upper Right product discussed in Chapter 8, was followed by a number of cheap imitations. Not one of these products offered any true innovation. None wanted to compete directly with the SnakeLight. They all used inferior material and lower quality manufacturing standards. The compromise of quality in materials and craftsmanship of rip-off products results in poor performance and short product life. These rip-off, low-cost companies are often sued successfully for design and utility patent infringements, costing the manufacturer far more in the long run than if they had tried to innovate in the first place.

Revolutionary vs. Evolutionary Product Development

Upper Right products can be revolutionary new products or evolutionary changes to an existing product line. Revolutionary products establish a new market or solution within a market. Evolutionary products typically begin in the Upper Right and remain there as new useful, usable, or desirable innovations address the dynamic SET trends. They require injections of new value to maintain the consumer's connection to the product. Revolutionary products enter in the Upper Right and remain there only by becoming evolutionary products that change with the SET Factors.

Figure 2.11a shows the perceived innovation of a product in a market and how a company introduces revolutionary changes to maintain the perception of cutting edge innovation and capture new portions of the market. As an example in the figure, Chrysler

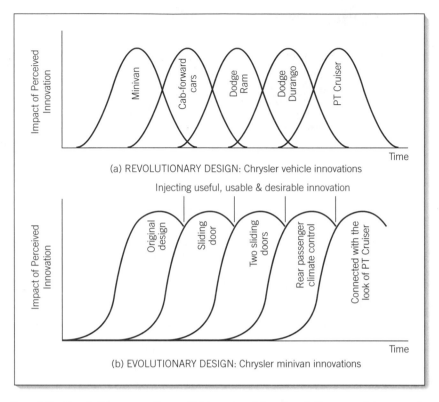

Figure 2.11 Revolutionary new Upper Right product (a) and evolutionary maintenance of an Upper Right product (b).

introduced innovations in their vehicles first with the minivan, then cab-forward design, then the Dodge Ram, next the Dodge Durango, and then the PT Cruiser. To keep the product in the Upper Right, new models must add innovations that meet the needs, wants, and desires of the market. Figure 2.11b shows how these injections of innovation keep the product line at its peek in the Upper Right. For this example, within the Chrysler minivan, innovation progressed through the introduction of a sliding door on one side, a sliding door on both sides, rear passenger climate control, and then consistent styling to capture the family look of the PT cruiser. Each of these innovations kept the company ahead of the competition and in the Upper Right.

The goal, then, is to become and remain a leader in the Upper Right by introducing revolutionary new products or evolutionary changes to existing products. To do so, the product must add significant value over the competition. Understanding value, not just trying to copy successful examples in the market, is critical to the success of the Move and is the focus of the next chapter.

Summary Points

- ❏ Throughout history, breakthrough products have succeeded by merging style and technology.

- ❏ Breakthrough products are found in the Upper Right of a Positioning Map indicating high style, high technology, and high value.

- ❏ Breakthrough products in the Upper Right maximize lifestyle impact, features, and ergonomics.

- ❏ Upper Right products lead or create new markets.

- ❏ Both evolutionary and revolutionary Upper Right products demand constant innovation.

References

1. Marcus, A., and H. Segal, *Technology in America: A Brief History*, HBJ College & School Div. Florence, KY, 1999

2. Porter, G., *The Rise of Big Business: 1860–1920*, Harlan Davidson, Arlington Heights, IL, 1992.

3. Norman, D.A., *The Design of Everyday Things*, Currency/Doubleday, New York, 1990.

4. Loewy, R., *Industrial Design*, The Overlook Press, Woodstock, NY, 1979.

5. Moore, G., *Crossing the Chasm*, Harper Perennial, New York, 1999.

Chapter Three

The Upper Right: The Value Quadrant

Breakthrough products are driven by a complex combination of value attributes that connect with people's lifestyles. This chapter examines the seven attributes of value and introduces a Value Opportunity Analysis process. We then apply this process to the case studies introduced in Chapter 1. Every product development team must conduct a Value Opportunity Analysis, which evaluates the current state of products in the market and projects areas where the new product requires significant improvement. This is an essential step in any new product program. Failure to thoroughly and thoughtfully complete this phase will have a negative impact down the line. The goal is to create a baseline reference for determining directions for research and subsequent concept develop-ment that brings clarity to the Fuzzy Front End of the product development process.

The Sheer Cliff of Value—The Third Dimension

As you look through the Positioning Map diagrams shown in Chapter 2, note how the Upper Right is separated from the rest of the quadrants. The reason is not just to highlight the importance of this quadrant. As mentioned in the previous chapter, the Upper Right has a third dimension, as shown in Figure 2.2 (repeated here as Figure 3.1). Unfortunately, it is not as simple as just putting a technologist and stylist together to Move to the Upper Right. Products in the Upper Right are there because they add value to a product; we illustrate this in the 2D Map by separating out the Upper Right quadrant. Adding value is not a trivial process—it requires a strategic commitment from the company to a user-centered iNPD (integrated New Product Development) process.

Figure 3.1 illustrates our theory that the third dimension, value, only comes into play in the Upper Right. Chapter 2 showed that products in the other quadrants, especially the Upper Left and Lower Right, do provide some value by addressing either image or features. The Upper Right products, however, maximize image, features, and ergonomics, targeting a *significant* level of value that meets the needs, wants, and desires of consumers without sacrificing usefulness, usability, or desirability. Thus, products that fall in the other quadrants are on a different, lower level of value. The shift to the Upper Right is a dimensional change that is not gradual; rather it is abrupt and significant. In many ways it represents a sheer cliff, which we call the "Sheer Cliff of Value." Ascending this cliff requires a strategic approach to ascend that begins with commitment and planning and

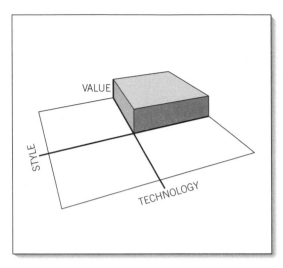

Figure 3.1 The three-dimensional Positioning Map showing the Upper Right Value quadrant.

ends with a user-centered integrated approach to product development. As discussed in Chapter 1, the product development process is akin to rock climbing. To create products in the Upper Right, you must climb the Sheer Cliff of Value.

In this chapter, we discuss customer-based value and show you how to use the concept of *Value Opportunity* to clarify a Product Opportunity Gap. Chapters 4 and 5 will then discuss the corporate strategy for committing to this process first by relating value to the corporate and product brand strategy and then by introducing a value-oriented product development process. The remainder of this chapter is devoted to understanding what value means in developing products for the Upper Right.

The Shift in the Concept of Value in Products and Services

■ Value in its true sense is lifestyle-driven, not cost-driven.

During the period of mass marketing, value was seen as the services or features a product provided for the price it cost. Good value was based on the lowest cost with the greatest number of features. The goal was to keep cost low, profits moderate, and sell in mass quantities. Products in the Lower Left are still driven by how many features can be delivered for the lowest cost. They are often sold in discount stores like Wal-mart and K-mart. Value in its true sense, however, is lifestyle-driven, not cost-driven. According to Webster's Dictionary,[1] value is the relative worth, utility, or importance of one item versus another; the "degree of excellence"; or something "intrinsically valuable or desirable." Relative worth does not mean cost, but rather the quality that causes something to be perceived as excellent. From the perspective of a product, the key terms are *utility* (namely, usefulness and usability), *desirability*, and overall perceived *excellence*. A product is considered *excellent* when it is ranked high in all appropriate aspects of value, when it delivers the qualities people are looking for. For the purpose of the development of Upper Right products, *we define value as the level of effect that people personally expect from products and services, represented through lifestyle impact, enabling features, and ergonomics, which together result in a useful, usable, and desirable product.*

So a product is valuable if it is useful, usable, and desirable. Though not directly recognized as a definition of value, these words were first applied to product development by Fitch, a design consulting firm headquartered in Columbus, OH, to describe aspects of a successful product. A useful product is one that satisfies a human need, is capable of being produced at reasonable cost, and has a clear market. A usable product is one that is easy to operate, easy to learn how to operate, and reliable. Finally, a desirable product is one whose technology, function, appearance, and market positioning make customers want to own it. *Products in the Upper Right are useful, usable, and desirable*, i.e., have value in that they are perceived as excellent in a number of factors.

▮ The cost to make a high-valued product increases less rapidly than the amount people will pay for it.

While cost is still an issue in the era of market segmentation, the more powerful factor is the consumer's need to connect their product purchases with their own personal values. When a product does connect, customers are willing to pay a higher price. People purchase products that enrich their experiences based on what is important to them, i.e., their values. The product must support that value base. The more the product does support that base, i.e., the higher its perceived value, the more people will pay for it. In the ideal case, and cases we have observed in practice, *the cost to make a highly valued product increases less rapidly than the amount people will pay for it!* In other words (as shown in Figure 3.2), the more value in a product the higher the price people are willing to pay, with the price increasing more rapidly than the cost. The profit is the price minus the cost, and thus the profit increases with higher value. The OXO GoodGrips adds so much value that consumers will pay several times that of the generic metal peeler. However the cost to produce it is not several times that of the generic counterpart, so the profit margin is significantly higher for the higher-valued product. This is also the case in SUVs. Although the SUV may cost twice that of the pickup truck whose platform it is built on, the cost to produce the SUV is not double that of the truck. The auto companies make significant profit on these high-value vehicles. (See Chapter 9 for a further discussion of SUVs.) This is the first way that Upper Right products lead to increased profit.

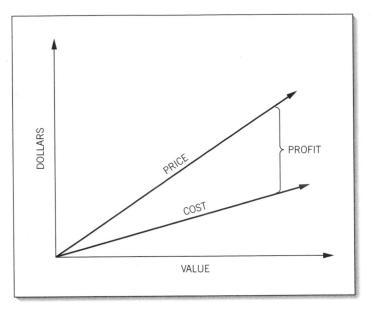

Figure 3.2 Price and Cost versus Value—Profit increases with added Value.

There are instances of high-value products that, due to manufacturing costs and the expenditure for emerging technologies, have a sales price that demands a lower profit margin compared to the cheap, poor-quality, competitor's product. But although proportionally they make less profit per item, they still make a large profit based on their increased sales price and resulting profit per item. This is the second way Upper Right products lead to increased profit. The Lower Left competitor or off-the-Map rip-off created by looking for the cheapest way to manufacture usually results in a poor quality product that may be churned out for a fraction of the Upper Right cost, but customers do not value their quality and will never pay a premium for this product.

The third way that Upper Right products lead to increased profit is by establishing brand, and thus customer, loyalty. Although not all Upper Right products will result in higher profit per item over competitors in the other quadrants, it is sometimes a strategic decision to produce an Upper Right product. This decision is made to establish a long-term relationship with the customer. Once an Upper Right product fulfills the expectations of a customer, he or she will be more likely to return to the brand for future purchases. As will be discussed in detail in Chapter 4, this happens because the product is the core of a company's brand strategy and the value of the Upper Right products help to establish strong brand equity. Strong brand equity means that customers are more likely to purchase your product over a competitor who has not established a core or appropriate brand identity. Not only will customers return to purchase the next generation of the product they enjoyed, but when they eventually seek out new products, or higher value products, they will return to the company with that Upper Right product. This was the strategy Volkswagen used in the introduction of the new Beetle. The features and style of the product met and generally surpassed the value expectation of their customer. Although VW did not charge an exorbitant amount for the vehicle, their goal was to move customers into future, higher priced lines, such as the Passat, with future purchases. The same was true for the Mazda Miata, the PT Cruiser, and the Ford Focus. It is the current approach of Apple with the iMac enticing customers to move up to the G4.

The fourth way an Upper Right product leads to increased profits is actually by charging *less* than the competition! An effective process of integrating engineering and design can lead to products with fewer parts and a more efficient process of manufacturing and use of finishes. These products end up costing less to produce than the previous solutions. Sharing that cost reduction with the consumer makes a strong statement for enabling market penetration. It also establishes a strong brand equity built on innovation and cost reduction. Although this enviable position is not easy to come by, the attention to detail that results from creating an Upper Right product can have surprising ramifications. Dell Computer developed a system for innovation in product customization and delivery that allowed them to acquire a strong share of the market yet keep their products at competitive prices.

Qualities and a Customer's Value System: Cost vs. Value

Consumers have come to expect a high degree of quality in the products they buy. Quality tools and programs such as TQM, QFD, 6σ, and ISO9000 have continued to raise the bar on the quality of manufacture and product performance. These attributes have become the expected baseline of entry into a market. What makes a product successful in the marketplace today, however, is determined by the qualities it represents and how these product qualities connect to personal values. Product qualities result from the combination of image, features, and ergonomics.

B. Joseph Pine and James Gilmore describe the emerging economy as the "experience economy," one where companies will succeed by producing or supporting experiences.[2] According to Pine and Gilmore, commodities lead to goods, which in turn lead to services that are now leading to experiences. These experiences are a new source of value for the consumer. What is striking in their research is that each progression has led to higher pricing of the product (Figure 3.3). Commodities provide the means to create goods that provide services that, together with goods, stage experiences. There is as much as an order of magnitude increase in price between goods and services and experiences. In other words,

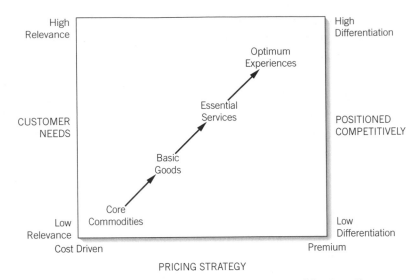

Figure 3.3 The progression of economic value from core commodities to optimum experiences (adapted from *The Experience Economy* by Pine and Gilmore[2]).

people will pay, and pay highly, for quality experiences. Figure 3.3 also shows how those companies that provide experiences differentiate themselves from the competition.

As stated earlier, it is no longer form following function. That has been replaced by *form and function fulfilling fantasy*. The shift from the industrial revolution to the information age is also the shift from the world of high work ethic and low fantasy expectations to the world of work as a means to provide for an ever-increasing array of fantasy expectations. Customers expect a product to enhance and fulfill their lifestyle, both physically and symbolically. In short, people want to fulfill their dreams. But what one group fantasizes about as an ideal product is different than another group.

In the 20th century, the entertainment industry has created a world culture of fantasy. Movies, television, books, vacations and products are all attempts to live up to customer dream expectations. Vacation resorts like Las Vegas and Disney World or cruises to natural settings bring fantasy into experience. People all over the world want to experience that level of fantasy. They want to extend that fantasy into every phase of their lives. Think about the influence of the *Star Wars* series, *The Matrix*, and *Star Trek* on products, fashion, and digital imaging. We now have products that look like three-dimensional cartoons (like Graves products for Target) and cartoons that look real (like the toys in *Toy Story*, where the Buzz Lightyear action figure toy is created from the same type of digital representation used to create the cartoon character in the movie). We can watch videos while driving, talk to anyone anywhere in the world, and we have on board navigation systems telling us where we are on the planet at any moment in time and where to go next to arrive at our destinations.

■ The Upper
Right repre-
sents the
products that
support the
new experience
economy.

In the Upper Right are those products that differentiate themselves from the competition by enhancing experiences. In other words, the Upper Right represents the products that support the new experience economy.

The argument for the experience economy is also presented by Rolf Jensen in *The Dream Society*.[3] Jensen argues that the information society will give way to the dream society (or we would say, the "fantasy" society). The future economy will be based on companies' ability to tell and sell stories. Our approach is to understand peoples' fantasies (or dreams) and to create products and services that create experiences closer to those dreams.

As consumers become more sophisticated in their ability to select products and their fantasy expectation increases, companies must learn to understand the new value structure of their core customers. Though aspects of this value system are deep-rooted, from religious and righteous beliefs, much of the system changes rapidly as people mature. Culture and trends shift faster and faster in more and more product markets. Thus successful companies must see the process as dynamic and constantly update their understanding of who their customer is. Connecting product qualities to the value system of customers is the new method for creating successful products.

Arguing for value-driven products over cost-driven products does not mean that price is never an issue. Pine and Gilmore state "no one repealed the laws of supply and demand. Companies that fail to provide consistently engaging experiences, overprice their experiences relative to the value received, or overbuild their capacity to stage them will of course see demand and/or pricing pressure"[2] (p. 24). In other words, people have a capacity that limits what they can afford. The point is that people will pay for value beyond what they pay for commodities. But the key is to understand what that limit is and what a given market looks for in a product, and then to add in the *right* features for the *appropriate* value.

We call this *psycheconometrics*. Psycheconometrics is the psychological spending profile of a niche market. It determines what people perceive is worth spending money on. The user experience is enhanced by the value people feel they are paying for.

Clearly the SnakeLight adds value and enhances experiences beyond the basic flashlight, Starbucks provides a richer experience than the local diner, the GoodGrips boosts the cooking experience beyond the generic peeler, and the Talkabout enhances communications beyond the walkie-talkie. People have paid a significant cost increase for the added value of these experiences. It has been argued that if there are two identical products on the market, then won't the one that costs less succeed? We respond that in practice there are no two identical value-oriented products on the market. Two different companies or divisions create differences in the products through brand equity, if not through differing features. Why do people shop at Tiffany's when they can buy similar jewelry at a lesser price in the local jewelry store? The answer is that

Tiffany's provides a shopping experience and a story for the customer to tell. The Tiffany's experience helps people feel better about themselves and people are willing to pay for that.

If, however, you are going to charge more than the competition, then the customer better perceive that the added value is worth the additional cost. If the product does not add value, then as a higher cost commodity it will fail. Manufacturing commodities is still an option, but it must be recognized that you are creating Lower Left products and price becomes the purchasing driver.

Value Opportunities

Value can be broken down into specific attributes that contribute to a product's usefulness, usability, and desirability, and connect a product's features to that value. Since products enable an *experience* for the user, the better the experience, the greater the value of the product to the consumer. In the ideal, the product fulfills a fantasy by facilitating a more enjoyable way of doing something. We have identified a set of opportunities to add value to a product, called *Value Opportunities* (VOs). These seven Value Opportunity classes—emotion, aesthetics, identity, ergonomics, impact, core technology, and quality—each contribute to the overall experience of the product and relate to the value characteristics of useful, usable, and desirable.

The VOs differentiate a product from the competition in the way that people's needs, wants, and desires influence the purchase and use of that product. The VO is a snapshot in time. What makes one set of VOs relevant today, due to the current analysis of SET Factors, may make the same VOs irrelevant tomorrow. Also, interpretation of the VOs is based on the SET Factors for a target market; what attributes one group finds important may be uninteresting to another.

The ergonomics, core technology, and quality Value Opportunities each address the satisfaction of the product during use; both immediately and long-term. The social and environmental impact, product identity, and aesthetics VOs each address lifestyle aspects of the consumer. The emotion VO connects most directly with the consumer's fantasy in using the product. Together these VOs define the third axis of the Upper Right, the value of the product to the consumer. In examining each of these in more detail, recognize that each affects a product differently. Although each is broken down into specific Value Opportunity attributes, this breakdown can be augmented as needed. For as cultural needs change, new value needs will emerge. This list, however, is fundamental and will generally support the analysis of value for most product classes, including all of the products discussed in this book.

The VOs are an extension of the breakdown of value in Chapter 2 as lifestyle impact, features, and ergonomics. Lifestyle impact represents the emotion, aesthetics, identity, and social impact Value Opportunities; features represent the core technology, quality, and environmental impact VOs. In the last chapter, we argued that all and only those Upper Right products are strong in all three categories. Although all Value Opportunities may not be targeted by an Upper Right product, at a minimum one relevant VO attribute that falls under each category must be targeted for a product to exist in the Upper Right. Of course, the more VO attributes that are targeted and maximized, the stronger the product's place in the Upper Right will be.

Emotion

The first Value Opportunity is *emotion*. All of the Value Opportunities support the product's ability to contribute to the user's experience, however emotion defines the essence of the experience; the emotion contribution defines that fantasy aspect of the product. For our purpose the emotion Value Opportunity is the *perceptual experience* of the consumer when using the product. Different fantasies distinguish different products. We break the attributes of emotion into:

- Sense of adventure: the product promotes excitement and exploration.
- Feel of independence: the product provides a sense of freedom from constraints.
- Sense of security: the product provides a feeling of safety and stability.
- Sensuality: the product provides a luxurious experience.
- Confidence: the product supports the user's self-assurance and promotes his or her motivation to use the product.
- Power: the product promotes authority, control, and a feeling of supremacy.

Think about the sensual feeling of sipping a cup of coffee at a Starbucks in Manhattan on a cool Fall day. Consider the feeling of confidence and security in picking small parts in a warehouse using the Crown Wave. Think about the sense of security and independence that families have when communicating with the Motorola Talkabout on the ski slopes in Tahoe. Products can utilize more than one emotional attribute toward value. This will be true for each Value Opportunity. Although some products succeed by focusing on key attributes, the more relevant attributes of each VO that can be targeted, the higher the likelihood that a product will add value to a target market. Each Upper Right product captures a range of VO attributes, as will be shown later in this chapter and in Chapters 8 and 9.

Aesthetics

Aesthetics, the second Value Opportunity, focuses on sensory perception. The five senses are all important attributes of this VO. Many products only focus on visual and tactile senses. However, stimulating as many senses as possible through the use of a product or environment builds a positive association of the product with its application. This provides an exciting opportunity to add value to a product if competitor's products lack this focus. The range of senses involved with aesthetics supports the emotion Value Opportunity, especially the sensuality attribute. The aesthetic attributes are:

❚ Visual: The visual form must relate shape, color and texture to the context of the product and the target market.

❚ Tactile: The physical interaction of the product, primarily focusing on the hand but also including any other physical contact between the product and user, must enhance the product experience.

❚ Auditory: The product must only emit the appropriate sounds and eliminate undesired sounds.

❚ Olfactory: The product must have an agreeable smell, providing appropriate aromas and eliminating undesirable odors.

❚ Gustatory: Products that are designed to be eaten, used as a utensil, or may otherwise be placed in the mouth (e.g., a child's toy) must have an optimum flavor or no flavor at all.

Product Identity

Products in the Upper Right make a statement about individuality and personality, expressing uniqueness, timeliness of style, and appropriateness in their environment. The identity of the product supports the emotion VOs and the consumer's fantasy in owning and using the product. The identity of the product also supports its brand identity (see Chapter 4). Three attributes of product identity are personality, point in time, and sense of place:

❚ Personality: The two main issues in a product personality are 1) the ability of a product to fit among yet differentiate itself from its direct competition, and 2) the connection that a product has to the rest of the products produced by that company.

■ In order for a
product to be
successful, it
has to capture
a point in time
and express it
in a clear, pow-
erful way.

■ Point in time: In order for a product to be successful, it has to capture a point in time and express it in a clear, powerful way. Point in time is a tricky combination of features and aesthetics.

■ Sense of place: Products must be designed to fit into the context of use.

Impact

A company has a number of ways to demonstrate that it can be a responsible manufacturer and respond to socially oriented issues. Social responsibility is connected with the customer's personal value system and, as discussed in Chapter 4, can often build brand loyalty. Charitable donations, safe work environments, and health- and family-oriented benefits all promote the corporate image. The company, however, can positively affect society through the product itself. Based on consumers' preference to buy products that benefit rather than hurt the environment or social groups, opportunities exist to add value to a product through social and environmental impact. Products can also have social impact by effecting changes in how people communicate and interact with each other. This Value Opportunity and its related social and environmental attributes are probably the least explored of all the VOs. Yet they continue to have a growing effect on product development.

■ Social: A product can have a variety of effects on the lifestyle of a target group, from improving the social well-being of the group to creating a new social setting (see sidebar).

■ Environmental: The effect of products on the environment is becoming an important issue in terms of consumer value. Design for the environment, or "green design," focuses on minimizing negative effects on the environment due to manufacturing, resource use of the product during operation, and recycling (see sidebar).

Ergonomics

The next Value Opportunity focuses on usability. Ergonomics refers to the dynamic movement of people and their interaction with both static and dynamic man-made products and environments. The terms *ergonomics*, *human factors*, and *interaction* are all related and will be discussed in Chapter 7. Ergonomics has both a short-term and long-term effect on the perception of a product. Consumers look for comfortable

Social Impact VO

Both social consciousness and social interaction provide opportunity for added value in a product. Three products highlighted in this book that have a strong effect on social well being are DynaVox's DynaMyte augmentative communicator, designed by Daedalus Excel, which enables people who can't speak to communicate (Chapter 8); the Baygen Freeplay Radio, which allows people in underdeveloped regions without electricity to use a radio to obtain news and health bulletins (Chapter 8), and the OXO GoodGrips, originally designed primarily for elders with arthritis. The GoodGrips, however, was designed and marketed for almost any individual to use. That objective is known as *Universal Design* (sometimes referred to as transgenerational design), an extension of the Americans with Disabilities Act (ADA). The ADA is usually discussed in terms of access to buildings and the ability to maneuver in public spaces. Designers like Pat Moore have crossed these bounds through the design of products and interfaces.[4,5] The goal of Universal Design is to make products useful and usable to the broadest range of users. The rule of thumb when employing a philosophy of Universal Design is that companies should never knowingly design a product that prevents a significant percentage of consumers from using it in normal operation of intended use. It is easier to design for broad use of a product if it is a priority in the early stages of a design. The reason OXO GoodGrips has been so successful is that it embodies the philosophy of Universal Design by clearly demonstrating that a product developed to respond to people who are physically challenged could work for everyone without stigmatizing anyone.

Other products may not target social conscientiousness directly, but still affect the interactions among people. Starbucks created a non-alcoholic way for people to meet and enjoy each other's company in a public setting. The Talkabout enables groups to stay in contact even when physically apart. The Crown Wave changed the attitude of the workers that use it; they now actually enjoy work that used to be stressful, tedious, and dangerous. And they are now in a better position to interact with, rather than avoid, customers in a warehouse environment. Even Harley-Davidson created an entire new subculture of social interaction. While the Harley was once associated with a criminal fringe lifestyle, the company has refocused its brand and extended its product line. Today white collar workers escape the 9–9, Monday–Friday grind and transform themselves on weekends by joining Harley Clubs that ride in full Harley attire. The Harley motorcycle, the core product, and all of its accessories create an environment that fosters a sense of comradery and escapism. (See the case study in Chapter 4.)

fit and intuitively simple controls in a new product, but a product must also hold up over time in comfort, consistency and flexibility in use. The ability of a person to interact with a product with ease, safety, and comfort contributes greatly to its overall value. These three attributes of ergonomics are also the attributes of the Value Opportunity:

▮ Ease of use: A product must be easy to use from both a physical and cognitive perspective. A product should function within the natural motion of the human body. The ergonomics of the size and shape of components that a person interacts with should be logically organized and easy to identify, reach, grasp, and manipulate.

Environmental Impact VO

Design for the environment, or "green design," presents an opportunity to improve product value with very broad societal implications. Black & Decker is beginning to make their products recyclable. Herman Miller, in chairs designed by Tom Newhouse, now lists materials in the recycling information on the bottom of the chair. Companies like Ford are openly struggling with the balance between their environmental concerns and the performance of their vehicles. Many companies in the U.S. lag behind Europe in terms of concern for environmental impact. Consumer attitude and government regulations, however, are both leaning toward more stringent requirements (government) and expectations (consumer) for environmental friendliness. This Value Opportunity, still ignored by many companies, provides another opportunity for differentiation from the competition.

In Europe, legislation towards mandatory take-back of durable goods at the end of their lifecycle requires companies to consider issues of disassembly and disposability. At the same time legislation that durable goods must be built with a specific recycled content (around 85% with an increase up to 95% scheduled) focuses the design of products with great reference to the environment. In the U.S., no such legislation exists. Thus use of recycled components and materials, and recyclable components and materials, are limited. In the U.S., however, autos do have a reasonably high (75%) use of recycled materials by weight, with steel and aluminum in particular being processed from scrap. Nonetheless, this decision in the U.S. is purely cost driven; it is cheaper for companies to use recycled steel rather than use virgin steel. The opportunity is here for more focus on green design and the related consumer awareness of the effort.

As Europe moves toward a higher percentage of recycled components in durable goods, they are exploring the idea of selling a service rather than a product. For example, car companies are considering primarily leasing or even just loaning cars that are mostly refurbished. Instead of trying to market a car as new that is mostly filled with re-built parts, they would provide the car as a service just as copier companies do with their machines. Rent, repair, and Web access are all means to make money off the service of the vehicle, and the problem of take-back disappears.

Bosch, an international company, makes automotive equipment, navigation systems, home appliances, industrial equipment, and power tools. The company is proud of its environmental approach to the design of its products. Their design strategy takes into account aspects of the environment such as choice of material, disassembly sequences, and separation of material in their products. One aspect of their business is the sale of refurbished power tools. Many customers like to trade up to the newest models introduced. Bosch will take back the older tools and either recycle them (since they are designed for disassembly) or resell them after refurbishment. It turns out that many tools have only been used for a short time. Those are the tools best suited for resale. Bosch has introduced a chip into the tool that records parameters indicating how many times a tool has been used and under what conditions. By processing that information, they can refurbish tools and sell them for additional profit, rather than dispose of them.

■ Safety: A product must be safe to use. Moving parts should be covered, sharp corners eliminated, and internal components shielded from users.

■ Comfort: Along with ease of use and safety, a product should be comfortable to use and not create undo physical or mental stress during use.

Core Technology

As aesthetics and personality target the style aspects of the Positioning Map, the core technology and quality Value Opportunities target the technology aspects. Technology alone is not enough, but technology is essential. It must enable a product to function properly and perform to expectations, and it must work consistently and reliably. People may want more than just technology, but they expect technologies to evolve at a high rate with a constant increase in functions that are better and more consistent.

- Enabling: Core technology must be appropriately advanced to provide sufficient features. Core technology may be emerging high technology or well-manufactured traditional technology, as long as it meets customer expectations in performance.

- Reliable: Consumers expect technology in products to work consistently and at high level of performance over time.

Quality

▌ Products should be perceived to be of high quality when purchased and they should meet those expectations over a long period of time.

The final Value Opportunity is quality: the precision and accuracy of manufacturing methods, material composition, and methods of attachment. Although related to technology, the focus here is on the manufacturing of the product itself—not the process, but the expectation of the process. Products should be perceived to be of high quality when purchased and they should meet that expectation over a long period of time. This value is measured by the sound a door of a car makes, the seams connecting two plastic parts of the computer monitor, or the way the rubber sleeve attaches to the head and tail of the SnakeLight. Although not an easy task, manufacturing technologies and assembly methods have progressed to the point that this goal is obtainable. A major argument of this book is that by spending the time up front to create a product that meets customer expectations, the downstream manufacturing detailing becomes more straightforward. By including manufacturing in discussions early in the process, potentially costly defects can be caught and dealt with early before economic investments in molds and assembly. The quality VO is broken down into two attributes:

- Craftsmanship—fit and finish: The product should be made with sufficient tolerances to meet performance expectations.

- Durability—performance over time: The craftsmanship must hold up over the expected life of the product.

Value Opportunity Charts and Analysis

We use the Value Opportunities to evaluate how products successfully Move to the Upper Right. Figure 3.4 shows a Value Opportunity Chart. The chart lists each Value Opportunity class and its attributes in a column. The values are measured in a qualitative range and are expressed as low, medium, and high for each attribute. If a product did not meet (or target) any level of that attribute, no line is drawn. (There is an assumption that if there was any intent to focus on an attribute, then there would be at least a low measure of success; if not, then the blank line indicates failure.)

Below the chart are listed *profit impact* (across the company), *brand impact* (on company brand), and *extendable*. Although not VOs, they are included in the chart because they indicate the overall success of the product. A product in the Upper Right produces profit

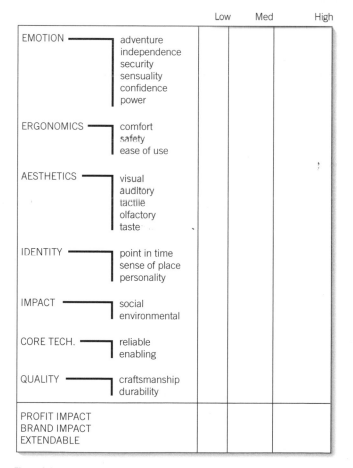

Figure 3.4 Value Opportunity Chart.

in a number of ways. The argument is that products may cost more but people will pay for value. Companies can increase market share and gain stockholder and investor confidence. They can generate sales that are greater than other products in the company or significantly add to the existing product lines. They can increase the equity of a brand and/or broaden the equity by moving into new desirable markets. Companies like Mercedes have always enjoyed greater profit margins. Sam Farber, founder of OXO, has stated that one of the major challenges a company has to meet is to determine the potential overall profit of a product that will cost more to produce and will need to be priced higher than the competition. It takes the combined insight of the team and management with the appropriate feedback from customers to make this decision. It has been said that only one company can be the cheapest; the rest have to compete using design. We would add that they must compete using integrated design that produces value.

People we have interviewed from various industries note that companies often make a "safe" decision and let spreadsheets and cost reduction become the primary ways to increase profit. While these approaches are sound, they can actually backfire and have a short-term payoff with a long-term negative effect. As price stays the same and profit is generated through reduction in parts, cost, labor, and steps in manufacturing, companies can start to lose the ability to be innovative. They lose sight of the competition and emerging trends. Companies have to learn to balance innovation risk management with conservatively tested measures of cost controls, carryover, and parts reduction. Developing a new product without significant innovation is a bigger long-term gamble than investing in an innovative product that brings new product attributes to the marketplace. Creating a stable platform and then using mass customization to create the proper style and feature interface is one method to accomplish this. Swatch Watch, Nokia, and VW have been successful with this approach. Establishing a consistent approach to product development and then applying it creatively in different products is another. OXO, Polaroid, and Tupperware have been successful developing new products with this technique.

■ A strong product and corporate brand means a higher likelihood of repeat business to the company and a higher price that the product commands.

Having maximized their Value Opportunities, products in the Upper Right have a strong brand identity and can have an even greater impact on the corporate brand. As stated earlier and discussed in more detail in Chapter 4, although there are many important factors that form the brand strategy of a company, the product or service must be core to the process. Upper Right products and services have a strong brand impact at the corporate level, while products in the other quadrants tend to either be nondescript (Lower Left quadrant) or have heavily biased brand impact from aesthetics (Upper Left quadrant) or technology (Lower Right quadrant). A strong product and corporate brand means a higher likelihood of repeat business to the company and a higher price that the product commands.

Products in the Upper Right often lead to expansions into other versions of the same product or other product lines. The GoodGrips handle is now used in over 350 products including pizza cutters, knives, and gardening tools. Starbucks has expanded in number of store locations, but also environments where their coffee is sold and product types (such as ice cream) that focus on coffee. Lack of extendability will not prevent a product from Moving to the Upper Right, but the Value Opportunity attributes are generally so strong that such extensions are natural.

■ Understanding how previous products failed, when focusing on the target market, allows you to discover how much better your product is—or should be.

The chart of a successful product is useful in trying to understand what Value Opportunity attributes the product team targeted and how well the product turned out. However, the chart is most useful as a comparison against competitive products. In the Value Opportunity Analysis (VOA), one chart indicates a pervious product or solution to a task, while the other represents the product of focus. In many ways, this analysis is easier than when considering a product alone. Understanding how previous products failed, *when focusing on the target market*, allows you to discover how much better your product is—or should be.

We now apply a Value Opportunity Analysis to the GoodGrips, Talkabout, Wave, and Starbucks.

VOA of OXO GoodGrips

First consider a Value Opportunity Analysis of GoodGrips versus the generic metal vegetable peeler (Figure 3.5). From a Value Opportunity perspective, the generic peeler ranks low in the emotions of independence and confidence, and meets a low level of each ergonomic attribute. The main things going for it are that it lasts forever (durable) and has reasonably good reliability and craftsmanship. Due to its cheap price, there is very little profit per item. Companies that make the generic peeler make money through high sales volume. Although the peeler has been around for over 100 years, its generic form is made by many nondescript companies and it has not led to any further product lines.

The GoodGrips excels in its ability to meet strong emotion VOs in independence, confidence, and even security, especially for the original target market of elderly or arthritic users. The product also excels in all aspects of ergonomics, identity, core technology, and quality. The GoodGrips has very strong social impact which stems from the success of the handle that enables people to hold the product with a greater sense of security. Finally, an additional part of its success is the result of the highly refined visual and tactile aesthetics. A comparison of the VO Chart for the GoodGrips and the generic peeler explains how OXO is able to charge several times the cost of a generic peeler with great success.

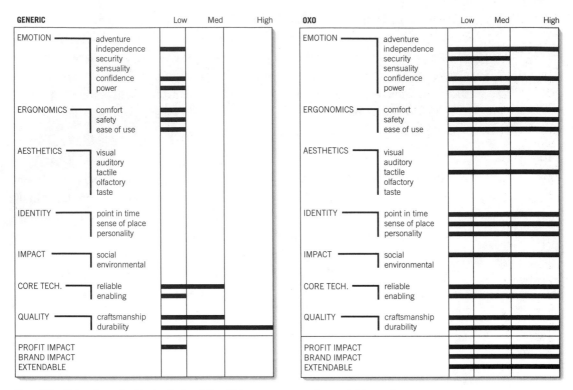

Figure 3.5 Value Opportunity Analysis of GoodGrips versus generic vegetable peeler.

While it is not clear what the per item profit is, it is clear why this product has become the first of a line of 350 and counting (See Figure 3.6). The sales figures put OXO in the black in the first year and the overall value and lines of the company have continued to grow during the last decade. Every company that produces products for the kitchen has been forced to play catch up. Instead of taking a cost reduction approach, OXO has chosen to create one new innovative product after another. The recent additions include a salad spinner that can be used with one hand and a line of hand tools that are well balanced, have simple and clean forms, and, of course, are more comfortable to grip. The product itself is core to the company's brand, with the featured black Santoprene handle becoming a part of the corporate name, "OXO GoodGrips."

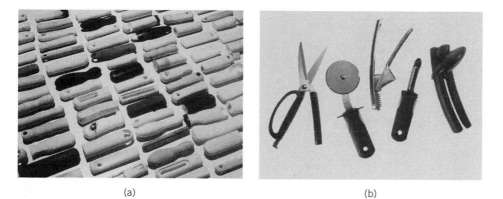

Figure 3.6 Studies for original handle (a) and extension of GoodGrips line shown through selection of handles and products (b). (Reprinted with permission of Smart Design.)

VOA of Motorola Talkabout

Next, consider a Value Opportunity Analysis of the Motorola Talkabout versus both the previous walkie-talkie and Motorola's own professional wireless communications products (Figure 3.7). The generic walkie-talkie did allow people to communicate while apart (giving medium adventure, independence, and security VOs) and they were reasonably easy to use. Their poor aesthetics and larger size, audible static with almost any interference, and lack of personality, however, limited their overall appeal and hampered their use. The poor manufacturing quality and limited styling and interface had no effect on the manufacturing companies' brands. The profit per item of the walkie-talkies was low and there was very little else you could do with them.

The Motorola professional products have strong VOs in the independence, confidence, security, and power emotions—they work well and consistently and people know that they do. They have very strong core technology and quality VOs and a strong auditory aesthetic. The previous professional products were reasonably comfortable and easy to use; they had a strong identity, though they did not adapt to any particular trend. Their use in mission-critical situations had strong social impact. Motorola certainly had high profit per item for their professional product. Their products had a strong brand impact, but areas of expansion for those products had reached a plateau. The team, however, needed to take advantage of the company's brand equity and technological expertise in developing the new consumer product.

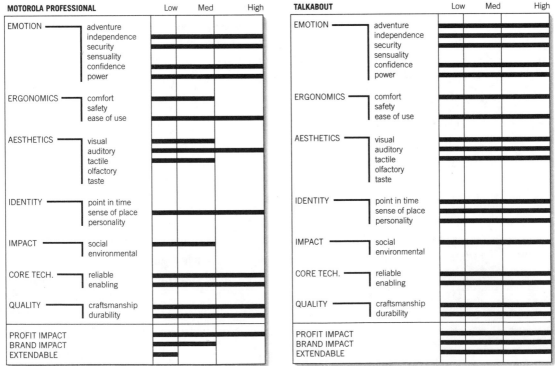

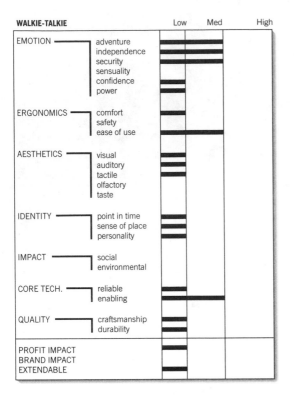

Figure 3.7 Value Opportunity Analysis of Talkabout versus walkie-talkie and Motorola professional two-way radio equipment.

The Talkabout maintained the perceived technology VOs (at least for the needs of the target market), but went after the identity, appropriate aesthetics, ergonomics, and emotion VOs. The product clearly went beyond the generic walkie-talkie in every value facet, and went beyond previous Motorola products by appropriately targeting the needs of the consumer market. Bruce Claxton, design director of the Talkabout project, stated that the design awards that Motorola received resulted in advertising worth several million dollars to the company. The value of this Upper Right product is reflected in the fact that the Talkabout has been awarded one of 12 Gold Design of the Decade Awards from the Industrial Designers Society of America (IDSA) and sponsored by *BusinessWeek*. It introduced Motorola two-way communication products to an entirely new consumer market and is now core to Motorola's brand identity. Today, millions of units are sold in a business that did not exist three years ago. The success of the product has produced line extensions that have built on the Talkabout's success. Sales of this product set a record for the consumer walkie-talkie industry and continue to climb. Motorola products now have primary shelf space in a greater range of stores. Departments in stores that carry the Talkabout promote Motorola quality and innovation in new ways. Motorola could have canceled this project as too risky for a company that has made its name in the professional sector. This one decision has opened up an unlimited range of new product opportunities and broadened the brand equity of the company.

VOA of Crown Wave

We turn now to a Value Opportunity Analysis of the Wave versus the previous solution: a rolling ladder (Figure 3.8). Although it is obvious that a higher-priced product would be more attractive than a simple ladder to perform a task, it took an analysis of what value and needs the potential (and resulting) product would fulfill versus a ladder to justify the development of the product. Although the developers did not directly use our method, the VOA is enlightening. The rolling ladder is cheap and lasts a long time, but there is no pleasure or security in using it. There had been several deaths from people using it in small parts pick environments. It allows a mundane task to be accomplished in a mundane and tedious way. Like the generic vegetable peeler, many nondescript ladder manufacturing companies make money through high volume versus high profit per item. And there is reasonable expandability from different sizes and features (such as extensions and trays).

The Wave creates a series of value-added attributes. It allows one person to work effectively, efficiently, and safely. It decreases worker mental and physical repetitive

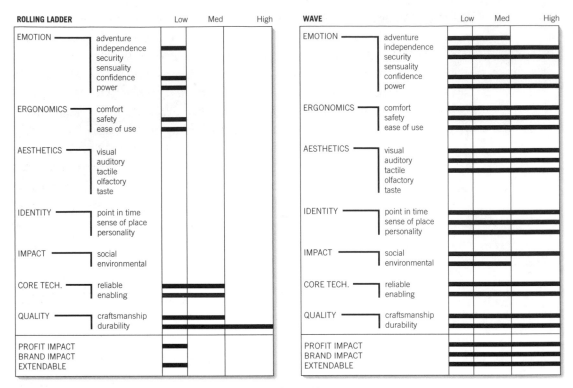

Figure 3.8 Value Opportunity Analysis of Wave versus rolling ladder.

stress and increases worker safety. It is easy to learn and fun to operate, increasing worker satisfaction and enjoyment on the job. In terms of VOs, the Wave promotes high independence, confidence, and adventure, with very high ergonomics, appropriate aesthetics, and a strong product identity. Although the product costs more, the technology is reliable, of high quality, and reduces injury. The product provides a new profit area for Crown. The new product brand strategy gives the parent company an identity that takes their products out of the warehouse and puts them into consumer environments, broadening the brand equity. This new area can be the beginning of an entire new product line for the company as they explore small part picking and retail store applications.

VOA of Starbucks

Finally, we turn to a Value Opportunity Analysis of Starbucks (Figure 3.9). Recall the SET Factors in Seattle and the target market of professionals with disposable income. The previous focal points for coffee and conversation were coffee shops (our choice of comparison), diners, and doughnut shops. The typical coffee shop had reasonably tasty and reliable food and a pleasant but often dated and nondescript atmosphere. Patrons gathered to socialize and eat, but didn't consider it a leisurely environment, particularly inviting, or the place to "be seen." Instead there was a level of independence with a focus on food, and often a sense of adventure to find the really distinct environment with the great specialties instead of the usual, mediocre fare. Coffee shops are reasonably profitable but typically lack any brand equity or ability to expand.

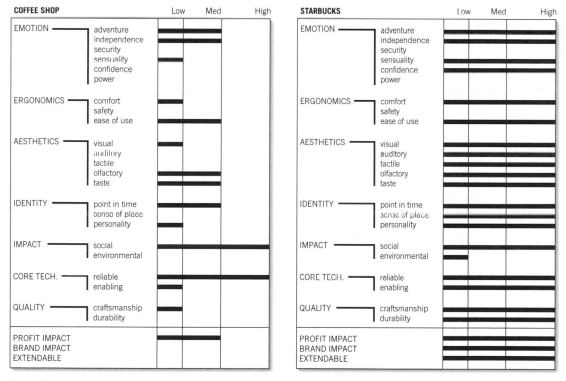

Figure 3.9   Value Opportunity Analysis of Starbucks versus a coffee shop.

Diners and coffee shops are as American as the apple pie they serve. However, as the SET trends shifted, the environment, atmosphere, and perceived quality of food and coffee diminished. Diners gave way to fast food chains that created increased speed and established a threshold of consistent value at low prices. As the cycle continued, fast food lost its perceived value and there was an opportunity for Starbucks to create a new solution that promoted coffee first and food second. Their standard was higher and so was the cost. The environment was changed to create an appropriate atmosphere for purchasing and experiencing a higher quality coffee than could be purchased at a fast food chain or at the few remaining diners. Starbucks saw the POG. They created the new experience for people, allowing them to take a few minutes out of their day to relax and enjoy the company of others or to read a good book.

Starbucks is a stark contrast to fast food and a shift from the classic diner. Here the emotion, ergonomics, *all* aesthetics, complete identity, core technology, and quality VOs are at a maximum. Their ability to capitalize on all Value Opportunities is an indication of their success. They even have strong impact VOs, with their creation of a social gathering place and their concern for the environment through recycled paper goods. The result is that Starbucks has high profit margin on their products (as of today, we pay between $2.95 and $4.85 for coffee and milk under such names as latte, cappuccino, and double espresso). Starbucks has clearly demonstrated how value and strong identity enabled their expansion into 2,500 stores in 13 countries, with products available in airports, turnpike rest stops, and supermarkets.

The Time and Place for Value Opportunities

Just maximizing the Value Opportunities isn't enough to guarantee an Upper Right product. There are two critical issues that must be considered. The first is that mechanically finding ways to just increase the VO attributes, as you perceive them, is doomed to failure. The VOs must be maximized based on the product end user's perception of value. Further, the VOs must work in concert to create a complete product in the Gestalt sense, not a set of features that each work in their own independent way to achieve an aspect of an experience. To enable a team to succeed in reaching a complete design requires a vision, and usually a visionary. There is often a core team or even an individual with the vision of what the product should be, not in the detailed sense but in the POG sense. In large companies, the visionary is often not part of the core team, but rather a manager in the position to fund and protect the core team.

Upper Right products don't just satisfy POGs, rather they satisfy the vision of how the POG affects society and the SET Factors.

The second critical issue is to recognize that VOs are a representation of the SET Factors, at a given point in time. SET Factors are dynamic. If the company does not keep a sense of the pulse of change in the target market as the SET Factors and VOs change, an Upper Right product today can easily become a Lower Left product tomorrow when a competitor recognizes the new SET Factors and creates a product to meet a more current POG.

VOs and Product Goals

Figure 3.10 shows specific goals for each VO attribute for the Wave. The VOA does not generically apply to the design of all products. Instead it provides the basis for developing product-specific goals. Each VO attribute needs to be interpreted within the context of the SET Factors and specific POG for a given market and user type. It would be easy to just claim that a new product will maximize all of the VO attributes. To be useful, the team must determine how the product will serve to maximize each relevant VO.

The Upper Right for Industrial Products

What is striking today is that Upper Right products that enhance experiences or fulfill dreams are emerging in all types of industries. Crown's Wave is one example of a product category that previously had no understanding of the need for style and value. The Marathon carpet cleaner in Chapter 8 is another. Electronic test equipment has found the value in adding style to an otherwise banal industry. Fluke's consistent yellow and gray styling, clear brand identity, and ergonomic design separates their product from the pack.

Even traditional commodity manufacturers are making the Move to the Upper Right. VistaLab Technologies manufactures pipettes used in various laboratory applications including sample preparation, reagent addition, and other precision liquid handling tasks (see sidebar). The company has been working closely with a major design firm to design ergonomic, styled products. The company recognizes that even in the conservative laboratory supply industry, adding value through style and ergonomics will add to the experience of using their product and separate them from the competition. By improving the balance and feel of a common laboratory tool, technicians can feel better about their work and themselves.

WAVE

EMOTION
- adventure – Continuation of the quality of experience expected of personal products (car, bike, motorcycle)
- independence – Freedom to move effortlessly through and up and down within work environment
- security – Feeling of safety and stability
- sensuality – N.A.
- confidence – Feeling of certainty to perform required tasks
- power – Ability to have control over one's work environment

ERGONOMICS
- comfort – Satisfying and enjoyable experience while using product in standing position when lifting and reaching; controls must be comfortable to hold
- safety – Operator must be securely enclosed in vehicle particularly when in lift position; product must not pose significant threat to others in warehouse/retail environment
- ease of use – Ingress and egress of vehicle must be accomplished through a few simple movements; operator controls must be easy to learn and easy to react to; vehicle must be easy to maneuver

AESTHETICS
- visual – Product should have appropriate look for lightweight lift vehicle that may be in retail space
- auditory – Product must be quiet when in operation and use sounds effectively for warning and emergency situations
- tactile – Interactive surfaces must have appropriate material and finish to promote effective use
- olfactory – N.A.
- taste – N.A.

IDENTITY
- point in time – Must establish a new visual aesthetic for the area of light duty lift assist products
- sense of place – Design must be appropriate to retail environments
- personality – Serious but fun and give the appearance of being light and nimble; must be a departure from the look of Crown's heavy lift equipment

IMPACT
- social – Should have a positive impact on the quality of worker experience and retention and be consistent with OSHA standards
- environmental – Must be produced with the environmental standards for other Crown equipment

CORE TECH.
- reliable – Product must perform consistently and be easy to service and repair.
- enabling – Product technology must fulfill claims of product by safely and smoothly moving and lifting operator to perform tasks

QUALITY
- craftsmanship – Must maintain the integrity of all Crown products, not being seen as cheaper but rather lighter
- durability – Must be able to maintain function and appearance appropriate in retail environment throughout life of the product

PROFIT IMPACT – Create new profit stream for Crown

BRAND IMPACT – Create a new brand identity that places product identity over company

EXTENDABLE – Capable of generating a variety of new off shoots from original design

Figure 3.10 Value Opportunity Goals for Crown Wave.

VistaLab Designs the First Ergonomic Pipette

For over 35 years, VistaLab Technologies has made pipettes and other liquid-handling products. Their original pipette is a 30-year-old product sold to the laboratory market, which is very conservative in buying habits. Many lab technicians were trained on the VistaLab product and they are still using it many years later (see Figure 3.11). The current market is competitive and cost-driven. VistaLab's original product is still made from metal while the competitors use plastic and tend to have much lower production costs.

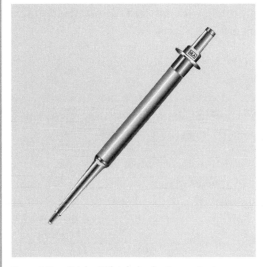

Figure 3.11 Original VistaLab pipette product. (Reprinted with permission of VistaLab Technologies.)

The VistaLab Product Development Team, led by Vice President of Product Development Jeff Calhoun, decided that instead of catching up to the competition, they needed to leapfrog the competition and "do something very different." The problem with most pipettes is that they are not ergonomic because the piston is in line with the pipette tip. When the thumb pushes down, its angle is unnatural and can be hard to control. The other extreme is fully electronic equipment where the technician controls the liquid distribution electronically, rather than with finger pressure. The design team discovered that lab technicians like to control and feel the liquid moving in and out of the tip themselves by pushing the piston. VistaLab rethought the process and decided to create an ergonomic pipette with a shape that was determined by the human anatomy, not design convenience. They also chose to use electronics to assist the technician in setting the adjustable volume rather than over-automate the liquid handling process.

The design team hired Frogdesign from New York (how else to leap*frog* the competition?) and worked closely with the firm to create the ergonomic pipette shown in Figure 3.12. The goal was a radical departure from the standard design, capturing a creature-like and emotional form that was easy to approach. The team performed a detailed ergonomic study (a task analysis discussed in Chapter 7) of the mechanics of using a pipette. They combined primary research with VistaLab's cumulative and intimate knowledge of the customer to create this Upper Right design. The company is clearly making a statement of how style and ergonomics can merge with technology to create a differentiating, high-value product. In 2001, the product won the Gold Industrial Design Excellence Award for the industrial and scientific equipment area by the IDSA and sponsored by *BusinessWeek*.

Figure 3.12 VistaLab's new ergonomic pipette. (Reprinted with permission of Frogdesign and VistaLab Technologies.)

Dave Smith, leader of the design of the Wave, comments, "When you design a product you don't change who the customer is. When you get up in the morning you use your electric razor and clean yourself by dispensing soap from the pump container. You go downstairs and get ice and water from the door in your refrigerator. You get in your car and insert your key and away you go." All of these products are designed to meet your value needs, wants, and desires.

Smith then says, "You get to work and all of a sudden you are supposed to change? It doesn't work that way. You have a basic expectation of product features and form. You evaluate your environment based on cumulative experiences."

So if you are a manufacturer of clamps or bolts, why should your customer have to sacrifice what is expected in their own personal purchases? Think about an ergonomic clamp or bolt, much like VistaLab has considered an ergonomic pipette. Creating such an Upper Right product could significantly differentiate you from your competition and raise the level of expectation of the customer who needs to assemble your product.

In addition to enriching the work experience on the assembly line, consumers are now demanding an aesthetic for the interior of products. The trend began with the iMac, where translucent exteriors means that the aesthetics of the interior of the product now matters. End users now see each and every component so the style of their assembly becomes critical to the overall success of the product.

The same is true in other products previously considered impervious to the issues of style. Engine compartments in cars must now capture the theme of the vehicle, even though the customer is likely to open the hood for the first and last time in the showroom.

From Original Equipment Manufacturer (OEM) parts to complete products, high value products are the leaders today. This and the previous chapter explained the characteristics that make a product Move to the Upper Right. The book now turns to a process of how to get there—strategic commitment, brand management, and a well developed user-centered iNPD process.

Summary Points

❏ Value is no longer the most features for the lowest cost. For breakthrough products, value is lifestyle-driven, addressing the qualities of a product that make it useful, usable, and desirable.

❏ Breakthrough products fulfill a fantasy by facilitating a more enjoyable way of doing something.

- There are seven basic Value Opportunities to differentiate a product and contribute to the overall experience of use: emotion, aesthetics, identity, ergonomics, impact, core technology, and quality.
- VOs are relevant at a point in time and within the context of a product opportunity. They provide the basis for developing product-specific goals to meet the needs at that time.
- All industrial products are candidates for the Upper Right by addressing ergonomics and lifestyle effects in conjunction with technology features.

References

1. *Webster's New Collegiate Dictionary*, G. & C. Merriam Company, Springfield, MA, 1973.

2. Pine, B.J., II, and J.H. Gilmore, *The Experience Economy*, Harvard Business School Press, Boston, 1999.

3. Jensen, R., *The Dream Society*, McGraw Hill, New York, 1999.

4. Pirkl, J., *Transgenerational Design: Products for an Aging Population*, Van Nostrand Reinhold, New York 1994

5. Covington, G., and B. Hanna, *Access by Design*, Van Nostrand Reinhold, New York, 1997.

Chapter Four

The Core of a Successful Brand Strategy: Breakthrough Products and Services

At the core of any brand strategy is the successful experience of using a product or service. Identity, advertising, and distribution cannot correct the failure of a product to perform as expected. Thus, as discussed in this chapter, all members of product development teams must understand and participate in brand development. Consumers purchase breakthrough products to support their lifestyle values. They also identify with companies that represent values compatible with their own. Developing successful product brand begins with understanding your customers' values and connecting that awareness to the broader goals of your company's values. Those values are then captured in a unified strategy. The strategy, often articulated as a mission statement, flows to programs, products, and satisfied customers. This chapter presents ideas and methods to build and support both corporate and product brands. Products that have been successful in achieving this are highlighted.

Brand Strategy and Product Strategy

We have established the fact that the best product opportunities materialize from emerging trends that are the result of changes in the SET Factors. These changes generate Product Opportunity Gaps (POGs) which must be broken down into Value Opportunities (VOs). VOs must be then translated into product features and style. The process of identifying VOs and converting them to product characteristics begins with a corporate and product brand strategy, the focus of this chapter.

■ If new companies establish their brand by accident rather than by design, it becomes expensive and difficult to reinvent or clean up the brand later.

One of the most powerful forces driving contemporary businesses today is the development and management of brand. While graduates in MBA programs study brand and many consulting firms are experts in advising companies on brand, other core disciplines in the product development process need to be aware of the relationship between a company's overall brand strategy and how that affects the new products it develops. In small, emerging companies, it is important to understand that the first products developed establish the brand of the company. If new companies establish their brand by accident rather than by design, it becomes expensive and difficult to reinvent or clean up the brand later. OXO started the right way and built naturally; Iomega did not, as will be discussed soon. Interdisciplinary teams need to have a shared vision of the brand when developing products. The vision needs to balance the everyday expectations of the customers in the intended market with the longer-term strategy and mission of the company. Imagine if Apple's electrical and mechanical engineers did not buy into the commitment to design a transparent iMac. It was equally important for their manufacturing engineers to commit to the quality needed to produce transparent and translucent parts without flow lines. Their industrial designers needed to design parts with a clear understanding of the visual effects of the interior components. All of these groups needed to work in unison to deliver an aesthetic result that was flawless in execution and that built on the brand history of innovation and user-friendly personal computers established by the Macintosh two decades earlier.

The brand decisions made by a company should be reflected in its products. The Aeron chair makes a major statement about the brand of Herman Miller. The company chose to produce a chair based on ergonomic comfort versus a chair based on a traditional office hierarchy (see Chapter 8). This decision is a clear statement that Herman Miller supports, literally and figuratively, the concept of lateral management and comfort over rank. The name Aeron, like the chair itself, is equally contemporary and ethereal.

Brand identity is described by D.A. Aaker as "a unique set of brand associations that the brand strategist aspires to create or maintain. These associations represent what brand stands for and imply a promise to customers from the organization members…by generating a value proposition involving functional, emotional or self-expressive benefits[1] (p. 68)." Aaker further shows how the product is core to the brand, yet the brand is more than the product alone.

Where does a company's brand value and identity reside?

- Is it in the goals and mission statements that flow from the CEO down through management to particular divisions, programs, and products?
- Is it in the products and services that a company offers and produces?
- Is it in the corporate identity, advertising, and public persona that a company adopts to communicate its message to the public through formal and informal media channels?
- Is it in the experience that a customer has when interacting with the product or service?
- Is it in the perceived success of the company by investors, stockholders, and the economic community at large?

The answer to all of these questions is, yes! Many companies, however, often focus on one of these over the others. They fail to see that the branding process is a cycle that must be constantly monitored and ready to react to change. A product or service is integral to maintaining the brand value of a company. When a company produces products that are consistent with the brand strategy, then all aspects of the brand work in unison to effectively compete in the marketplace. However, the failure of a product to communicate the brand value of a company to a customer can negatively affect the brand image and no other channel can effectively offset that effect. A strong advertising campaign cannot offset a bad product, nor can updating an identity program overcome a poorly conceived product. If a company learns to build a message around the relationship between its customers and its valued product (the product experience) everything else flows from that. The brand, values, and relationship to the customer should all be represented in the mission statement of a company and in the brand identity of its products.

Brands must build on a core tradition and adapt to the current SET Factors. Heinz recently changed the color of their ketchup to green and designed a new package that encourages children to decorate their food when applying the ketchup. The brand once known for its quality of "anticipation" is now a friendly fun food accessory for kids. The company reacted first to the on-the-go generation by packaging their ketchup in squeezable containers; people had no time to "wait" for ketchup. More recent trends in food for kids, from fruit rolls to candy worms, have introduced color, texture, and participation into the food experience. Heinz reacted to this trend by introducing squeezable green ketchup, a product so successful in its introduction that the company had trouble keeping up with demand. Continuity in the brand is maintained by communicating the emerging trends in food condiments through color and packaging, just as originally done with the Heinz red-colored ketchup, unique glass bottle, and keystone label. Heinz had to make the change to make their product appealing to kids and parents; the traditional look had become old fashioned. While this change was made for kids, the original bottle remains available for adults and keeps the original brand message intact.

▌ A successful product must connect with the personal values of customers.

A successful product must connect with the personal values of customers. A product experience includes both the expression of the product and the interaction with the product. Customers are looking for three basic things from a product that will improve their lives: 1) Is the product useful, does it enhance some activity, or allow them to accomplish an activity that is important to them? 2) Is the product easy to use and does it stay consistent in use throughout the expected life of the product? 3) Is the product desirable? Does the product respond to who the customer is as a person and complement how he or she wants to project themselves to others? Americans like to add a variety of things to their food; a product that enhances the flavor of food is *useful*. A container that fits in your hand, is easy to squeeze and dispenses a thin controllable line for decorating food is very easy for kids to *use*. Designing a package that a child can use independently and giving it and the ketchup a vibrant green color makes the product contemporary and highly *desirable* for kids and their parents. These same issues exist in complex products. A car is *useful* if it allows you to get from one place to another whenever you want. Some cars are easier to *use* than others; some have controls and settings that are easier to adjust to particular sizes and preferences. If you owned a VW Beetle in the past, you may *desire* to relive that experience in the present. If you have a large family, then a van or SUV is more *desirable* than a sports car. If you have disposable income and can afford an extra car, you may *desire* a sports car just for the driving experience.

The more complex the product and the larger the company, the harder it is to deliver on these three simple objectives. Developing a useful, usable, and desirable product that creates a meaningful connection between the identity (brand) of a company and the personality and needs of a customer is hard enough. Creating that relationship and making a profit is the major challenge. Finding the position between mass production with low margin and smaller-run niche markets at higher profit margins is a challenge companies must contend with. How low can Mercedes go with the cost of their cars before they negatively affect their brand of exclusivity? How can Saturn get into the higher-price markets and extend their brand out of economy? The Motorola Talkabout was a success even though they refocused the technology in comparison to their professional products.

The product, the customer, and the product experience must be the core throughout the whole company. For teams to succeed they must:

- focus on a shared, consistent understanding of who the customer is;
- respect one another and recognize how each area of the company contributes to the product experience for each and every stakeholder;
- recognize that their approach, attitude, and end product all form the basis for the product and corporate brand;
- recognize that the value-base and affiliated qualities the customer seeks must drive the product development process.

Corporate Commitment to Product and Brand

The development of products and services in the Upper Right requires a commitment at all levels of the company, from the CEO to middle management all the way to the engineers, designers, marketing and finance personnel, and others responsible for actually creating and producing the product. As shown in Figure 4.1, there are four fundamental levels to this commitment that feed back and continuously refine the

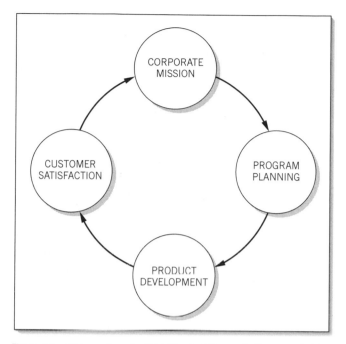

Figure 4.1 The cycle of product development from corporate mission to customer satisfaction.

process for the company. First is the corporate mission itself, the strategic goals that drive the company's long-term and short-term goals. From that mission statement, program planning takes place, where the goals and resources of a product development program are defined. Next, product development takes place, with the outcome a product or service that will be sold to a target customer group. If the product meets or succeeds customers' expectations, then they will be satisfied. And if customers are satisfied in a true sense—the product is useful, usable and desirable—then the product will sell and make money for the company, fulfilling and reinforcing the main goals of the corporate mission.

If the process succeeds, and customers are satisfied, then shareholders and investors make money and they, too, are satisfied and further reinforce the corporate mission. If the process fails, then investors, often impatient and unforgiving, may require a change to the corporate mission and management. All too often, companies focus on cosmetic changes to keep shareholders happy. Ironically, those companies that instead focus on the product, in a way to create a highly valued product, maintain the *long-term* satisfaction of the shareholders.

The program planning process is critical to the overall process. It is this level of middle management's responsibility to translate the goals of the CEO or president into a successful product in the marketplace. When programs are over budget, late, or fail to meet profit targets, it is usually this level of management that is to blame or given the blame. Thus, a coherent process and approach to managing that course of action will improve the chances of a product succeeding in the marketplace.

■ To develop a product within the mission of the company, the entire organization must have a consistent view of the brand strategy.

To develop a product within the mission of the company, the entire organization must have a consistent view of the brand strategy. Since there are a number of individuals and levels in a company that affect the brand message, it is easy to have a break in the continuity of communication. Product planning groups at the upper level of a company may not have a clear communication channel to the teams developing the products or the customers they are designing for. Outside consultants can be in conflict with internal working groups. Advertising companies may design the look and feel of an ad campaign without contact with the product team. A consulting firm may design a logo, website, or support literature without any contact with people working directly with the product. We cannot emphasize how important it is to have a shared vision of the company and the customer and to maintain an open dialogue early in the process. It is also important to keep key decisions consistent and sequenced appropriately. Deciding on a name or graphic identity may be premature until the product characteristics are clear. Committing to an arrangement and number of features may occur too early and force major engineering changes downstream. The visual aesthetics cannot be decided until it is clear that the form connects with the lifestyle image of the intended customers. All of these decisions put tremendous pressure on middle management to regulate the flow of information up and down the levels of a company and into and out of the company between inside groups and outside consultants and suppliers. It also puts pressure on a process of creating parallel decision paths that must integrate at each critical phase.

The corporate mission to customer satisfaction process begins with a corporate strategic commitment to the process found in both the philosophy of and structure for product development. The philosophy is found in the brand identity of the company and its products. The structure is found in an *integrated* New Product Development (iNPD) process that puts the user in the center.

Corporate Values and Customer Values

A company's brand identity relates to the values it represents and how they resonate with their customers. As discussed in Chapter 3, consumers need to connect their product purchases with their own personal values. When a product does connect, customers are willing to pay a higher price. There are two distinct types of value systems that everyone has. One is on a broad social level and the other is personal. While they are often connected, they need not be. In general, a company's overall actions connect with the broad social values, while the products and services it provides connect with the personal values. Chapter 3 discussed the Value Opportunities that enable a product to enhance a user experience with the product through personal values. However, a company's values can also have impact on the perception of its products. Nike went through a tough period not because the products lost their value but because Nike lost its perceived value as a result of its cheap labor practices. Kathy Lee Gifford's clothing line was attacked for the same reason. Tobacco companies are trying to impress customers with their altruistic commitments to offset their public image. Many anti-smoking factions felt that the Virginia Slims Tennis Tournament was hypocritical by supporting both women's independence and promoting a product that many consider to be the fastest growing cause of death in women. Being a good corporate citizen helps create a broad context that supports a positive feeling in consumers. People purchase products that enrich the experience based on what is important to them, i.e., their values. Both the product and the company must support that value base.

As discussed in Chapter 3, people are dynamic and their value system is too. The most successful companies learn to anticipate trends and make changes while staying true to their core mission and identity and can maintain or increase customer loyalty. These companies understand how interconnected these brand attributes are. The better the brand attributes are coordinated, the better the company performs. A successful brand strategy integrates the profile of the company with its products and creates a customer experience that is consistent with the corporate message and inspires brand loyalty. Any message that a company communicates through formal advertising, or through cultural interaction and support, must also be consistent with the core company–customer relationship.

Managing Product Brand

Building an Identity

In some cases, a product becomes the basis for a new company, while in other situations, new products are developed within an existing company. There is a variety of alternative strategies that companies can consider when developing a brand identity for a new product. These include:

- how a new product can become the basis for a new company
- how a new product in an existing company can spawn a new division or line of products
- how a company can develop a new and broader identity
- how a company can use a flexible identity connecting a core across all products but also making each product unique
- and how a company can develop an aesthetic that becomes so powerful it spills out into other markets

The case studies referred to in this book represent many of those approaches. In the case of OXO and Iomega's Zip Drive, a new product can become the basis for a new company. On the other hand, Motorola, Crown, and Black & Decker were each established companies that spawned a new division or line of products with the development of the Talkabout, Wave, and SnakeLight, respectively. Iomega and Starbucks brought attention to their product or service through an entire identity system across the company. In the case of Starbucks, a flexible identity allows each coffee roast to take on its own identity while keeping a constant core logo and style across products. Many auto companies produce a product to introduce a customer to the entire company, as was done with VW and the Beetle, Mazda and the Miata, and Chrysler and the PT Cruiser. VW's approach takes a secondary product, such as the laser-cut key, and creates a symbol by bringing it through the entire line of VW and Audi creating a strong identifier for the company, much like the Coke bottle is for Coca-Cola in the soft drink industry. Herman Miller and Tornardo each developed a new and broader brand, Herman Miller with the development of the Aeron Chair basing its design on size rather than management hierarchy and Tornardo emphasizing ergonomics and ease of use in a traditional market of carpet cleaning where style was previously perceived to be irrelevant (see case studies in Chapter 8). Other companies have been effective in creating such a powerful aesthetic that it spills into other markets. For example, the Apple iMac created a trans-industry trend of translucent plastic around technology. Now every time a product is seen to resemble an iMac, even if not made by Apple, it reinforces the brand value of, and generates free advertising for, Apple. Some of these approaches are explored more fully below.

Company Identity vs. Product Identity

When developing new products, the relationship of the look of a product to other products produced by the company is critical to consider. In doing so, a company may choose between two options, one to maintain a strong role in the product identity or the other to allow the product brand to overshadow the company identity. SnakeLight is a good example of a product with its own brand identity that overshadows the parent company, Black & Decker. The design of the SnakeLight is unique and promotes the product attributes and style apart from the look of other Black & Decker tools. The distinctive head and the flexible core give the product a unique brand identity within the category of flashlights. The look is also unique within the line of Black & Decker products. A benefit of a clear product identity supports the legal defense of a successful product. The brand identity of the SnakeLight has helped Black & Decker defend itself against companies that have attempted to rip off the look of the SnakeLight. Through the use of Trade Dress and Design Patent infringement in complement to Utility Patent infringement, Black & Decker has successfully sued a half dozen companies that have produced rip-offs.

Dewalt products, on the other hand, have a consistent use of graphics, color, and finish across the entire line. All Dewalt products use yellow, black, and silver. Most of the products have yellow as the primary color, silver as the second, and black for the logo and details. A few specific products reverse the emphasis for effect and use black as the primary color to promote their unique attributes. The products are instantly recognized in stores. The Dewalt brand identity in contrast to Black & Decker extends the trade dress protection to an entire line of products rather than one as with the SnakeLight. Yet Black & Decker owns Dewalt. The parent company strategically uses its branding approach dynamically to optimize corporate and product sales.

The product graphics, packaging, instructions for assembly and use, and any digital interaction screens must fit into a brand identity that complements the product and extends the brand. When Crown developed the Wave, they chose to give it a unique identity to fit the context of use. The name, Wave, is the primary identity. The Crown logo, also used on all their other lift products, is downplayed (see Figure 1.12). Wave is actually an acronym that comes from the more technical development name, "Work Assist Vehicle." The name Wave was chosen to give a less serious identity to this new line of products. The graphics, manuals, video and website are all built around this decision. The color of the vehicle is primarily white and gray with the option for bright colors for details. The Wave logo is also portrayed in a more vibrant color and expressive typeface. This is also a departure from the subdued colors of the other Crown products. Crown has also added a new sales force specifically for this product.

The brand identity of the OXO line of products is based on the interrelated ideas of a comfortable and strong grip, universally accessible products and a sculpted handle of black Santoprene, which becomes the signature material that expresses the brand. All of the OXO products are designed using a contemporary aesthetic that combines visual sophistication with perfect tactile properties, which create a secure, comfortable, and confident experience. The logo is clean and simple, easy to recognize from a distance, easy to remember, and reads the same way backwards and forwards. OXO has developed its reputation primarily by word of mouth, the most cost-effective and positive type of advertising.

The Motorola Talkabout is an example where the brand is separate from the company's primary line of professional two-way walkie-talkies. The name Motorola is still the primary identifier; however the use of a more customer-friendly and accessible secondary brand identifier, the compressed word Talkabout, and the look of the product have established a new market for the company. This decision by Motorola is very similar to Sony's choice of the word Walkman. In this instance, the company maintains the strength of the parent company's established competence, high-technology performance, but uses the secondary identifier to connect to the new market. This hybrid identity extends the brand of the company and maintains an active relationship in the mind of the consumer between the parent company and the new product.

Another approach to maintaining a separation between products but a core connection to the parent company is through a flexible identity. Here a theme is maintained between products with a strong reference to the parent company, yet each product is also given its own unique attributes and identity. Starbucks uses this approach to differentiate each of its roasts with a clear statement that they are all part of the Starbucks family. Each roast is given its own name and a unique logo is designed for each roast, but under the same basic style. The roast logo is placed on the same lower part of the bag of coffee with the company's Starbucks logo consistently on the top.

A recent approach to constantly updating products to stay with current trends is the use of what is being called *postponement*. The traditional approach to product development is to determine up front all varieties of a product that will be offered. Once the molds are made and the colors decided, the product remains unchanged until the next model is produced. With the emergence of rapid manufacturing techniques and the ability to make shorter manufacturing runs affordably, detailing decisions can be postponed until just prior to the product's release. In doing so, style details can stay current on a continual basis. The approach also allows for changes in products much more frequently. Swatch began the trend with interchangeable watch faces, bands, and hands. Nokia uses the approach to allow customers to choose from a wide variety of covers on their cell phones. Motorola is using the approach to produce different models of the Talkabout. Postponement allows for different product models within a core product and brand. The variety of styles available to the customer allows for each user to customize the product to their personality. This feature tends to add considerable value to a product, pushing it further to the Upper Right. People will pay for value and so, in addition to allowing for variety within a brand, postponement tends to command high profit margins for these interchangeable features.

Building Brand vs. Maintaining Brand

■ Relating the company and product brand to the core needs, wants, and desires of the customer can convert a failing company into a market-leading success.

Brand must be built and maintained. Connecting to the customer enables both to take place. UPS has long-standing brand identity; they have made the right changes to keep up with or ahead of the competition. FedEx is a relatively new brand that had to establish itself right away. It went from obscurity to high international recognition in a relatively quick period of time. While you can easily recall the brown trucks of UPS and the bold purple and orange of the FedEx logo, you use their services because you can rely on them to deliver what you send on time and to the intended recipient. In comparative terms, UPS is the seasoned professional and FedEx is the young upstart. Both are equally respected. One has quickly built a powerful brand identity and the other has successfully managed long-term brand equity. We will examine the brand strategy of UPS further in Chapter 8.

This subsection examines two case studies, one in which a brand is built up, the other in which an established brand is maintained. In both cases, relating the company and product brand to the core needs, wants, and desires of the customer converted a failing product or company into a market-leading success.

Starting from Scratch: Iomega

The development of the Iomega Zip Drive (Figure 4.2) is an excellent example of building a new brand identity. Iomega has become one of the most recognized brand names in the computer industry. While the core technology was impressive, the original Zip drives did not fare well in the marketplace until Iomega created a strong brand that merged visual graphic identity with distinct product forms and colors.

The Iomega Zip Drive is a classic case of tech transfer, such as discussed in the book *Crossing the Chasm* by Geoffrey Moore.[2] Iomega wanted to transfer its core technology from military applications to consumer markets. The initial attempt failed miserably, causing the company to go back to the drawing board. The main competitor was SyQuest. The SyQuest cartridges had less than half the memory capacity and were inherently unstable and bulky (Figure 4.3). Iomega had addressed those limitations and problems. The core technology and compact size had tremendous promise. However, the company had failed to understand how to design a product interface that made it easy for consumers to use it. The Zip Drive also needed a strong product and company

Figure 4.2 Current Iomega Zip Drive and disk. (Reprinted with permission of Iomega Corporation.)

Figure 4.3   Packaging for SyQuest cartridge versus Zip disk.

brand identity. Iomega turned to Fitch to give them the right look and feel. They took a useful product and made it usable and desirable.

There were two SET Factors in this case. First was the consumers' demand for inexpensive peripheral products that could significantly and affordably allow them to store and transfer large files. Second was the increased sophistication of computer hardware and peripherals. Mac, Compaq, Dell, HP, Gateway, and IBM are constantly competing for the personal and office computer market. Style has played a major part in the competition. A company entering this market had to understand the need to compete in style and technology to fit into the existing office and home desktop environment. If the product worked on both levels, price would not be an issue.

The need for more computer memory is always growing. Having a relatively inexpensive and highly reliable peripheral product would be an instant success. An anonymous black box would not be accepted regardless of how well it performed. Iomega initially tried to borrow a look from a different market and developed a design that resembled a Sony Discman. It was more confusing than helpful.

Fitch, a consulting firm with offices in the U.S. and England, was hired to create a competitive product for the next product launch at the upcoming Consumer Electronics Show. In six months, Fitch redesigned every aspect of the product except the core technology. The logo, packaging, Zip Drive, and the Zip disc were all redesigned to give Iomega a clear brand position in the computer peripherals industry. The bold indigo color created a distinct product in an industry of non-color, which would highlight an aggressive brand identity.

A simple design element was the use of a window to allow consumers to see the inside. Thus the logo on the disc was always visible. Even during use, a window on new technology is always a good idea. It helped sell washing machines and dryers and, as vividly described in *The Right Stuff* by Tom Wolfe, even the astronauts requested a window in the first space capsules.[3] Whether you are looking out or looking in, a window is a comforting feature that makes the product more friendly and accessible. The product was designed to stand on one side or lay flat. It looked good in both orientations, rubber feet giving it stability on its side and becoming a contemporary detail when the product was lying flat. Figure 4.4 illustrates the details of the features that integrate style and technology.

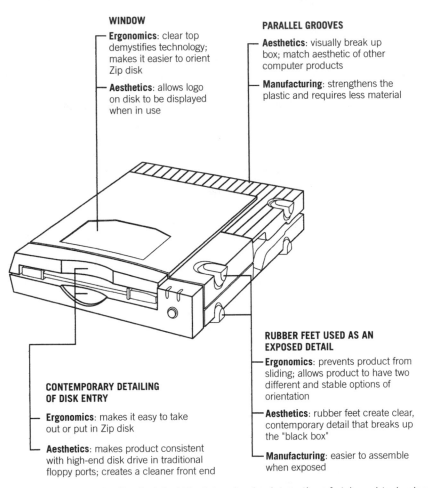

WINDOW

Ergonomics: clear top demystifies technology; makes it easier to orient Zip disk

Aesthetics: allows logo on disk to be displayed when in use

PARALLEL GROOVES

Aesthetics: visually break up box; match aesthetic of other computer products

Manufacturing: strengthens the plastic and requires less material

CONTEMPORARY DETAILING OF DISK ENTRY

Ergonomics: makes it easy to take out or put in Zip disk

Aesthetics: makes product consistent with high-end disk drive in traditional floppy ports; creates a cleaner front end

RUBBER FEET USED AS AN EXPOSED DETAIL

Ergonomics: prevents product from sliding; allows product to have two different and stable options of orientation

Aesthetics: rubber feet create clear, contemporary detail that breaks up the "black box"

Manufacturing: easier to assemble when exposed

Figure 4.4 Product details of original Zip Drive showing integration of style and technology.

Soon consumers became attached to the brand and carried their Zip disks with them with confidence and pride. Sales grew exponentially, and companies approached Iomega with the goal of integrating the Zip Drive *into* their computers. It is interesting that with technology shrinkage, the identity of the Zip Drive became hidden again inside computer towers. This happened, however, after the brand became established and the disk itself still connects users with confidence and security to the durable technology and up-to-date aesthetic. When the iMac came out, Iomega responded by making their external product in translucent colors consistent with those of the iMac, again placing the product on the computer desk and on the leading edge of aesthetic trends.

Maintaining an Established Identity: Harley

The Harley-Davidson motorcycle is synonymous with the American ethic of individual freedom and escape. It is not just a product, it is a lifestyle and is representative of a global subculture. The life experience of owning a Harley can be complemented by owning the apparel that goes along with it. Once Harley understood the connection, the company became a lifestyle company with a motorcycle as its symbol. A couple in France won a contest that allowed them to pick any location in the world for their marriage. They chose to be married at the Harley-Davidson Corporation in Milwaukee, Wisconsin. It was not too long ago that Harley faced extinction. During the last decade it has risen like a phoenix and has forced every other motorcycle company in the world to respond to its classic design features. These features (shown in Figure 4.5), which include the fenders, the 45° V-twin, four-stroke engine, the seat, and the handlebars, have been codified by Harley owners. Harley does not chance a bolt on its design without full support of its customers. The company stays in constant contact with its loyal customer base by holding major rallies annually where the company employees mix with its customers. This form of customer connection, a type of ethnography discussed in Chapter 7, involves everyone in the company, not just marketing. Harley's problem was the exact opposite of Iomega's. They had a product that had a strong identity and poor record of performance. By slightly adjusting the identity from "rebel without a cause" and biker violence to freedom and escape from the 9–9 rat race, the company responded to a new trend in society. By taking ownership of their manufacturing process, Harley employees were able to reinvigorate brand identity and produce a higher quality motorcycle. They managed to improve performance and keep the original look and feel.

Figure 4.5 1994 Harley-Davidson FLHR motorcycle. (Reprinted with permission of Jim Dillinger; photo of Dillinger with his 1994 Harley-Davidson FLHR by Larry Rippel.)

Harley does not just manufacture motorcycles. The motorcycle is the core of the company brand and has generated a range of lifestyle products that consumers use to reexperience the feeling of owning and riding a Harley. Harley stores were redesigned to sell clothing and gear. They have been so successful that the company makes more profit from their lifestyle products than they do by selling motorcycles. Honda, BMW, and all the other competitors have been forced to create their own version of the Harley Hog. A design created over 50 years ago is outselling all the ergonomic, aerodynamic forms developed in the last two decades. When a biker rides a Harley alone or in a group, they partake in a fantasy experience. The sound, the wind, the look and feel of the Harley, combined with the attire, projects an unmistakable message about the values of the rider. Brando, James Dean and Peter Fonda are always out there with them.

Brand and the Value Opportunities

■ Value Opportunities must be integrated with a company's existing and future brand strategy.

Remember that a brand is communicated to the customer through a value proposition. This communication must ultimately be articulated through the semantics of the product, i.e., the attributes and personality of the product as seen by the user. The way a company chooses to develop and implement the Value Opportunities ultimately defines the semantics of the product and its associated brand characteristics, resulting in that value proposition. All products can be measured using the VO attributes we have presented in Chapter 3. It is important to note, however, that all of these opportunities are in constant flux as the SET forces change. As one company interprets the SET Factors and considers the VOs during product development, another company may have a different interpretation and develop a very different product. It is not enough to identify the Value Opportunities and then try to respond to them individually; rather they must be examined as a set in the context of the SET Factors. Each POG that evolves shifts the relationship and possible interpretation of the VO attributes. The VOs must be integrated with a company's existing brand strategy, and it must be recognized how their interpretation changes the future strategy. Interpretation of the VOs is part art and part science. It requires the development of insightful concepts and the testing and refining of those concepts against the issues established in the research phase with core customers. Integrated teams create integrated concepts and can more easily interpret and modify concepts in a coordinated way that synthesizes the style, features, ergonomics, technology, manufacturing, and cost. As the product defines the brand, so the VOs define the product. Thus Value Opportunities are closely tied to the brand identity of the product.

Computer terminals were initially covered in bent sheet metal. Apple Computer changed the whole look of computers with their large, one-part, aesthetically refined plastic covers. Most were gray with a few black ones interspersed throughout the industry. Then the iMac pushed the concept of plastic to a new level by introducing the use of clear and translucent colors. This was driven by advances in molding and affordability of emerging methods, competition, and social interest to make computers fit into everyday life in the home and office. The VOs for the iMac include:

- strong emotional, attributes of independence, confidence, and power
- visual, auditory, and tactile aesthetics
- comfort and ease of use in the ergonomics VO
- a very strong point in time, sense of place, and personality identity
- social impact in its ability to more readily connect people to the Internet
- strong core technology and quality VOs.

All of these VOs are akin to people's perception of the iMac and together they define the brand.

The brand of a product (as opposed to a company) needs to be developed based on the character of the product and how it communicates value to the intended market. This involves the look and style of the product as represented by the aesthetics and identity VOs, the physical interaction with the product (the ergonomics VO), the psychological interaction with the product (the emotion and impact VOs), and the performance features through the core technology and quality VOs. The product must communicate brand value throughout the short-term and long-term life and use of the product. The initial impression and interaction with the product drives the short-term interest to purchase, while the long-term comfort, performance, interaction, and satisfaction are the forces that build brand loyalty. A product's style, the correct set and location of features, the initial comfort, and confidence in technology are the attributes that customers look for initially. Durability, flexibility, reliability, and service are the features that promote long-term satisfaction and are an expected baseline quality attribute of all products. The Value Opportunities affect both the short- and long-term satisfaction and are critical to brand equity.

An effective product development process will tie the corporate mission and brand to the product and customer. All of these activities must resonate with the company's goals and broader public identity. All of the stakeholders in the company need to be on the same page relative to the product and its relationship to the competition and the rest of the company's expressed values. But the process is not easy. The team must understand the essence of the user, the desired user experience, and how that understanding translates to product criteria. The company must understand how teams of disciplines that think differently and initially have very different, and often conflicting, goals can work together to create a successful product that meets those criteria. Finally, management and the workforce must understand how all of this integrates into a new product development process with goals, deadlines, and clear objectives. And that is what we turn to in the next chapter.

Summary Points

- ❏ Breakthrough brand strategies are tightly coupled with products and services.
- ❏ Corporate brand success is linked between corporate mission, program planning, product development, and customer satisfaction.
- ❏ Consumers support companies that have personal values compatible with their own.
- ❏ Brand within a product is communicated through the Value Opportunities.

References

1. Aaker, D.A., *Building Strong Brands*, The Free Press, New York, 1996.

2. Moore, G., *Crossing the Chasm*, Harper Perennial, New York, 1999.

3. Wolfe, T., *The Right Stuff*, Farrar, Straus & Giroux, New York, 1983.

Part Two

The Process

Chapter 5 A Comprehensive Approach to User-Centered, Integrated New Product Development

Chapter 6 Integrating Disciplines and Managing Diverse Teams

Chapter 7 Understanding the User's Needs, Wants, and Desires

Chapter Five

A Comprehensive Approach to User-Centered, Integrated New Product Development

Companies need to structure and navigate the Fuzzy Front End of the new product development process. In this chapter, a four-phase integrated process is introduced, which begins with opportunity identification and ends with the realization of a well-developed product concept. At the end of this process, a product will be ready for "go/no-go" program approval and intellectual property protection. By effectively structuring the early stages of the process and embracing more qualitative approaches, down-stream activities become more efficient and less error-prone. This leads to a greater chance of success in the marketplace.

Clarifying the Fuzzy Front End of New Product Development

■ The most successful products surpass the original target market and appeal to a broad range of customers.

In the first four chapters, we established an argument that constant changes in local, national, and global Social, Economic, and Technology (SET) Factors produce Product Opportunity Gaps (POGs), and that POGs can be expressed in terms of Value Opportunities (VOs). VOs must then be translated into a product solution that integrates the appropriate style and features that anticipate emerging needs, wants, and desires of consumers. Products are successful when they are deemed acceptable by customers because they are useful, usable, and desirable. The most successful products surpass the original target market and appeal to a broad range of customers, often transcending age, economics, and national boundaries.

In this and the next two chapters, we will discuss the core of this book, how to Move to the Upper Right. We will give you an approach so you can take these ideas and put them to work for your company. In this chapter, we provide a method for structuring the early phase of new product development, what has become known in industry as the "Fuzzy Front End." In Chapter 6, we discuss how to manage this approach and in Chapter 7, we provide an in-depth discussion and description of qualitative methods used to gain a deep understanding of the target user and translate that understanding into product criteria. The most powerful new area of product research is in an emerging field called *new product ethnography*. This form of applied anthropology takes traditional ethnographic methods and blends them with new technology and interdisciplinary research teams to turn a descriptive process into a predictive field that helps to determine Value Opportunities. New product ethnographers must go beyond observation; they need to deliver "actionable insights," namely insights into behavior and lifestyle activities and preferences that lead to product attributes. Through these descriptions their work becomes of value to other members of the product development team. The results of new product ethnography complement, and often occur prior to, traditional marketing analysis.

A New Way of Thinking

The integrated New Product Development (iNPD) process is not just a set of methods that can be plugged into an existing company structure. It is a way of thinking that combines three key elements:

1. A truly horizontal and interdisciplinary structure

2. A commitment to maintain a focus on what customers and other stakeholders value

3. A system that begins with an emphasis on qualitative methods of discovery and development and evolves toward quantitative methods of refinement and manufacture

▌ Team members must trust each other, have mutual respect for the value of all the fields involved, and learn to appreciate the value in having a variety of methods to bring to the table.

The team that is assembled for this process must be representative of the three core competencies needed to deliver products: marketing research, engineering, and design. The team should include additional areas of expertise that reflect the nature of the product. The core team should be relatively small and should stay together throughout the process with expertise added and subtracted as needed. It is often the case that each discipline involved in the program sees its own area of expertise as the most important and that the methods of their discipline are superior to methods used by other areas. The primary bias that must be addressed is discipline-specific importance. Team members must trust each other, have mutual respect for the value of all of the fields involved, and learn to appreciate the value in having a variety of methods to bring to the table. Team members must be good listeners, advocates for their own point of view, and not feel threatened by criticism. The most important attribute they must have is to learn to place their expertise at the service of the customer.

Team members always have their own opinions on the products they develop. Making sure that the end customer is always considered is an important way to prevent personal bias from influencing a program. Many personal insights are valid but must be confirmed by a good understanding of the customer. The success of the team is dependent on knowing how to integrate insight and shed bias. A product that is driven by an overemphasis on either aesthetic expression or technological process will not succeed. Translating customer requirements into the right core technology, and type and placement of features, combined with an appropriate set of sensory aesthetic choices, can only be made with a good understanding and continued dialogue with the people who will use the product.

The hardest aspect of this approach is the use of qualitative methods. Early in the process as the team is attempting to find direction and then gather knowledge, it is important to not get bogged down with large statistical surveys and to not start identifying and detailing solutions. The use of qualitative methods allows for broad investigation with little investment and these approaches are easier to summarize, evaluate, and communicate within the team, to stakeholders, and to management. Team members that come from technical fields find it very difficult to do this and often fail to trust the process.

iNPD Is Only Part of the Process

It is essential to recognize that the four phases outlined in this chapter represent the front end of the overall product development process shown in Figure 5.1. If used correctly, it will significantly reduce downstream development problems in parts integration, manufacturing quality, and missed opportunities in the style and features of the product. The process starts after strategic planning and ends with program approval to develop and manufacture the product. After program approval (and after the focus of this book) are the more detailed refinement stages of the process, where designs are refined, production prototypes built and tested, and then the product is brought to launch. Every company uses a subtle variation of this process. The length of the total product development process varies significantly as well. In the auto industry, it can take several years. In the development of digital hand-held products that process could be as short as six months.

It is becoming harder and harder to find time for the issues raised in the Fuzzy Front End. The use of quantitative methods and fear of manufacturing errors make it easier for companies to commit time and resources to the back end of the process. The challenge all competitive companies face is finding the time for effectively managing the front end and giving programs the proper start. This is because companies usually do not have a clear methodology or champion for this process.

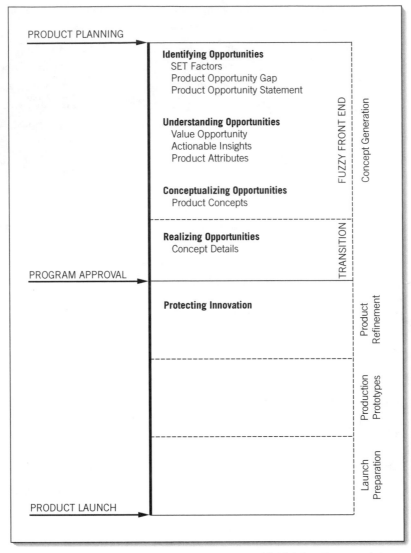

PRODUCT PLANNING

Identifying Opportunities
   SET Factors
   Product Opportunity Gap
   Product Opportunity Statement

Understanding Opportunities
   Value Opportunity
   Actionable Insights
   Product Attributes

Conceptualizing Opportunities
   Product Concepts

Realizing Opportunities
   Concept Details

PROGRAM APPROVAL

Protecting Innovation

PRODUCT LAUNCH

FUZZY FRONT END

TRANSITION

Concept Generation

Product Refinement

Production Prototypes

Launch Preparation

Figure 5.1 Complete product development processes highlighting the span between product planning and program approval.

User-Centered iNPD Process

The user-centered iNPD process is presented in four phases: Identifying the Opportunity, Understanding the Opportunity, Conceptualizing the Opportunity, and Realizing the Opportunity. Many consider only the first two phases, identifying and understanding the opportunity, as the Fuzzy Front End. They do this because they quickly target a project solution and spend conceptualization time refining the basic idea. As shown in Figure 5.1, in our iNPD method all four phases are part of, or affected by, the Fuzzy Front End. The first three phases constitute the primary parts of the Fuzzy Front End where the problem definition is uncertain and vague. The fourth phase is a transition phase into the more concrete and analytical stages of product development. The Fuzzy Front End still extends into the fourth phase because its iterative, uncertain characteristics require customer feedback and insights gained from the first phases to bring the product toward resolution.

The focus of the process, at least initially, surrounds the management of options. The process is much like a series of funnels (as shown in Figure 5.2), where opportunities are expanded through a gathering process and then filtered down to one or a few ideas based on the team's analysis and interpretation. These remaining ideas are then expanded again in more focused depth with one investigation (gathering, analyzing, and interpreting of information) leading to the next area of focus. The process is critical in that the many pieces of information generated provide inspiration and understanding as the emerging idea develops. Some companies save these discarded pieces of information for use or idea generation in future projects. Figures 5.1 and 5.2 show where many of the tools introduced in this book fit into the process. As you read further into this chapter, these figures can be referenced to help bring the process together.

The first phase focuses on the *identification* of, and selection of, product opportunities. The main tool used in this phase is the SET Factors presented in Chapter 1. For those seeking new product opportunities, this phase is critical. For those who have already identified a product opportunity, or for those involved in the modification of an existing product, this phase can still lend insights into directions to take to refine and specifically define the opportunity.

The second phase focuses on the *understanding* of the product opportunity. A POG was identified in the first phase, but how does that opportunity translate into criteria for a product? The focus of this effort is the user. The main tools to understand what the user needs, wants, and desires center around a set of qualitative research techniques that present an in-depth understanding of the typical user, rather than a statistical overview of a mass population. These qualitative techniques are the focus of Chapter 7 but will be introduced in this chapter along with complementary approaches that together define the context and characteristics of the developing product.

The third phase shifts into the more traditional product development process by introducing techniques for product *conceptualization*, with the outcome a single concept to be realized in the fourth phase. Our approach to this phase builds on standard approaches found in the literature on product development. What differentiates us from these standard approaches are:

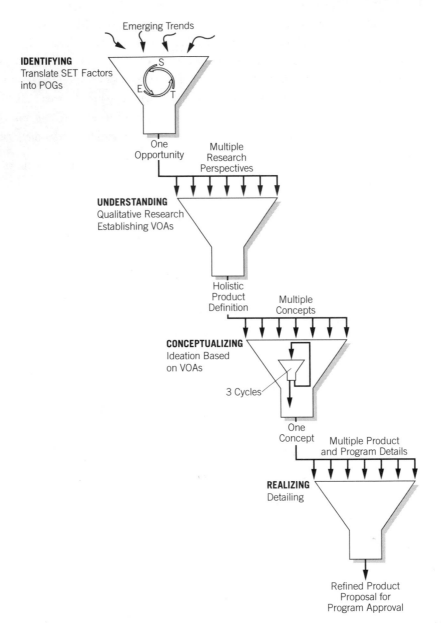

Figure 5.2   Structuring the Fuzzy Front End as a series of funnels: The Four phases are Identifying, Understanding, Conceptualizing and Realizing the Opportunity.

1. *The connection to the user:* At each step of the process we guarantee that the evolving concept meets the early product specifications, and we constantly obtain feedback directly from the core user and expert group. Engineers in particular

■ No one
will buy a
well-made
product that
they don't want.

often ignore the first two phases and disregard the significance of a user-based definition of the product prior to conceptualization. The result is often a process that compromises success by focusing too early on the detailed development of a product that misses its target in the marketplace. Therefore, while we take into account the importance of approaches like 6σ and DFM (Design for Manufacturing) and further find these methods critical to the long-term quality-of-manufacture success of the product, we argue that these approaches are only effective if, and are actually meaningless unless, the product concept itself is effective in meeting the needs of the user; *no one will buy a well made product that they don't want*!

2. *The product definition:* We begin conceptualization from a powerful position of having *defined* what we are trying to develop based on substantial user research; to do so makes the process more efficient, again with fewer design changes and conflicts emerging downstream and with a higher likelihood of market success of the product. We have found that by taking time from the downstream phases of the development process and allocating it to the early phases (especially Phase II), the process becomes more efficient and effective, with higher quality products in concept, and an easier time meeting quality manufacture specifications later.

3. *The integrated framework*: We introduce tools and methods to overcome discipline bias and conflict. Team support and intra-team respect improve the environment for interdisciplinary product development. Negotiation tools that meet everyone's needs and expectations work within that environment to make the process more efficient and satisfying to the team members. Chapter 6 will explore issues in team performance and interests-based negotiation strategies critical to success within interdisciplinary teams.

The fourth phase is the *realization* of the product, a proof of concept phase. It takes the single concept that results from the third phase and details the concept to result in a working functional model, a form model, a justification of the integration of the function and form models, a manufacturing plan, and an initial marketing plan, including initial financial figures and a possible roll-out strategy. The goal of this phase is to prove feasibility of the product, have buy-in of the customer, understand the potential sales and profit of the product, and articulate function and form innovations that differentiate the product from the competition. The result is enough information to judge whether or not the product is likely to succeed in the marketplace and whether the company should commit resources to move the product to market. This commitment can be significant in terms of both financial expenses and personnel resources. Also, with the timeframe to bring the product to market, the company is committing its future reputation for creating successful products. The effective use of this process, however, increases the likelihood that a product will succeed at both this critical juncture and in the marketplace. By articulating the innovations at this time and supporting that argument through prototyping, the second result of this phase is to begin the patenting process for both utility and design patents.

Further phases that occur after concept sign off, including 6σ approaches, manufacturing detailing, integrated prototyping, product layout, part reduction, sales and marketing, and lifecycle concerns, will not be discussed in this book. Instead references to the literature will be provided. Of course many of these issues cannot be ignored upfront. As argued in Chapter 7, any secondary stakeholders with a significant effect on the development process should be included up front in the development team, either by inclusion of the stakeholder or by detailed specification of his or her concerns. These secondary stakeholders have an effect on, and react to, the product design, but are often not the primary driver in its development. Secondary stakeholders often include manufacturing, environmental and lifecycle engineers, distributors and point-of-purchase sales units, and user support personnel. By taking these concerns into account up front, the efficiency of the downstream process increases significantly. There are fewer design changes downstream where any major change is a significant cost and time drain on the process. However, the details of many of these processes still occur after the design concept is completed, where there is an abundance of literature to connect to our process.

Phase I: Identifying the Opportunity

Goals

Product:
- Develop a significant number of potential POGs
- Choose most appropriate POG

Team:
- Develop team communication morale
- Move from being conscious of the team's incompetence toward unconscious competence

Results
- A product opportunity stated as an attempt to mediate experience
- An initial scenario
- Identification of potential customers
- Identification of potential advisors and stakeholders

Methods
A variety of qualitative methods for identifying and selecting an appropriate opportunity:

- Scanning SET Factors to identify POGs
- Brainstorming
- Creating, qualitatively evaluating, and reducing lists
- Weighted matrices
- Beginning to open different research paths:
  Primary research — users and stakeholders
  Secondary research — literature
- Team-building exercises

The biggest challenge in starting a new product development program is preventing preconceived ideas from driving the process. The team must learn to look at a new product as a new field of knowledge to investigate. Some of the stumbling blocks that prevent this from happening include:

- Fixation on a detailed solution to what is really a not yet well-defined problem;

- A heavy-handed management approach that details the program description and preliminary direction, and directs the team without allowing the team members to own the project;

- A team member that may have a bias against, or ignorance of, different disciplines on the team, and tries to design the product from a particular discipline perspective, feeling that that team member's field is the most important and must direct the process;

- Management sending a clear message to team members that, while they may be on an interdisciplinary team, their future is in the silo report structure of their own discipline.

■ Teams with unresolved problems will often break down and the needs of the customer will become lost in the discussion.

If any of these issues develop and are not addressed early, they will have a negative effect on the program. When the most stressful periods occur, teams with unresolved problems will often break down and the customer will become left out of the discussion. Personal issues take over and most decisions are made through power plays that usually require going out of the team to call on upper management to resolve issues. The interest of the customer is abandoned and at best a routine or safe solution is chosen.

If the team is to become comfortable with each other and their relationship with management, then they must become comfortable moving from general and vague ideas to more focused decisions using a shared decision process that involves using their expertise in concert with the knowledge acquired during the process and their understanding of the user. Team members should welcome feedback early, look for problems, and not become defensive or overly protective of their ideas. The team must become an environment that supports each member, allows for "mistakes," and supports out of the box thinking.

The first two phases of the iNPD process should be full of learning and surprises as teams develop possible paths and insights that they would never have imagined before the project. If teams are just cruising on what they know and lack a sense of discovery and excitement, then they are not being positively aggressive and open in exploring and exchanging ideas. Teams should get to know each other and trust each other in the first phase. They should engage in team-building experiences and should have such an event outside the workplace. Any group of people from different disciplines that opens up to each other, and to the new set of information that the other disciplines bring, should be able to make a significant improvement on the current state of any product. A highly functional team will soon develop a shared expertise that is greater than any management insight. They will become the experts of the new product context as it evolves. The developing team needs to be understood and respected as the evolving experts.

The first step to developing a product is to identify the opportunity for that product. It may be that the competition, or the upper management of the company, provides the step for you. However, it may be that you are part of team whose job it is to come up with the next breakthrough product for the company. Or it may be that you are a small company looking for a new product, or even your first product. In these cases you must come up with an insight that will make it worth your while to spend the next several months, or years — and to spend significant company resources — developing a new product concept.

In the first chapter we introduced the SET Factors, those of Social trends (S), Economic forces (E) and Technological advances (T). We saw several examples of how scanning the evolving state of these factors helps identify product opportunities. Scanning these factors is done through secondary sources such as current popular press and newspapers, specialized magazines, and technical journals. Discussions with primary sources can also be revealing along with individual insights. The initial primary research for this phase, however, is quite qualitative, based on informal conversations and observations. The result of understanding the evolving state of the SET Factors is the identification of Product Opportunity Gaps, or POGs. These POGs specify all major paths that the team might take in developing a product.

The goal is to first generate as many opportunities as possible in a short amount of time, to filter the ideas down to a few of more serious interest, and then to investigate each at a cursory level to enable the generation of an initial scenario. The generation of ideas merges initial SET scans with structured ideation. Techniques of brainstorming and ideation are used to generate ideas.[1,2,3,4] We typically tell teams to generate upward of 100 opportunities. Of course, for targeted product areas, this number may be difficult to achieve. However, the more POGs identified, the better the source for opportunity selection and the better the likelihood that you have scanned broadly enough to select the right one to focus on.

The list of 100 or more POGs must be filtered down to a reasonable number. The initial filter will be a combination of common sense, an understanding of the potential resources that might be available to pursue an opportunity, the potential for a useful, usable and desirable product, and buy-in and potential contribution from the team itself. Obviously a housewares company would not (yet) find much of a market in designing kitchen goods for use in outer space, a toy company would not have the expertise or financial backing to develop an automobile, and a team of mechanical engineers and industrial designers would not be the most appropriate group to design a new computer chip. If there are months allocated for the complete product development cycle, then a limit in potential complexity would make sense. The idea here is *not* to envision or conceptualize potential solutions, but rather to establish the boundaries and scope of the problem. Concept ideation is not required to pass judgment on the feasibility of thinking further about many opportunities; if there is doubt, but enthusiasm, toward an idea then it is worth keeping it alive at this point.

■ Make an informed decision about which opportunity has the most potential for your company.

The purpose of the initial filtering is to bring the number of ideas down to about a dozen. The team, at this point, should then take these dozen ideas to the next round, where an individual, or pair of individuals, spends one or two days exploring each opportunity in more detail. Try and find an expert or a potential target user. Ask them about the problems they have doing a task and how effective they find current solutions. Characterize who the target market might be and roughly how big it is. Read the literature that targets the issues surrounding the opportunity. In general, spend this time gaining as much expertise as you can in each area so that, as a team, you can make an informed decision about which opportunity has the most potential for your company.

The goal of this process is not to gain personal buy-in in any one area. Rather your job is to remain unbiased and to share your findings with the team as a whole. Personal commitment to any one project at this point can make your contributions ineffective. Instead you must view your effort as an extension of the team. Even if the opportunities you explore are not selected, your effort was not in vain. Instead, your energy and diligence may save the team from wasting a significant amount of resources. One effective method is to make sure that the team members who propose a given idea *not* be the ones who investigate it.

Once this period of due diligence is completed, the team reassembles and each person or subgroup presents their findings about each project. The team can now make a more informed decision as to which opportunity seems to have the most potential. Again, the team must judge each opportunity based on time and financial resources, the potential for a useful, usable and desirable product, the potential market size, potential contribution from each member of the team, potential creativity in solving the problem, and excitement from each team member. Other criteria may evolve out of specific needs of the team or infrastructure of the company.

We recommend using a weighted matrix (Figure 5.3) to help filter these dozen ideas down further. The weighted matrix is a simple idea, where each column represents an opportunity and each row represents criteria used to judge the opportunity. Each opportunity is rated from 1 (low) to 3 (high) in each category. Each row can be further weighted from 1 to 3 as to the relative importance of that category versus another. Scales and range of weights can vary, however it is important to remember that these are very qualitative decisions used only as a filter to remove the clearly less preferred opportunities. Once each opportunity is rated, then its value is multiplied by the weight for a given row. Columns are then summed to give an overall numeric value for comparison. The opportunities with the higher total values are the ones the team is more interested in. The ones of lower value are of less interest and should be removed from further consideration (or saved for future products).

CRITERIA	WEIGHTS	opportunity #1	opportunity #2	opportunity #3	opportunity #4	opportunity #5	opportunity #6	opportunity #7	opportunity #8
		OPPORTUNITIES							
time and financial resources	3	2	1	3	3	3	1	2	1
potential for a useful, usable, and desirable product	2	2	1	2	2	1	1	3	1
potential market size	1	1	3	1	3	1	2	2	1
potential creativity	2	2	2	2	3	3	1	3	2
potential contribution from team members	3	3	3	1	3	2	3	3	3
TOTALS		24	21	21	31	24	18	29	19

Figure 5.3 A sample weighted matrix.

The weighted matrix should never be used to conclusively choose a single opportunity based only on its numerical outcome; the process is subjective and qualitative. While recent research in the literature argues for the unscientific and possibly conflicting results from these types of analyses when attempting to reach a definitive conclusion, rather than a comparative overview, we have found weighted matrices quite useful in filtering out inferior concepts and stimulating discussion within the team.

The process may take two steps: first filtering the dozen ideas down to two or three and then, possibly after further investigation, bringing the selection down to a single best opportunity. It is also possible that the team brings the list of opportunities down to two or three and management is brought in to examine the details of each and make the decision of which one the team will pursue. This last approach is recommended *only* if the team is excited about each of the remaining ideas. If the team now hesitates about any idea, then it should be removed from consideration. At the end, regardless of who makes the final decision, the team must buy in to the opportunity. Not doing so will cause downstream problems. Everyone will spend a significant amount of time pursuing the evolving product. The most successful product results from a team that enjoys the process and project of focus.

At the end of the process, the team develops a single scenario, using the method presented in Chapter 7, that captures the essence of who the user is, what need the product fills, why it is needed, how it will make a difference to the user, and when it will be used. Again, there is no concept ideation and no specific ideas of what the product will be, look like, or how it will function. All that exists is the notion that if a product existed to fill the void in the user's life then it would be a viable product for the market.

For those teams given the POG by management, the initial qualitative exploration of the opportunity remains important. Further, the team should still go through the exercise of evaluating the POG based on the criteria laid out above. The team must still buy into and get excited by the opportunity and evolving project. It is important to do this from the beginning to enable a focused effort in the next phase. Early in the process is the appropriate time to make sure that all team members buy into the project. Shifting personnel early in the process is much easier than later in midstream.

■ The product opportunity must be stated in general terms and be based on the product experience instead of product criteria.

At the end of Phase I, there are two results: a description of a product opportunity and a scenario. The product opportunity must be stated in the most general terms and be based on the product experience instead of product criteria. It describes the product opportunity in terms of the gap without describing specifically how the product will fill the gap. The challenge is to find the right balance between an opportunity that is stated in terms that are too specific and one stated in a way that is too general. The goal is to let the statement and scenario set up Phase II. For instance, saying you are going to improve the way elderly people use an oven is a general statement that leaves too much variation. Saying that you are going to design a tool that electromechanically lifts food out of an oven is too specific. A balanced statement would be more like this: The product opportunity is to improve the way elderly women lift things out of the oven.

The scenario that follows would sound like this:

> Mary is 70 years old and lives alone. She loves to bake and often entertains her family for holidays. She has developed arthritis and is no longer comfortable reaching into the oven to lift things out. Losing the ability to bake things has been very depressing for her to contemplate. Mary is hesitant to have her family over and no longer feels confident entertaining in her home.

Here are the components of the scenario:

> The product is for older women who have lost the strength and flexibility to lift. They become the core market. Review of the literature should focus on this group. The expert advisors for this program are health care workers who work with the elderly and doctors that work with seniors and are experts in rheumatology. It is also important to know about ovens, specifically the type of ovens that older women might own. It also requires looking at ADA guidelines. Other stakeholders are people who install ovens and sell appliances, organizations that promote products for seniors, and doctors and healthcare workers that might prescribe this for patients. The primary customer base is the women themselves; it is important to find women that fit in this category. Some may have already developed naïve but novel ways of addressing the opportunity. Although applicable to men as well, the majority of the elderly population is female. Any particular issues for woman may make the product better meet the majority needs, wants, and desires of this population.

Through the combination of the statement and scenario, the team now has the directions of where to look for gaining a better understanding of how a product may improve this situation. However, there is no clear sense of what the product might look like, how it should be powered, and what material it would be made out of. The opportunity statement and the scenario will be revisited to make sure it is being adhered to and it serves as the core of the team's understanding of the program. Both the opportunity statement and scenario continue to evolve after each phase.

Phase II: Understanding the Opportunity

Goals

Product:
- ▌ Through primary and secondary research, create an understanding of the Value Opportunities
- ▌ Translate VOs into general product criteria

Team:
- Maintaining healthy team dynamics
- Developing conscious competence
- Becoming a high performing team

Results
- A set of guidelines that help to take actionable insights and turn them into product concepts
- An in-depth understanding of the user:
    Clarification of intended market
    Clear list of value expectations from core market, expert users, and advisors
- Further develop and detail scenario
- List of product characteristics and constraints

Methods
Methods for obtaining and analyzing information from core market and expert users and advisors

Primary research:

- New product ethnography
    Interviews
    Observation
    Visual stories
- Scenario development
- Task analysis

Secondary research:

- Human factors and ergonomic analysis
- Lifestyle reference
- Research databases

Approaches to integrate team into highly functional entity

In Phase II, a high-performance team breaks into subgroups to research the paths suggested by the product opportunity and scenario. The goal is to cast as wide a net as possible and then focus on the ones that provide the best insights. Here the team will interview and observe expert users and, in combination with secondary research in the literature and primary research in interviewing stakeholders and expert advisors, will start to generate directions for the team. Teams need to model the experience for the user and identify the Value Opportunities. The goal is to develop a model of behavior that reflects an understanding of the lifestyle and relevant activities of the core user and the human factors and ergonomics that underlie the human action during the experience. If the experience is a woman lifting things out of the oven then the process of baking in the oven needs to be understood.

■ Understanding
how a product will
be purchased is
also important to
know.

As awareness begins to grow, the team produces models of the experience and starts to develop an understanding of the Value Opportunities for the product. The factors of importance that will make the product useful, usable, and desirable start to emerge. The scope and perceived need must be quickly established to prove that this product opportunity could truly benefit the user and that a sizable market exists. An understanding of how a product like this would be purchased is also important to know. For example, determining the patterns of use of the oven and how people bake determines how to make the product useful. Understanding the aesthetic needs of women and others who might purchase this product helps to frame out the issues of desirability.

A very large part of the process of understanding the opportunity is in understanding the user, which is the focus of Chapter 7. Techniques such as task analysis that break down the user's interaction with a product or activity, ethnographic research that observes and models the behavior of a target market, lifestyle reference that summarizes the cultural and social interests of the user, human factors research that articulates the ergonomic interaction of the user with a product, and further scenario development that tells a story of how a customer might use a product each help to define the specifications of the product. Identifying key experts to provide a more holistic view of the user as part of a group can be an effective means of broading the scope of people interviewed. They also can provide a conduit to identify appropriate users to target in the qualitative research. Physicians and therapists can provide expertise while groups of patients (with their permission) can provide feedback in health and medical product design. Instructors in adult education courses can provide expertise in certain hobbies and a pool of potential users through their classes. Specialty store owners and can provide knowledge of habits and activities in areas such as cooking, clothes buying, and furniture trends, for example.

Three other aspects of the opportunity are considered at this point. The first comes from scanning and understanding technology. Competitive products and patents begin to describe the state of the art. Understanding technologies available or emerging but used in other types of products broadens the team's understanding of what a product might be, and what is feasible to consider in developing a product.

At this point rough prototyping also begins. How can you prototype a product if you have no concepts to build? The prototyping at this point is at the block level, helping to understand bounds on the size of the product, and initial studies on how a person might handle a product of a given size or proportion. Figure 5.4 shows some block-level prototypes of a hand-held augmentative communications device designed by Daedalus Excel. They are early models leading to the DynaMyte device discussed in Chapter 8. These Phase II models are weighted with lead to allow end-users to start "using" the product, at least at a conceptual level. They also help the team bound the size and weight of admissible technologies and understand the possible limits in sizes and features.

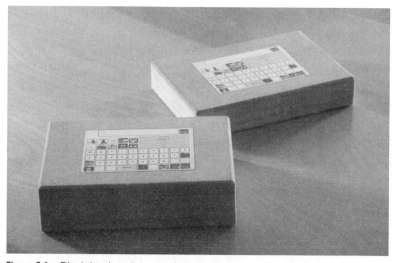

Figure 5.4 Block-level prototypes that are precursors to the DynaVox System's DynaMyte Augmentative Communications Device designed by Daedalus Excel Product Development. (Reprinted with permission of Daedalus Excel.)

Finally, a more refined scenario is developed that captures the essence of the product opportunity in a short story that focuses on a potential user. As will be discussed in Chapter 7, the scenario helps ground the process and keep it focused. Along with the development of the scenario comes initial market research into the size of the market, the buying habits of the target user, and the financial capacity of the target market. What type of products does the customer purchase. How many potential customers might there be in this market? What income levels do the target users make. Where do they spend their money now?

There are several ways to begin to understand the characteristics of the market. Traditional demographics tend to be irrelevant at this point in the process. Rather, marketing databases that augment our understanding of the culture and lifestyle issues are most useful. Through our collaboration with Prof. John Mather from Carnegie Mellon's Graduate School of Industrial Administration, we have used Stanford Research Institute's Values and Lifestyles (VALs) database in our own work. VALs breaks the U.S. consumer market into eight different segments based on financial capability, values, beliefs, and point in life. VALs was developed through detailed surveying of close to 5000 respondents, exploring not only issues of age, income and education, but also key psychological attributes including energy level, self-confidence, level of consumerism, and more. The result is a multi-volume enumeration of the buying distribution of the eight market segments including everything from trucks to movies to magazines to clothes. Even information on purchasing trends with individual brands is available. In our interactions with teams, we have observed that the VALs segmentation helps to bridge perceptual gaps from marketing to design and marketing to engineering. It gives engineers information that they can translate into features and it gives designers lifestyle references they can use to determine appropriate product forms. There are other such databases that focus on lifestyle segmentation, including PRIZM by Claritas Corp., and we have found that such broad statistical understanding of detailed purchasing trends can nicely supplement ethnographic research to provide a rich picture of the targeted market. Such databases, however, should be used with caution and only to supplement in-depth qualitative research of target users, but not replace it.

■ The result of all this research is a growing understanding of the user experience and the emotion surrounding the experience.

The result of all of this research is a growing understanding of the user experience, the emotion surrounding the experience, the product attributes that enable the emotion, and realization of those attributes through physical design and definition of market resources. This realization can be described through the Value Opportunities. The VOs of a POG, supported with an analysis of the particular POG against the current competitive environment, suggest a deeper insight into the target user, the product opportunity, and the differentiation needed to move the product to the Upper Right.

The result of this phase is a behavioral model of the target user, a detailed understanding of his or her needs, wants, desires, dislikes, and resource capacity. The scope of technology available is understood. Bounds on the overall dimensions of the product are also known. The VOs on the product that will be used to develop product concepts, and to judge the effectiveness of any concepts generated, are understood. This rich level of understanding of the product opportunity up front enables a more targeted and efficient approach to the next phases of product development.

It is important that participants from all disciplines (and for small product development teams *all* members) participate in this process. Historically, marketing alone has defined the product characteristics and specifications. Although marketing's participation is important, it alone is not sufficient. The methods we present go beyond, and complement, traditional marketing. They result in a deep and broad understanding of the context for a future product that the team will develop, a context that all key team players must understand. It is difficult to transfer that context to the design team. We have often observed in the traditional approach that the design team interprets the description from marketing, with each person interpreting it in his or her own way, and the tie to the user is lost. An analogy is the children's game of "telephone operator," where one person whispers a phrase to his neighbor who whispers it to her neighbor. By the time it gets to the end of the line, the phrase has completely changed. So too here. When engineers and designers interpret a description that a marketing person wrote as an interpretation of user data, the connection to the user is lost. For larger teams it may be impractical for all team members to spend time researching in depth the lifestyle and essence of the customer (for example, in the auto industry where teams reach more than 200 in number). Even with these teams, however, it is not unreasonable for all members to participate in short interviews, customer discussions, or observations. All team members should be trained on the importance of this technique and or proper execution of the methods.

At the end of Phase II, all team members should have a shared understanding of the requirements of the product. They are starting to become the experts. They have developed models and diagrams of the product experience. By the end of this phase, the team has a vague sense of what the product will be like. If this was compared to human embryonic development, the cells will have differentiated and the parts of the body are there but there is no sense of what the baby will look like. The high-performance teams start to lose their discipline-specific roles and a lot of crossover behavior results. Marketing research, visualization of ideas, and developing technical feasibility are often shared activities that are invited and seen as non-threatening by the group.

The scenario established early in Phase I would be developed further and the product opportunity statement would be clearer. The scenario would sound more like:

> Mary has arthritis in the lower spine and shoulders that limits her range of motion. She also has lost strength in her back and arm muscles. A device is needed that fits in the context of a standard oven that will compensate for her limited motion and reduced strength and allow her to easily put in and remove a variety of pans and baking dishes in the oven. The device will have to lift items that range in weight from a 1–15 pounds.

The product opportunity statement may now sound like:

> The team will develop a product that will integrate with a standard oven and will be easy to install and clean. It must have a simple mechanism and must cost no more than $50 to buy and install. Any installation should be easy enough for a family member to do. While the primary market will be senior women with arthritis between the ages of 70 and 85, the primary purchasers may be family members.

At this point, the scenario and product opportunity statement are complemented by a series of models, diagrams, facts, and statements gleaned from research documents, which frame out the issues that will serve as the guidelines for assessing the concepts developed in Phase III. For example, the size of standard ovens will be known and the team will also know that a typical oven hasn't changed in size in close to 50 years. The Value Opportunities are also framed out and must be interpreted into product characteristics. The security, safety, and independence emotion VOs and the ergonomics VOs are critical to the acceptance and use of the product. The social impact VO separates this potential product from most other kitchen appliances. The opportunity for a unique visual and tactile aesthetic, and related identity, can create a new market. Finally, the quality and core technology VOs will need to be clearly articulated to target an elderly user and her family. A task analysis and ethnographic research, all covered in Chapter 7, will provide a detailed model of how an elderly woman uses the oven and compare this to a younger, more agile and strong woman. The analyses will also provide insights into how a product that fulfills the opportunity would improve the task for the elder user.

Phase III: Conceptualizing the Opportunity

Goals

Product:
▮ Turn Value Opportunities into product concepts that are perceived as useful, usable, and desirable
▮ Generate many concepts and, through iteration, reduce to one

Team:
▮ Use interests-based negotiation strategies
▮ Overcome perceptual gaps
▮ Keep conflict focused on product needs

Results
▮ A product concept that is:
    represented as a rough visual aesthetic
    technically feasible
    perceived as useful, usable, and desirable
▮ Visual prototype
▮ Functional prototype
▮ Clear market definition

Methods
Cycles of modeling/representing prototypes tested for validity with core market, expert users and advisors:
▮ Brainstorming
▮ Pugh charts
▮ Focus groups
    Drawing
    Visual prototyping
    Engineering prototyping

▮ The goal is to test as many concepts as the team can.

While Phase III starts to resemble a product concept phase in any program, there are two main differences. First, the concepts are the result of healthy team interaction and stakeholder insights. Second, the concepts are tested against criteria established in Phase II through focus groups composed of users and expert advisors. The goal in this phase is to develop a series of evolving prototypes representing the concepts. The team continuously tests as many concepts as it can, starting with simple representations and moving to more detailed versions through the phase. This process should be iterative and go through as many cycles as possible, completing at least three cycles. The emphasis is on getting feedback, turning the feedback into a new generation of prototypes, and then testing again. Some companies use rapid prototyping, some use virtual prototyping, while others use blue foam models. The emphasis is on speed of turnaround. If rapid prototyping is expensive and time consuming, then use simple methods. The feedback is more important than the method. This is particularly true in the early rounds.

The feedback to the team through these cycles is invaluable. It is often not viewed as a part of product development research and often hurried or hidden, rather than respected and supported. The difference between Phase II and Phase III is that the second phase develops an understanding of the opportunity while the third phase develops an understanding of the product itself. It is during this stage that the team becomes truly expert. By the end of this phase, they will have a solid understanding of stakeholders and knowledge of the aesthetics, features, materials, and technology that will induce a customer to buy the product.

This phase requires a return to brainstorming methods to generate as many physical concepts as can directly or indirectly meet the criteria set up in Phase II. Once the team combines concepts and reduces the number down to a reasonable level (say 8–10) based on how likely they will meet the expectations set up by the specifications, then each concept can be explored in more detail. Each concept is visualized by sketches and rough form models, that begin to capture the essence of the product. High-level functionality is specified, including mechanisms that might enable the product to behave as desired.

At this point the team returns to the user group for more quantitative feedback. Here more traditional focus groups and surveys help the design team understand what aspects of the concepts potential users like or dislike. This is also an opportunity for the users to help the team design the product by asking them for suggestions of how to improve the product. When presenting each concept, all sketches, form models, and functional specifications should be presented at the same level of specificity. To have one design better fleshed out than another will shift the preference scale towards the more detailed concept by default. Prototypes do not have to work and many details can either be ignored or represented graphically. However, the prototypes should be neat and should clearly represent the features that the team is focusing on at this stage of the development process.

The key to the quick prototyping and feedback is to enable several iterations (again, at least three) in the development process. The team should take the feedback from the first round and use that to again brainstorm on ways to evolve and refine the product.

At each iteration, user feedback will reinforce what aspects of the product are working well and what need to be changed. The surveys and focus groups augment the specifications laid out in the second phase, which are used to judge the success of the concept.

In parallel, this phase includes the process of reverse engineering of competitive products or technologies of interest. Reverse engineering is a useful way of making sure the team stays on top of the evolving field. Most larger companies already reverse engineer their competition. For example, automobile companies constantly take their competitors' products apart to understand what new features they are introducing, what new technologies they are using, what manufacturing processes and materials they select, and what aspects of the product fail. The process of reverse engineering first requires breaking apart a product to understand how it works and how it is made, and then using that analysis to understand how the current product can be improved. Details on reverse engineering and function analysis can be found in Pahl and Beitz[5] and Otto and Wood.[6]

Knowledge of technology derived from the reverse engineering process is then fed into the concept development process, helping to shape and add detail to the evolving product. Mechanisms begin to take form. Technologies begin to be specified. As the iterative process continues, the technical features become more refined. In this phase, manufacturing considerations become relevant. How will the product be made? What materials will be selected? What are the cost implications? Does the state of manufacturing need to be pushed (as was done with OXO and Apple)? At the same time, the designers are developing the look and feel of the product, refining the details as the process evolves. Marketing is beginning to think about pricing, distribution, and roll-out strategies.

The process must remain integrated. If engineering works alone on their functional design while industrial design works alone on their form and marketing makes assumptions on features or aesthetics, then it is likely that the three will never integrate. We have observed many teams in trouble because each discipline does their own thing. Only after the three parties sat down together and talked through a solution did a successful concept emerge. As product tensions mount, so do tensions within teams. The tools and methods from Chapter 6 are critical to managing conflict in the team. Tension in the development process is natural and important. One aspect of a design solution causes problems for other parts. For example, mechanisms might need to be conceptualized, but as one type of mechanism is selected, its proportions and space requirements may affect the initial form studies. Negotiating product-based conflict is an effective way to determine successful product solutions. However, the conflict should be based on meeting the interests of the user rather than personal, power-based struggles, and the negotiation must be managed in terms of time and emotion.

Weighted matrices used in Phase I are again of use here; now the columns represent each concept and the rows represent criteria derived from the specifications of Phase II. The weighted matrix becomes even more useful in this phase, providing a means for each discipline to articulate their views of the product in a form that team members can discuss. Thus the weighed matrix becomes a support tool for interdisciplinary communication. Note that as the product concepts becomes more refined, and the criteria more specific, the weighted matrix takes the from of a Pugh Chart, developed by Stuart Pugh,[7] as a means of comparing competing concepts based on technical considerations. Now one concept or standard solution is chosen as the datum to which all other concepts are compared and scored as better (+1), worse (–1), or the same (0). As with the use of weighted matrices for opportunity identification, no concept should be selected based entirely on the numeric outcome of the matrix. Rather the matrix should be used to filter out the inferior concepts and to enable the team to discuss the pros and cons of each preferred concept.

Focus groups will help define the market. Alternative approaches for the market will be considered, formulating an argument of why the new product will be superior to the current state. A better understanding of the lifestyle and expectations of the market, for example through segmentation tools, and the costs of competitive products will all lead toward an initial marketing strategy and price target.

> The opportunity to improve Mary's ability to bake might lead to concepts that attach to a counter or lift from a floor. Other options might include permanent attachments in the oven, or better yet, attachments that fit into a standard oven using the guides for current racks. The latter concept, being the most inviting from a usability and cost analysis, would lead to further ideation on how to get a rack from inside the oven out and up to a counter height while still supporting the weight of a casserole dish. This might include assist devices from outside the oven, and innovative mechanisms from within. At the end of this phase, a good understanding of one or two primary mechanisms will be known, a basic aesthetic for the user group will be identified, and a cost target will be known.

Traditional methods for conceptual design, product refinement, and market planning can be found in books such as Otto and Wood,[6] Ullman,[8] Ulrich and Eppinger,[9] Urban and Hauser,[10] and Wheelwright and Clark.[11] Readers not familiar with these processes should read these texts. However, the tie to the user and the requirement that user-based specifications, developed in Phase II, must be met, along with an iterative, refining process of continual feedback from the user and stakeholder groups, differentiates and ties together our approach from traditional, more discipline-specific methods.

A single concept emerges, as the product of the team, at the end of Phase III. The concept meets the look, feel, and technical expectations of the target market. What remains are the details: the material and color, the sizing and packaging of parts, the curves and flow of the shape, the product name and logo, the manufacturing specifications, the detailed marketing roll-out strategy, and the final cost of — and expected profit from — the product.

Goals

Product:
- Get program approval for full ramp up to manufacture and market roll out
- A complete product concept that is deemed as useful, usable, and desirable
- A product concept that is patentable

Team:
- Continued interests-based negotiation
- Constant communication through product integration

Results

Refinement of appropriate aesthetic values, features, material and manufacturing core technology
- Form model
    Function model
    Manufacturing plan
- Clear marketing plan for product
    Financials
    Marketing roll-out strategy
    Possible logo and name
- Intellectual property protection
    Utility and design patents and trade dress (brand identity)

Methods
- Stakeholder reaction to refinement of concepts from Phase III
- Detailed visualization and representation in 2D, 3D models digitally, and physical models in three dimensions
    Detailed design of aesthetic components
    Detailed design of technical features and interface
- Rapid prototyping
- Market testing with focus groups and interviews
- Research and selection of core technology
- Research and selection of materials and manufacturing processes
- Costing of product

In this final phase, the product concept is refined to the point that it becomes a real product. The form is refined, again through user feedback, to capture the semantics and style laid out in Phase II. The mechanics of the product are specified and sized, meeting the functional requirements of the product. The market is examined in more detail, with a strategy to move the product to market and, eventually, make money. The results of this phase are a detailed form model; a detailed, working, functional prototype; a manufacturing plan; and a marketing plan with financial information specified. The approaches used to develop these prototypes are standard (see the references given in the previous section). However, again, the user-focused specifications from the second phase are a constant check on the success of the process. Often the process breaks into more discipline-oriented activities: designers make the form models, engineers the functional prototypes, and marketing the marketing plan. Marketing also must determine what *value* the product has to the customer to determine an initial price point. Although not preferred, the skills of team members might require such a breakdown to keep the process efficient. The team still functions, however, as an integrated, high-performing unit that stays intact and in constant communication. It is critical that the team has matured to the point that it works as an integral unit so that as team members each pursue their discipline tasks, they only do so through consideration of how their decision impacts those of all the other team members and how the Phase II specifications and scenarios affect the process.

At the end of this phase is a major milestone, commonly referred to as a "go/no-go" decision point. If the form and function models differ then, at a minimum the team must present a design on paper (or computer) showing how these models will integrate. Management may want to see an integrated prototype before final commitment for the program. Often, however, individual models drawn on paper or CAD will suffice. The quality of the prototypes is critical to the decision-making process. Form models do not have to work, but they must show each feature in sufficient detail to capture the overall theme and feel of the product. Function models do not have to look like the final product, but they must be neat and clearly illustrate how the product behaves.

> The oven aid will have a detailed mechanism designed with all parts specified. A function model will prove that the device is effective in sliding out of the oven and up to counter height while carrying a casserole. It will then be able to be brought into the oven with the same load. The mechanism will also need to illustrate how a weak elderly woman can lift the weight without dropping it. The form of the product will be specified enough to capture the semantics of ease-of-use, security, and safety, with a contemporary look and feel clearly articulated and represented. The approach to distribution and sales for the targeted elderly women will be specified as a cost of $49.95, purchased where appliances are sold, and advertised in *Modern Maturity* and in doctors' offices.

At this point the company can decide whether the project should move into the development-to-market phase. Major costs are committed for tooling. Plans for manufacture and quality assurance are developed and implemented. Marketing costs are committed for distribution and advertisement.

At this point, as well, patents can be applied for. Both design and utility patents should be considered. Patent protection is an important step toward protecting not only the functional innovations, but the product form and identity as well. Trade secrets are another

■ Brand is hard to build; technology is hard to develop. Patent protection is the only way this investment can be protected.

route best used for manufacturing processes and chemical compositions. Mechanical and electronic products are readily reverse engineered and should have a distinct look and function that can be protected through patents. Schmitt and Simonson in *Marketing Aesthetics*[12] nicely summarize the benefits of patent protection as a way to support the product and company brand. Brand is hard to build; technology is hard to develop. Patent protection is the only way this investment of the company can be protected.

At the end of this phase, a company must decide to commit significant human and economic resources to realize the product opportunity. In some companies iNPD may take weeks while in others it may take a year. There is no magic formula. However, companies must realize that investing 20–25 percent of the overall product development program in the four phases outlined here will save significant time and money later. Many companies have a final phase where a limited run of actual products are produced and evaluated. Mistakes late in the process are extremely difficult to fix and require significant time and cost to resolve. Many products limp into the market with last-minute repairs that become apparent soon after purchase. Once a company fails to adequately fill a Product Opportunity Gap, it is extremely difficult to recover with subsequent products. This can have a significant impact on the brand of the company. The iNPD process is a wise investment to make sure the gap is successfully filled the first time.

This is the point of product commitment, where all of the sweat and energy of the team, and the investments in money and time of the company, pay off. This is also the point of departure of our book. As the process moves forward from here, the tie to the user cannot be lost. Further, in the next phase of *design refinement* the battles between cost and feasibility often lead to compromises and frustration. The critical task is to protect any innovation from the earlier phases. To minimize compromise and maximize integrated solutions, it will be critical to maintain appropriate respect and negotiation practices from these earlier phases, as will be discussed in Chapter 6. The ability to identify and prioritize primary users' and stakeholders' concerns, determined in Phases I and II (and further developed in Chapter 7), help to maintain the integrity of the initial product concepts.

Resource Allocation

Before looking at tools to understand the user, team collaboration, and management of the process, this chapter will end by discussing the planning of the process through resource allocation. Allocating resources is a challenging and often daunting question for a company. This section addresses the support of the user-centered iNPD process through time, money, and people. Which types of people should be put on the team? Should consulting firms be used or should the company invest in their own personnel? How long should this process and each phase take? How much money will the company spend on the process? How do these methods apply to small versus large companies? This is all part of the early planning effort for the process. The quick answer, repeated throughout the book, is that the more time you can give the early part of the process, the more cost-effective and efficient will be the downstream processes.

Resources come in many forms. The most obvious is money, and of course everything the company does ties in to finances. Time is money. People are money. It makes the most sense, however, to explore each of these topics separately (time, money, and people) to make tangible decisions on how much of each should be allocated and when they must be allocated. In examining each topic, note that the bottom line is that this is not a science. We cannot (at least at this time) give you a formula that will tell you for any given product how to make these allocations. We have seen over and over again that companies that try to use a fixed formula end up with projects that are always over budget, and late, and with teams that are overworked. We also note that the distribution of resources varies by industry and product type. The design of a vegetable peeler takes a significantly different (lesser) resource allocation than the design of a vehicle. Several people and several thousand dollars are sufficient for a product like the GoodGrips and several hundred people and several hundred million dollars are involved in just the early design conceptualization process for a car. These allocations are also influenced by the experience of the company. As individuals build expertise and the company builds a base of user understanding, the earlier phases may go faster, at least for re-design efforts.

■ The more time, money, and people you can steal from downstream and move to the front end, the better the process will become for you.

It takes experience in the process and an understanding of what is possible in an industry to sufficiently make allocation decisions. That said, our experience has given us rules of thumb in each of these categories, rules that seem to nicely scale with increased resource allocation, which we will share with you. The bottom line is that the more time, money, and people you can steal from downstream and move to the front end, the better the process will become for you. Often companies try and compress the front end to have the resources to fight deficiencies downstream. Our position is that the allocation of more resources to the front end will lead to a better-executed product with fewer downstream catastrophes. If you are new to the process, it is a gamble, but our experience and the experience of companies that use the methods discussed in this book have all shown that the gamble is worth taking. It takes as much resources to develop a mediocre product as a great one! A properly executed and supported user-centered iNPD process will lead to a successful product in the marketplace.

Allocating the Time Resource: Scheduling

The Talkabout took 6 months to design from concept to manufacturing (well past the fourth phase of this book). The newest Ford F-150 took three years (36 months) to design through detailed design alone. The timeframe of different products depends on the complexity of the product: the level of technology, the number of parts that must be integrated and the level of coupling between the parts (both geometrically and functionally), the number of people that contribute to the design, and the amount of diversity in the product development team. Our experience is that the more time that can be allocated early in the process, the better the end product. Our initial rule of thumb is to be generous with the early phases but build up the percentage allocation as the process progresses. One recommendation to allocate the time for the four phases is to spend roughly 20 percent of the time for Phase I, a bit more for Phase II, close to 30 percent for Phase III, and again slightly more for Phase IV. Note that because a sufficient effort was put into defining the product, the later phases become more efficient, not requiring huge time allocations. The reasons are that the process reduces uncertainty and the resulting design changes that come from cutting short or even ignoring the Fuzzy Front End of the process. By allocating sufficient time and using the methods of this book, the front end becomes directed rather than uncertain.

Allocating the Cost Resource: Financing

The deeper into the product development process you get, the more money it's going to cost you. The increase is not linear, but rather increases exponentially as more commitment is made and the process gets closer to manufacturing. To get started, however, does not take a lot of money. As a matter of fact, if the product is relatively simple, then it can be developed for a few thousand dollars (prior to commitment to development of the manufacturing processes). Inexpensive form models married with functional prototypes that work can often capture the excitement of a product. Each of the after-market truck bed products discussed in Chapter 9 were developed for under $1000 (not including personnel and overhead).

As products gain complexity, even the prototyping costs increase significantly. For those products that are evolutionary, in that they are built off of a previous platform or keep components from a previous product, then those parts can and should be re-used in the prototype. For those revolutionary products with newly designed components, then as parts integrate into a unit that begins to look like the final product, reused or off-the-shelf parts become less desirable. Instead, individual prototype parts must be detailed and made, usually by a manual process. Even in our fourth phase, where product concepts are realized but not detailed to the point of manufacturing, integrated prototypes can become quite costly. Again, we cannot a priori in a book determine what finances will be required to develop a product. One rule of thumb is to examine how detailed a prototype will be required. If separate function and form models accompanied by arguments of how to integrate the two models into a common platform are acceptable, then the process can be done with very little financial commitment toward hardware. If a working product is required, then the financial commitment increases significantly.

Allocating the Human Resource: Team Selection

Companies don't make products; people do. But the company picks the people to join the team to make a product. Teams should be composed of appropriate disciplines. Stakeholders within the team should have the capability to work through the four phases and develop the detailed product concept. The core team must be picked up front. The process is dynamic, however, and the team must be as well. New players must be brought on board as early as possible as the product definition unfolds. However, not all team players need to be employed by the company. Large companies such as Ford, GM, Chrysler, Motorola, Hewlett-Packard, Apple, Whirlpool, and Nike hire enough core players to have expertise in all areas of their product development. Even there, suppliers, who are not employed by the company, are often an integral part of the team. Smaller companies often find it difficult to afford to hire all participants. They rely on consultants to help develop their product. For example, in the design of the GoodGrips, OXO went so far as to partner with Smart Design, an external consulting company, throughout the whole process. Consultants differ from suppliers in that suppliers actually produce parts for the product while consultants assist the company in designing the product, but are not responsible for producing any parts.

The question of who to hire full time and whether to look in-house for product design versus looking toward suppliers or consultants falls back on defining the core of your business and your financial capacity. If you are a small operation that focuses on technology, it may be difficult to hire an industrial designer onto your staff. Instead, you may look at many of the several hundred product development firms across the country and around the world to assist in the process. As you look more seriously toward user-centered products, it would behoove you to hire at least one designer. Not only can the designer speak the language of the design consultant but also the language of the user. Further, the designer can bring a different perspective and focus on the application and further development of your technology. If user-centered design is your focus, then a connection to the user should be considered a core corporate competency. For further information on industrial design services, contact IDSA at www.idsa.org.

Summary Points

- ❏ The four-phase approach to the Fuzzy Front End enables clarity and control.
- ❏ The iNPD process increases the likelihood of program approval and intellectual property protection.
- ❏ Resource allocation is critical to success in the Fuzzy Front End.

References

1. Osborn, A.F., *Applied Imagination*, 3rd ed., Charles Scribner & Sons, New York, NY, 1963.

2. Adams, J.L., *Conceptual Blockbusting: A Guide to Better Ideas*, Addison-Wesley, Reading, MA, 1986.

3. Michalko, M., *Thinkertoys*, Ten Speed Press, Berkeley, 1991.

4. E. De Bono, *Six Thinking Hats*, Little Brown & Co., New York, 1999.

5. Pahl, G., and W. Beitz, *Engineering Design: A Systematic Approach*, (K. Wallace, ed.), Springer-Verlag, London, 1977.

6. Otto, K., and K. Wood, *Product Design: Techniques in Reverse Engineering and New Product Development*, Prentice Hall, Upper Saddle River, NJ, 2001.

7. Pugh, S., *Total Design: Integrated Methods for Successful Product Engineering*, Addison-Wesley, New York, 1990.

8. Ullman, D.G., *The Mechanical Design Process*, McGraw Hill, New York, 1996.

9. Ulrich, K., and S. Eppinger, *Product Design and Development*, McGraw Hill, New York, 2000.

10. Urban, G.L., and J.R. Hauser, *Design and Marketing of New Products*, Prentice Hall, Englewood Cliffs, NJ, 1993.

11. Wheelwright, S., and K. Clark, *Revolutionizing Product Development*, The Free Press, New York, 1992.

12. Schmitt, B.H., and A. Simonson, *Marketing Aesthetics: The Strategic Management of Brands, Identity and Image*, The Free Press, New York, 1997.

Chapter Six

Integrating Disciplines
and Managing Diverse Teams

At the core of the product development process are engineers, designers, and market researchers, with each group viewing the product from a distinct perspective. In this chapter, we present research that demonstrates the inherent gap in perception between these different players. Integrated New Product Development (iNPD) teams must overcome these gaps and seek to become high-performance teams. To do so, the interests of the user must drive effective negotiation strategies between team members. This chapter introduces tools and provides guidelines that will enable you to integrate disciplines and manage diverse teams. The goal of the process, from both the team and management perspectives, is to foster teams that maintain a consistently high overall performance. The process of developing a product should be as rewarding for the team as it is valued by the person who buys it.

User-Centered iNPD Facilitates Customer Value

Moving to the Upper Right requires an integrated approach from different disciplines including design, engineering, and market research. Although each discipline brings their knowledge to the process, the team must integrate to create a product that is useful, usable, and desirable to the user. In contrast, the more traditional approach keeps each discipline independent and isolated (as shown in Figure 6.1). In the traditional model, marketing focuses on product concepts based on marketing criteria: Who wants to buy the product, what will they pay for it, how will it be distributed, and what will it cost to get it to market? Design focuses on product concepts based on the visual appearance or human factors: What should the product look like, how should it be used, and what are the best materials for the right interaction and look? And engineering focuses on product concepts based on technological innovations: how should the product work, what technology is best, and how should it be manufactured? Marketing traditionally has defined the product, while engineering and design have iterated between themselves based on their respective, and usually differing, interpretation of the marketing criteria.

In looking at the commonalities among the three disciplines, design and marketing tend to both focus on desirability of a product — the brand and lifestyle images, ease of use, and costs to take into account the aesthetics. Marketing and engineering both focus on usefulness of a product — the functional features, platform upon which the product is

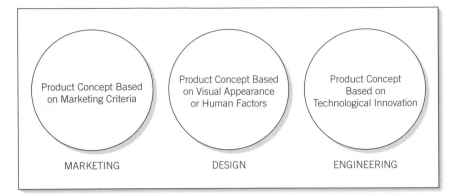

Figure 6.1   Traditional model of product development — independent disciplines.

built, safety and reliability issues, and production costs. And design and engineering both focus on usability of a product — the ergonomics, interface with the product, the integration of the different features and associated costs, the selection of material, and manufacturing. Each overlap is secondarily also concerned with the other two value attributes, but the primary driver of the interaction is as indicated. The point is that the usefulness, usability, and desirability of the product stem directly from the interaction between the disciplines. Thus, it is the overlaps between disciplines that define the value of the product to the consumer, the value that leads to success in the market and profit for the company (as shown in Figure 6.2).

▋ Although the need for integration seems obvious, it is not an easy thing to do.

Although the need for integration seems obvious, it is not an easy thing to do. People often find that the path of least resistance is the one that is most comfortable, that of falling back on working within their own discipline. When engineers work with engineers, or designers with designers, they speak the same language, think the same way, and use the same tools. If different disciplines have different ways of thinking about and approaching a problem, then the overlap of disciplines shown in Figure 6.2 could be difficult. When engineers and designers work together, for example, they often find themselves frustrated, feeling like the other party could care less for their concerns. These feelings can turn into conflict, which significantly affects the design process.

▋ Teams will perform at their best when individuals are inspired, empowered, and given the respect and trust of the people they are working for.

Managing a group of people that comes from various educational and professional backgrounds is exciting and challenging. Schools and corporations do not teach or even recognize the difference between managing within an area and managing across areas. All of our experience managing teams and conducting primary and secondary research about teams, has given us insights into ways to help optimize interdisciplinary team performance. Teams will perform at their best when individuals are inspired, empowered, and

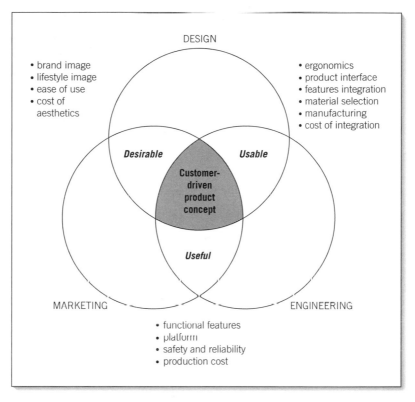

Figure 6.2 Overlap of disciplines leads to value: User-centered iNPD.

given the respect and trust of the people they are working for. In the current climate of new product development, finding and keeping the talent to build successful teams is a challenge. If people are not treated well, they will leave the company. Product managers must have a range of abilities to effectively manage integrated design teams.

For teams to be empowered they must:

■ recognize where differences lie and why those differences exist;

■ be given tools to work through difficulties in an efficient and productive manner;

■ be placed in an environment that supports integrated New Product Development (iNPD).

This chapter focuses on the integration and management of interdisciplinary teams, first exploring the differences between diverse disciplines in the product development process, and then introducing tools and management techniques to help teams overcome those differences and be empowered. The goal is to move from the traditional structure shown in Figure 6.1 to the iNPD structure shown in Figure 6.2. We begin by introducing the concept of *perceptual gaps* between different disciplines to provide a foundation on which to understand how differently each discipline perceives a product. The discussion is highlighted through our research on product perception among design team members. Next we characterize high-functioning teams and strategies for conflict negotiation within those teams. Since all parts of a complex product cannot be designed by all members of the team, a new classification system is introduced to help teams and managers determine what parts must be designed in an integrated fashion and what parts can be championed by a single discipline. We then provide guidance on how to manage interdisciplinary product development teams based on our experience with teams in a variety of settings.

Understanding Perceptual Gaps

To understand the root challenges in team integration, we first examine how different these disciplines really are. We worked closely with a major automobile company to explore this issue. One part of the research focused on a qualitative study of studio designers, engineers, and marketing people to elicit their perspectives on the product development process. There were multiple parts to the study. Here we review one part of the results; we will refer to other aspects of the study later in this chapter. For further details of the study, see Cagan, Vogel and Weingart.[1]

In this part of the study, we chose to focus on a set of colanders, very simple products that are independent of the auto industry. Each of the three colanders shown in Figure 6.3 has its own characteristics. The colander in Figure 6.3(a) is a stainless steel colander, that in Figure 6.3(b) is a two-piece plastic molded colander from Tupperware that won the 1995 Gold IDSA Excellence Award in Consumer Products (sponsored by IDSA and *BusinessWeek*), and the one in Figure 6.3(c) is a cheap, one-shot injected molded colander. To each participant, we asked: "If you owned a company, which colander would you prefer to sell and why?" Participating in this study were three studio designers, three from marketing, five engineers, and two suppliers (who happened to be trained as engineers).

The results, shown in Figure 6.4, were significant. All of the designers selected the stainless steel colander. All but one of the engineers, including the suppliers, selected the cheap one-shot plastic colander. And no one chose the award-winning Tupperware colander. Marketing had a mixed view of the products; their contribution to other parts of the study that focused on their industry was more definitive.

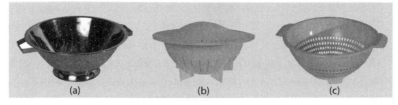

Figure 6.3 Three colanders used in study.

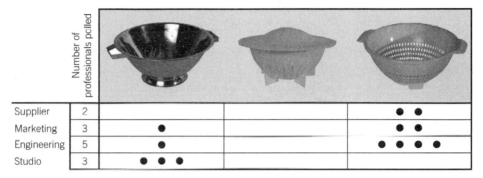

	Number of professionals polled			
Supplier	2			● ●
Marketing	3	●		● ●
Engineering	5	●		● ● ● ●
Studio	3	● ● ●		

Figure 6.4 Overall results of colander study.

It is interesting to note that the one engineer that preferred the stainless steel colander was known for his sensitivity to styling issues and was even identified by the other participants even though the results were anonymous. In following that engineer's performance in the company, we found him one of the best at negotiating solutions between suppliers, engineers, and designers. In one instance, he led the effort in developing an innovative solution to a problem previously considered routine, which positively affected many other parts in that subsystem. He was seen as someone able to bridge the impasse in perspectives. His identification clearly indicates that team members are aware that differences in perception typically exist, and that those who overcome them stand out.

When we asked the participants why they had made their preference choice, the designers felt the metal colander was indicative of qualities such as simplicity, durability, and good value and was in keeping with current styling trends, saying, "Chrome is in!" Chrome had come back in vogue in the auto industry. In contrast, they felt that the one-shot plastic colander was "cheap and ugly looking," was "not elegant," and had "an unresolved shape." The designers, up on current trends, rejected the Tupperware colander as "over styled," recognizing that tastes and trends change (what was trendy and award-winning five years ago is no longer the current style).

The engineers had a different view of the products. They found the stainless steel colander an "old-fashioned" aesthetic, and "complicated and intricate" due to the multi-step manufacturing process, thus directly affecting manufacturing costs and quality control. The plastic one, on the other hand, was affordable ("cheap") and easy to manufacture. For them, the two-piece Tupperware colander was "confusing," with the purpose of the top unclear.

■ Perceptual gaps are the differences in perspectives that team members have that stem from discipline-specific thinking.

Behind the different preferences between designers and engineers is a more fundamental difference in approach. For the designers, shape and aesthetics drive the decision process; for the engineers, cost and complexity drive the process. These differences in perception are what we call *perceptual gaps*, a model of which is shown in Figure 6.5. Perceptual gaps are the differences in perspectives that team members have that stem from discipline-specific thinking and prevent teams from developing an integrated interests-based conflict resolution process. These gaps make negotiation and collaboration strategies difficult.

Perceptual gaps come from several sources. One stems from differences in education. Engineers are trained to know what is "right." They use physics and math to model, understand, and eventually control their environment. They recognize what can be done and what can't be done, based on their understanding of how the world works. They think in terms of function; form is often secondary. They focus on performance, quality, and manufacturing. Designers, on the other hand, are primarily visual thinkers, trained to explore and think about what should be, not what is. They are limited only by their imagination and influenced by the human side of the world around them. They have a good understanding of manufacturing but are comfortable pushing the limits if doing so allows them to better express their forms. They think of quality as aesthetics and emotional impact.

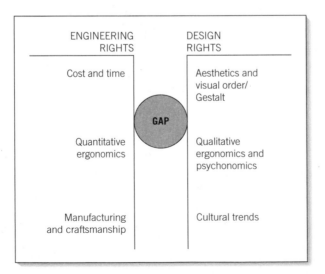

Figure 6.5   Perceptual Gaps model.

Another source of perceptual gaps is the inherent personality of an engineer versus a designer. Engineers tend to be black and white — things are right or wrong. They are comfortable with math and use statistics to reach consensus and conclusions. Designers are more comfortable with uncertainty. They view the world around them as evolving and indecisive. Engineers like to get to specifics early while designers like to leave options open late.

We present three particularly relevant examples of perceptual gaps that we witnessed in industrial settings. The first was an interaction between a designer and engineer discussing a 15 mil gap that occurred between the body of a car and the bumper. There were two alternative designs. The designer had felt that they had worked hard to achieve a preferred design, if only the engineer would get rid of that gap. The engineer, however, was frustrated because the designer didn't understand the complexities involved in removing the gap. It wasn't easy. First there was the need for structural re-inforcement, which would add weight to the vehicle and added complexities to manufacturing. In addition, the manufacturing machines in the intended plant were not capable of producing a part that would meet the designer's needs. The engineer's view was "this cannot be done," while the designer had heard that all before from engineering.

The second example involved an engineering manager that had to work with a design manager who never seemed to meet cost targets. The engineering manager said the process was similar to bringing a child to a candy store and telling that child to pick out the biggest, best, most impressive basket of candy he could. The child gets very excited and really works hard to pick out the best candy that he could. And when he comes up to the register his parent says "Wow, that's great, but you have $200 worth of candy and we only have $20 so you will have to put most of it back." The engineering manager saw himself as the parent and the design manager as the child. No one wants to tell their child that they can't have what they want, but the fact is the money is limited. And he will work with that child to make sure the child gets the things he really wants. But he sees the child kicking and screaming and getting upset, which does no good because he still will not be able to get all that he wants. He understands that it's hard to put that candy back. But if the child had let the parents walk around through the store calculating the sum from the beginning, there wouldn't be this hurtful scene at the cash register. But the child (designer) does not want him to do that.

The designer's view is quite different. The third example came from a design manager discussing his interactions with engineers. To him, the form of a product was like a bowl of gourmet soup. All the ingredients are there for a reason — it tastes good! Although you can take the pepper out or reduce the amount of salt, doing so will sacrifice the taste. But you can't really say why. If you keep going you end up with a bowl of water. Designers are like chefs; they understand how everything fits together into a great tasting soup (or product). The engineers keep trying to cut costs by taking out a little of this and a little of that until the soup (product) tastes (looks) bland.

Differences in perception are an important and positive part of the design process. These differences help provide the trade-offs that make products innovative and yet affordable and produced on time. However, these gaps may also be disruptive to the process if each player does not respect the other (as with the second and third examples). Each player must appreciate the alternative perspectives (lacking in the first example). All too often disciplines feel superior, leading to roadblocks in the design process and preventing group consensus. At times, this leads to personal conflict with lasting effect. Often different players will work together repeatedly, but if early encounters are negative, it will be hard to develop trust and respect in future projects.

Team Functionality

Individuals from diverse disciplines face perceptual gaps when they come together to work as a team. In addition, teams must navigate their own diverse personalities. We turn now to the literature and our own experiences with team functionality, especially in the design process, examining aspects of collaboration, negotiation, and performance.

Team Collaboration

Since conflict within a team exists, it must be managed. Weingart and Jehn[3] argue that collaboration is the key to managing that conflict. The first step is to identify whether the intra-team conflict is based on the task at hand (*task* disagreements) or personality-related issues such as political views, social activities, hobbies, and opinions about clothing or hairstyles (these types of conflict are called *non-task conflict*). Our view is that task conflict can often be beneficial to the design process. The goal of iNPD is not to remove conflict but make it productive and focused on the task at hand. Non-task conflict tends to be detrimental to the team as a whole, interfering with the project, taking valuable time away from the effort, and at times exacerbating personality differences that prevent team members from communicating at all. The goal is to minimize non-task conflict and manage it outside the project environment. When teams are formed, we recommend that they take time outside of their work environment to get to know each other through a social activity. For example, one of the most highly functional teams we have observed went spelunking. It is also important to realize that team members don't need to like each other. Rather they need to respect each other professionally and focus on the task to get the job done. We observed one team whose members clearly didn't want to be in the same room together. By focusing on the project and using our user-centered iNPD method, they were able to produce a fantastic design. Of course, the preferred state is for team members to work out their non-task disagreements and enjoy the process.

Once the focus is on disagreements about the task at hand, collaboration can take place. Through collaboration, disagreements can be altered into joint gain. The idea behind collaboration is not to compromise; compromise means that each party in the process "gave in" and left the process disappointed. Rather, collaboration implies more mutually beneficial results based on more effective communication. Weingart and Jehn describe three techniques to support collaboration, which we will summarize.

The first is to create a group atmosphere that supports team focus, the capability to solve the problem, trust among each other, and open conflict communication channels with which to discuss conflict. In many ways, we see trust as the most critical. Trust is hard to build and easily broken down. Trust must evolve slowly through positive interactions and responses. Trust may be slow to build, but we have seen high levels of trust lead to very efficient and productive design processes.

■ Once a conflict takes on a personal or competitive tone, it is very hard to disperse.

The second technique to support collaboration revolves around group member behavior. The goal is to look for and act on opportunities for joint gain, those situations where both parties can win. It is critical that team members exchange truthful information. Factual information keeps team members aware of each other's needs and helps substantiate each person's position. Similarly, exchanging information about one's priorities can facilitate trade-offs across different issues. If some issues are more important to one party than another, then making concessions on the less important issues may enable each party to gain on other more important ones. In addition, this increases insight into the other party's viewpoints, which may make future collaborations more efficient. Once a conflict takes on a personal or competitive tone, it is very hard to disperse. Instead people tend to "one up" each other and the conflict gets worse and more personal. The key to success is to recognize that this is happening and try to respond with a new tact, a direct response that brings the conflict into the open, or a more integrative and collaborative response that might shift the process back on track.

The third technique to support collaboration focuses on the mindset of the team members. Many people approach resolving conflict as a win-lose situation, that one party has to win while the other comes out on the short end. This of course does not have to be the situation. Rather, an attitude of cooperation and collaboration and an openness to creative thinking can often lead to win-win situations. We have observed both types of attitudes where the win-win view usually leads to innovative, superior solutions. Finally, collaboration requires interdependence on other team members. Negative emotional outbursts and attitudes such as frustration and anger tend to interfere with collaboration. These emotions need to be kept in check and resolved as non-task conflict outside the scope of the project.

Negotiation in the Design Process

Now that strategies and techniques are in place to set up collaborative efforts, the team needs to focus on approaches for negotiating solutions to conflicts that emerge in the design process. We turn to a discussion on the use of interests, rights, and power as discussed in Ury, Brett, and Goldberg,[4] and our investigation into their use and effectiveness in the design process done in collaboration with Prof. Laurie Weingart at Carnegie Mellon's Graduate School of Industrial Administration.[2] As people choose to use interests, rights, or power, they significantly affect the tone, atmosphere, and effectiveness of the negotiation in design.

Interests-based negotiation addresses all of the concerns, desires, and needs of each player in conflict. People's preferences and priorities can be learned and trade-offs found to overcome barriers, where everyone wins. This implies that people exchange information, that all relevant stakeholders are included, and, in particular, the interests of the user are considered. The result can be innovative solutions to difficult problems. This is the ideal approach to conflict negotiation in the design process.

A *rights-based* approach uses standards, precedence, and views of what is right and wrong to resolve a conflict. Here there is either a winner and loser, or compromises must be made, indicating that a better solution probably was available. Often prior solutions, industry averages, and traditional profit or cost targets and analyses are the basis for such negotiation. Although rights has its place in the design process (as discussed later in this chapter), solutions based on precedence alone are often routine or mundane and can be ineffective.

Finally a *power-based* approach is one where a person is forced to do something they wouldn't otherwise do. The result is one where people feel bad about each other and the losing party often enters future engagements looking for revenge. Power-based techniques include strong-arming, threats, invoking the boss' power, and hoarding information.

Figure 6.6 shows three concentric circles with interests in the center, rights in the middle ring, and power on the outside.[4] As shown in the figure, interests-based negotiation may be the central goal, but such negotiation is realized only by understanding that one or more parties could retract to rights or even power if the process doesn't have complete buy-in from all parties.

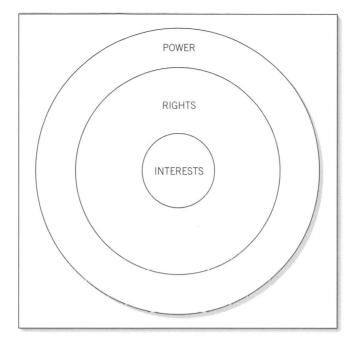

Figure 6.6   Interests, rights and power (based on Ury, Brett and Goldberg[4]).

This is particularly relevant with full-service suppliers who participate in the design of a system or part (discussed further in Chapter 9). Although each player should express his or her interests and be aware of the interests of others, fundamentally the company that hired the supplier could very well fall back on the position of threatening to look for another supplier. Also, this is relevant within a team where one person is more highly ranked than the others. Although the middle or upper manager could easily unilaterally make a decision, doing so would undermine the cohesiveness and attitude of the team. Participants might think "why should I bust my butt to save money or improve the quality or aesthetics of a part if my effort is just going to be thrown away by the manager."

Figure 6.7 maps the concentric interests, rights, and power circles of Figure 6.6 onto the Perceptual Gaps model of Figure 6.5. The common situation is that there is no basis for interests, often due to perceptual gaps. Instead team members rely on rights to argue for their perspective. In the end, upper management decrees a decision from above. Clearly, for an effective iNPD process, team members must overcome these gaps and use an interests-based approach to negotiation. To maintain an interests-based stance is to recognize the long-term gain from a cohesive, collaborative team. By driving the process based on the user's interests, i.e., the needs, wants, and desires of the customer, then the process remains focused and all team members can bridge their perceptual gaps by focusing on a common argument of why decisions are chosen (as shown in Figure 6.8).

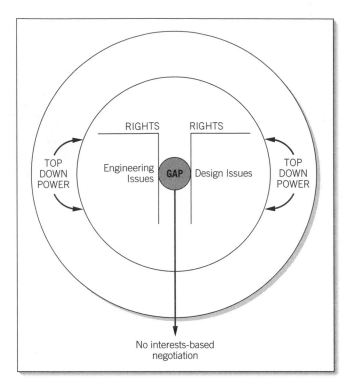

Figure 6.7 Typical Perceptual Gaps and the dysfunctional use of interests, rights and power.

When teams use the collaborative techniques discussed in the last section in conjunction with interest-based negotiation, we have seen the design process become more effective, less emotional, and — overall — more successful. We turn now to an understanding of what is considered a high-performing product development team.

Team Performance

The goal, according to Katzenbach and Smith in *The Wisdom of Teams*,[5] is to develop and manage high performance teams. High performance teams

- are self-motivated, accept criticism, quickly establish an atmosphere of mutual respect and integrate different perspectives;

- function horizontally, rather than in a hierarchy, and shift leadership roles as appropriate;

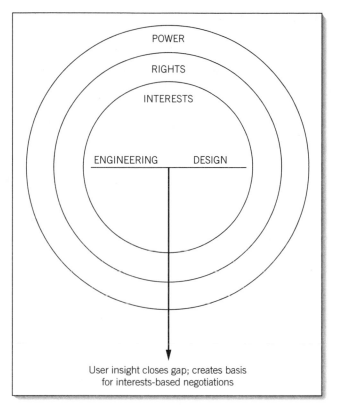

Figure 6.8 iNPD Perceptual Gaps Negotiation Model — the user's interests help bridge the gaps.

- actively seek advice and input from managers, expert advisers, and potential customers;

- want to identify and correct flaws rather than become overly defensive;

- have a clear rationale for their decisions;

- tend to have a sense of humor as a group and use it to shed stress;

- quickly become experts in the subjects needed to develop insights into the product opportunity;

- accept the fact that they are mutually responsible for the work of the team; and

- develop the Gestalt dynamic where the team is greater than the sum of the individual capabilities of its members.

The ideas expressed by Covey[6] and Kao[7] are consistent with these points. Covey points to looking for win-win decisions and stresses learning to master the art of hearing and being heard. Perhaps the most important aspect of Covey's principle is the shift from being independent to understanding the value of interdependence. While most of us are taught that independence is the goal to shoot for, Covey considers this only the beginning. Realizing that your success is inextricably linked to the input of other team members makes you able to get the most out of a team experience. Kao compares successful teams to a performance of improvisational jazz. When musicians are "jamming," all the players know where they are going without requiring a clear vision of the end and they respond and play off one another, building as they go. No one is reading sheet music and they are not playing from memory. Applying this approach to product development requires trust and listening and is based on the belief that the best results will unfold naturally as work progresses. True innovation is not developed from preconceived notions. Innovation is developed as a result of the maturing of the wisdom of the team to see the direction and move with it.

An ideal high-performing team evolves quickly and therefore makes the most of each phase of the program. If teams take time to mature, they do so at the expense of the process. If a team is not functioning effectively early, they may fail to identify a true opportunity. Their research of the opportunity may not be as deep, preventing them from identifying true insight that leads to Value Opportunities. If, as Covey points out, team members have achieved the level of self-confident independence, they are more able to adapt to the challenges required to work in an interdependent team atmosphere. Teams that have members that lack the first level of Covey's personal development often need to learn to trust and share ideas.

The challenge for managers is to get teams to a high performance level as quickly as possible. A manager must expend the most energy early in the process getting the team up to speed and must stay with the team until it shifts into high-performance mode. Once that state is achieved, less time is spent questioning the team's insights and decisions. The role of managing shifts to supplying the team with resources, clearing obstacles for the team, and serving as a check on the process.

In the book *Flow*, Mihaly Csikszentmihalyi[8] contends that individuals (and we believe teams as well) work best when challenge and ability are both set at the proper level to achieve maximum performance and satisfaction, namely, a "state of Flow." When teams achieve this state, their dynamics are positive, team focus is heightened, and they are able to shut out distractions. High performance teams achieve a state of Flow more naturally. Managers have to work harder to help lesser functioning teams reach the state. There are several advantages to helping teams achieve a state of Flow:

1. the positive atmosphere increases the potential of creating breakthrough products,

2. team members enjoy the process as well as the satisfaction of seeing the end product, and

3. positive team performance extends to future experiences within the company.

We have observed a variety of teams in our work. We have learned that teams can evolve quickly in a managerial atmosphere where the communication is clear, consistent, and constant with a structure provided that helps support the team's development. A team can lose direction, and if left undiagnosed for any length of time, it can be very difficult to reverse the trend. As we have fine tuned our approach we have been able to get teams up and running quickly in the first phase. Figure 6.9 illustrates five team profiles over the product development cycle. Team 1 is the ideal team, able to quickly move to a high-performing team and produce a truly successful product concept. Team 2 is somewhat typical in that it gradually becomes functional and then high-performing, with possible ups and down as its members gain trust in each other and the process. Teams 3 and 4 are examples of how teams should not function. Team 3 is barely a functional team, only achieving success at design reviews at the end of each phase. Team 4 is every manager's nightmare. The team does not follow the iNPD process and, due to personality conflicts within the team and inappropriate discipline participation, the team never functions well and produces at best a mediocre product. Management must restructure the team to allow the members to achieve at least a functional level of performance. Finally, Team 5 is an interesting dichotomy. The team members do not like each other and have strong personality conflicts — the dotted line shows the team performance based on personality only. But unlike Team 4, they follow the iNPD process and are able to produce a high-quality product as a functional team, and, at the end, even achieve high performance status, as illustrated by the solid line. This last team shows that even if the team members don't like each other, if they respect each other's abilities and follow the process outlined in this book, then they can still produce a high-quality and highly valued product.

Part Differentiation Matrix

Not all parts of a product should be designed the same. That may seem obvious but it isn't to most companies. Rather, companies tend to think about a system and its components in the same way. We have found in our collaborations with industry that there are two characteristics that most affect how parts should be designed.

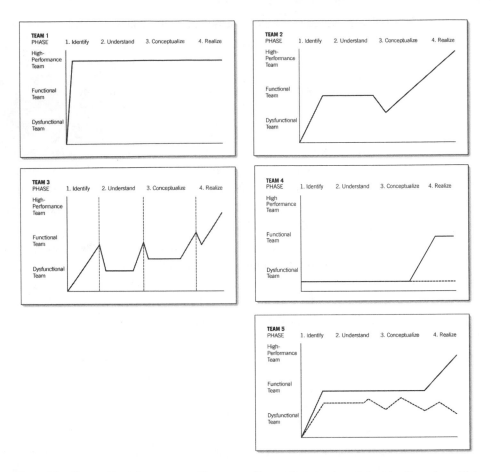

Figure 6.9 Five team performance profiles across the product development cycle: Team 1 — High performance team from beginning to end; Team 2 — early dysfunction evolving into high performance; Team 3 — Team peaked for Phase reviews; decreases in function in between reviews; fails to maximize process; Team 4 — Dysfunctional throughout; management needs to restructure team to achieve functional team level; Team 5 — team performance is functional; team dynamics are up and down; team respects process and works through to high-performance result.

The first is the lifestyle impact, those parts that capture the essence of the fantasy of the product to the customer, making the product desirable, especially at point of sale. Any parts that a customer sees or touches have primary lifestyle impact. These parts have the biggest effect on the product brand. Any parts that affect the performance of the product but are not visible and tend to merely satisfy a level of expectation of the user have secondary lifestyle impact. These secondary lifestyle impact parts do affect satisfaction, especially long term, but aren't critical to the semantics of the product and its statement about who the user is.

The other characteristic is the complexity of the part or system. By complexity we mean the inherent coupling of features within the part and its interdependence with, or impact on, other parts of the product. In other words, how connected is a part to other parts both by physical connectivity and functional connectivity?

These two characteristics can be mapped against each other in a two-dimensional matrix, shown in Figure 6.10, which we call the *Part Differentiation Matrix* (PDM). In the PDM, the top cells represent primary lifestyle impact components while the bottom cells represent components of secondary lifestyle impact. Complexity is represented through the horizontal axis — high complexity to the right and low complexity to the left.

It is clear that for more complex products of multiple systems and subsystems, a company would not have the resources for *every* part, down to the nuts and bolts, to be designed by complete, integrated teams. Such an approach, though theoretically ideal, is not feasible in practice. The PDM lends insights into just how integrated a team should be to design a given part and what negotiation strategies are most effective for an efficient design process.

The lower left cell of the PDM represents commodity or OEM parts, namely parts that are not highly interdependent or complex and that have little influence on brand or point of purchase sale. These are parts that the customer doesn't see and doesn't generally care about. There are numerous suppliers who manufacture these parts, and as long as they meet some minimum quality standard, it doesn't matter who makes them. Integrated discipline design is not necessary except for the specification of the part. Rather, cost is the

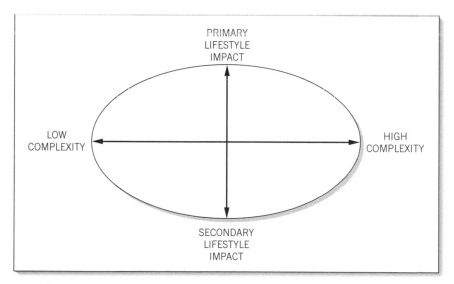

Figure 6.10 Part Differentiation Matrix.

only factor that would influence the selection of one manufacturer over another. The minimum quality standard cannot, however, be taken for granted, for failure of these parts will place blame by the customer on the manufacturer of the product, not the component.

On the other hand, in the lower right cell, that of high complexity but secondary lifestyle impact, are parts that won't directly influence the purchase of the product but will influence the reputation of the product and the likelihood that a customer will return to buy another of your products. This is the platform and core technology of a product. These are the parts that most influence long-term customer satisfaction based on the quality of the product's engineering. The influence of these parts on sales are subtle. The customer has a basic level of expectation about performance of these parts at point of purchase but, as long as that expectation is met, the parts will not influence sales. Often company reputation is the most critical part of satisfying customer concerns for these parts. Here engineering will take the lead in part development. The design group, however, must still buy in on the design. The details of the platform and system integration have important implications on how parts with primary lifestyle impact can be designed. For example, attachment points, overall size, and potential weight limitations are all determined or at least influenced by the design of these lower cell parts. So, though it would appear that the engineers alone should design these parts, it becomes clear that some level of team integration is needed.

The upper left cell, those parts of low complexity but primary lifestyle impact, has a similar interaction between disciplines. These parts are primarily driven by visual aesthetics and have minimal function. Instead they are critical in their support of the brand identity of the product. These components help sell the product and are the most visible aspects of the product at the point of purchase. They are part of the soup referred to earlier where you aren't sure why they belong but if the design works then every one of them has a purpose. Here design will take the lead, yet engineering must deliver the part at a sufficient cost and quality. As with the lower right cell, development of the parts in the upper left cell also requires some level of team integration.

The upper right cell, that of primary lifestyle impact and high complexity, represents parts that merge features and resulting technology with style and resulting brand image. These parts are critical to the look and feel of the product, its performance, and the effect the product has on the customer that leads to a sale. These parts (usually subsystems) require strong input from all players in the development process. In particular, design and engineering must work together in an integrated fashion in order to create part systems that meet identity, technology, and feature requirements. User buy-in to the product depends on the success of this process and, of course, a user focus is required for the process to succeed.

The PDM was developed through our research in the auto industry in collaboration with Prof. Weingart.[1] As shown in Chapter 9, the matrix is quite effective in focusing integrated effort and resource allocation in the vehicle development process. What we learned from the auto industry clearly transfers to any product that holds a reasonable level of complexity, requires user interaction, depends on styling and identity, and utilizes sophisticated technology. What is interesting is that the PDM can also lend insight in very simple, straightforward ways to all manufactured products. Further, the PDM supports the infastructure of the service industries. We now examine its application to the Wave, Talkabout, GoodGrips, and the support products for Starbucks.

First consider the Crown Wave, the most complex product of the four we are examining. In some ways the Wave is a vehicle with many of the trade-offs of a car, yet it is still simpler than the development of the Xterra or PT Cruiser. The PDM for the Wave is shown in Figure 6.11. The upper right cell focuses on the operator area, the region where the operator stands and where the controls are housed. This area in particular is complex and has the most effect on lifestyle value of the product. The upper left cell contains the external trim on the base, which develops the identity for the product. The lower right cell is the hardcore technology, the electronic drive and lift mechanisms. These features are the core functionality of the vehicle. The lower left cell includes the batteries, tires, and miscellaneous hardware.

The Talkabout is a much simpler product than the Wave, yet this is still a high-tech product and the trade-offs between lifestyle impact and complexity make the PDM

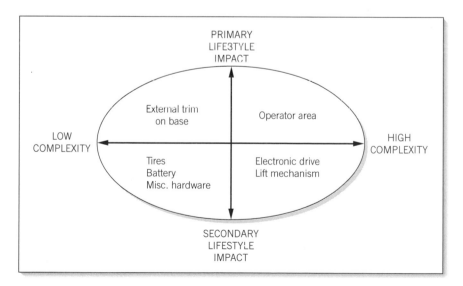

Figure 6.11   Part Differentiation Matrix for Crown Wave.

relevant (as shown in Figure 6.12). Here the upper right cell contains the housing and controls — the interface between the technology and the user. The technology itself is the majority of the parts of the Talkabout and is represented in the lower right cell. The lower left cell includes the individual electronic components and batteries. The upper left cell houses the logo for the product. This is very much a product designed through integration. Although the designers captured many features in the shape and style of the housing, they had to work closely with engineering to guarantee that the technology would integrate into the form.

The OXO GoodGrips is clearly one of the least complex products, in terms of number of parts, that could be designed. It contains a total of three parts: the handle, the blade, and the blade shield integrated with the plastic core. The PDM (shown in Figure 6.13), however, still helps to differentiate which parts the engineers can focus on (lower right: the blade), which features the designers can focus on (upper left: the potato eye remover and hole in the handle), and which require a joint effort (the upper right: the handle and plastic core/shield).

Starbucks, a service product, also can benefit from the PDM (as shown in Figure 6.14). Here the PDM decomposes all aspects of the support structure for the service environment and product line for Starbucks from the perspective of style and complexity/technology. The core players are not necessarily traditional product designers or engineers. The personnel at Starbucks fulfilled the roles of engineering, design, marketing, planning, and finance. In many ways this case study shows that discipline background is not critical. Rather, what is needed is the ability to fulfill the multiple roles needed to create a product

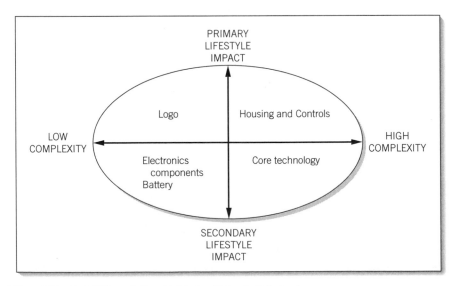

Figure 6.12 Part Differentiation Matrix for Motorola Talkabout.

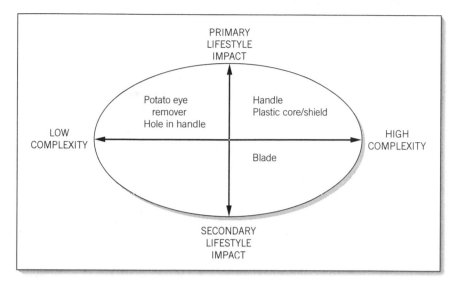

Figure 6.13 Part Differentiation Matrix for OXO Goodgrips.

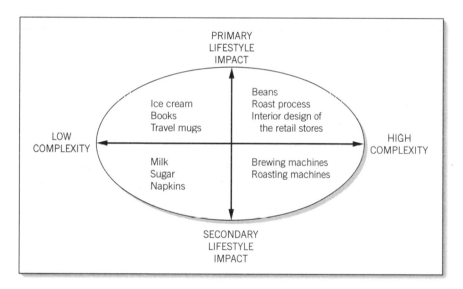

Figure 6.14 Part Differentiation Matrix for Starbucks.

or service in the Upper Right of the Positioning Map. The upper right cell of the PDM (as opposed to the Positioning Map) is the core product, namely the beans, roast process, and interior design of the retail stores. These cores are the focus of the designers, the engineers, and the marketing and planning group. The lower right cell is the core machinery: the coffee brewing and roasting machines that are standard for the industry. The lower left cell houses the extras such as milk, sugar, and napkins. In the upper left cell are the peripheral products including ice cream, books, and travel mugs. The peripheral products are designed by the designers and farmed out for production. The roasting and brewing machinery is specified by Starbucks and supplied by vendors. As Starbucks has grown and diversified, they have continued to maintain their core standards, that is, Starbucks coffee consistently uses top quality beans, roasted with precision, with coffee served in a warm, inviting environment. The recognition of this core product in the upper right cell of the PDM keeps the company focused on their strength even through their rapid growth.

▌ In the ideal world, all parts of the design would be developed in an integrated fashion, but time and financial resources limit the feasibility of such an idyllic process.

For all types of product development, then, the PDM helps the team understand how to allocate resources between focused, discipline-driven design, and integrated part development. Again, in the ideal world, all parts of the design would be developed in an integrated fashion, but time and financial resources limit the feasibility of such an idyllic process. The PDM, however, does not imply that engineers alone should design parts in the lower right cell and designers in the upper left. Not only do engineers have to produce the parts the designers create, and the designers have to build on the platforms subject to constraints imposed by engineers, but the basic axiom of iNPD is that all members of the process are part of an integrated team. As such, each team member brings perspectives and expertise to the process that must be welcomed and appreciated. Thus all team members should be encouraged to comment on the design of all parts and verify their integration into the overall functionality and theme of the product. Part design cannot take place in a vacuum.

▌ The goal is to add the right features for the appropriate cost.

As a last comment on the PDM, note that the lower cells tend to be more science driven and costs are more predictable. The upper cells, however, are more emotionally driven, and, as with emotion, costs are less predictable. Many companies try to set cost targets up front on all parts of the product. Although a reasonable goal, it must be realized that until the lifestyle issues of the product are understood and integrated into the design, predictions for costs of upper cell parts are just estimates and flexibility will be required. Cost-driven and lifestyle-driven processes must work in balance. There is a limit on how much a consumer will or can pay for a product. The goal is to add the *right* features for the *appropriate* cost and the PDM tells us which features directly affect sales and can support added costs. Using the typical cost-driven approach for the design of all parts often causes team conflict — and rightly so, as discussed in the next section.

Team Conflict and the PDM

By examining the PDM in the context of perceptual gaps, it should seem obvious that unproductive conflict is inevitable without a proper iNPD method. Conflict in the upper left (primary lifestyle impact and low complexity) and bottom right (secondary lifestyle impact and high complexity) cells occurs because one group needs to take the lead but the other still must influence the part design. In the upper right cell (primary lifestyle impact and high complexity), conflict emerges because each party fights for their own perspective within a challenging design framework. Recall earlier in this chapter that we engaged in a study on perceptual gaps among product development practitioners in the auto industry. As part of that study, we focused on perceptual gaps in the primary lifestyle impact (upper) cells of the PDM. We found stark contrast in the types of gaps and conflicts that emerged from these two cells.

The auto industry, like other industries, is challenged by constant time-to-market pressures; the conceptualization, detailing, and integration of a large number of parts; limited space; limited budget; and a variety of government regulations. As studio designers complete part designs, engineers must determine their cost to manufacture and begin the design of molds, usually in conjunction with a supplier. The more parts that can be completed early, the less pressure towards the end to get every part finalized and integrated. To the engineers, the parts in the upper left cell of the PDM are relatively simple parts that should be completed early in the design process. To the studio designers, these parts should certainly be envisioned early in the process, but there is no way that a part can be specified until much later in the process, because it must fit within and help express the brand identity of the vehicle. Engineers do not want to consider the cost of brand identity, but, as discussed earlier, designers do not tend to consider the complexities in manufacturing of even such simple parts. Thus the upper left cell parts (exterior side molding in our study) can cause conflict because of a difference in perspective of when a part can be designed and how complicated the part should be.

Parts in the upper right cell introduce different challenges and conflicts into the process. By examining a primary lifestyle impact and highly complex system (that of the design of the door system), it became clear that all participants understood the difficulty and complexity of the design task. Challenges included goal conflicts (between disciplines and trade-offs among design requirements), styling, human factors, component packaging (whenever a component is moved it affects the placement of many other components around it, much like the placement of pieces in a jigsaw puzzle...except here there is no clear "correct" answer), and craftsmanship, or fit and finish. When participants (engineers and studio designers in particular) were asked what the primary challenge was in designing the system, however, each discipline said their own was the biggest challenge. In other words, each discipline fell back on their own world as the driver of the process. Thus upper right cell parts of the PDM are challenged by the sheer complexity of the process and the need for each individual to get their own job done.

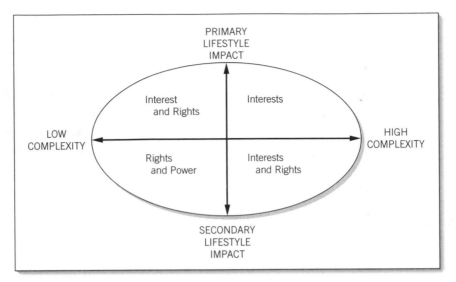

Figure 6.15 Part Differentiation Matrix and the application of Interests, Rights and Power.

It is interesting to see how our discussion of interests, rights, and power applies to the PDM.[2] As shown in Figure 6.15, the upper right cell requires the use of interests and only interests in solution negotiation. It is critical that the interests of each discipline are taken into account. Further, since this team will likely work together for a reasonably long period of time, any other approach will cause distrust and long-term problems for the team's dynamics. The cross diagonal cells of the upper left and lower right also should be mostly based on interests, but here rights will also come into play. Since one discipline takes the lead in these cells, their previous approaches or standards for designing the part will become more prevalent. In the lower left cell, interests are not needed. Rather rights and power can be used to get the best price and delivery time for the commodity parts.

PDM and the Role of Core Disciplines

It follows, then, that there must be balance between team integration and discipline-specific activity. The goal of iNPD is *not* to neutralize individual discipline expertise, but for each individual to bring to the table the strength of their knowledge. Engineers are the only group trained to perform analytical simulation such as finite element or computational fluid dynamics analysis. Engineers tend to be the people trained in details of manufacturing. Designers tend to be the players trained in human factors (at least through a qualitative sense), aesthetics, and 3D physical modeling. Marketing and finance tend to be trained in cost structure and market characterization.

Engineers and designers can bring a unique perspective to market research, designers and marketing researchers to feature definition, and engineering and marketing researchers to user preferences. Each discipline, however, will still be responsible for details in their area. Thus it is important in companies where teams co-locate and integrate that individuals maintain their training in their fundamental area. Further, each individual is best suited to understand advances in his or her area in other programs in the company. Thus, you would be well advised to encourage individuals in a discipline to interact in some formal or informal setting with people of the same discipline from other areas of the company. This could take place, for example, through seminars where people present discipline-specific details of their team's product.

Issues in Team Management: Team Empowerment

Integrated design teams are difficult to manage. Many managers feel that they are supposed to be the expert and that they are supposed to have all of the answers. Some even go so far as to think that they are supposed to make all of the design decisions. Typically this will just not work. The reason companies need interdisciplinary teams is because no one individual has all of the answers. The reason companies make the effort to hire the best people into those teams is because they believe in their employees' talent. The best approach to managing an integrated team is to give the team direction and stay back, taking on the role of advisor rather than micro-manager. In many ways, the manager is like a coach, guiding and training the team, however, the team must win the game. Like the coach, the manager is typically not in the trenches, observing and understanding first hand the needs, wants, and desires of the user. The team members are and they must produce the product that succeeds in the marketplace.

The two main challenges to the manager are:

1. How to foster creative problem-solving within limitations of time and economics.
2. How to manage the team's particular needs at any given point in the process, keeping in mind the broader issues and goals of the entire program.

This section describes approaches and insights to meet those challenges and manage interdisciplinary design teams. We have gained these insights through management of, and discussions with, a variety of teams in a broad base of settings. Although this team empowerment approach may be difficult at first, most participants tend to step up to the plate and excel in the product development process.

Understand the Corporate Mission

Recall in Chapter 4 the four levels of corporate commitment to product and brand: corporate mission, program planning, product development, and customer satisfaction. It is the program manager's job to translate the corporate mission into a successful product in the marketplace. It is often the case that a program can get lost in detail and small problems and start to move away from both the customer focus and the strategic plan. It is the manager's responsibility to make sure that the team understands and stays true to the corporate mission and to understand the impact of brand strategy on the process. As the team develops new insights into customer trends, the program manager is the conduit to feed back that information to upper management.

Serve as a Catalyst and Filter

The manager needs to maintain a balanced view as neither a "company man" with a top-down approach nor an over-protective manager with a bottom-up focus. Supporting a top-down management can be an effective way to gain advancement in a company. Making sure you are always doing what your superiors say and then telling those under you what the rules are is a safe way to manage. However, this approach often stifles a team and limits innovative solutions. Becoming overly defensive and protective of a team is another style that is used. This "champion of the little people" approach makes you a hero with your team. However, it also creates negative relationships with upper management and isolates the team. It is a far less effective approach for achieving advancement than the first method. Maintaining a balanced point of view is important. Teams are often right and insightful. The program should create possibilities and new ideas that management needs to mediate and at times allow to alter pre-program strategies. Knowing when to push upper management for more time resources or a shift in focus is more art than science. However, successful managers trust their teams and must be able to separate the normal tendency of a team to want to do things a different way with true insights and breakthroughs.

Significant product breakthroughs usually have a cost attached to them. The original cost targets may be challenged when a breakthrough idea emerges. The program director must make a decision to argue for increased cost or to tell the team to make it work in the program cost structure. It is a matter of understanding the dynamic tension between constraints and variables. Every program has areas where change and experimentation are required (variables) and other areas where rules must be adhered to (constraints). For instance, if a product must debut at a tradeshow in 12 months, that is a constraint that cannot be ignored. Missing an external deadline could throw a program off an entire year. Finalizing the aesthetic features prior to understanding the lifestyle desires of the customer, however, is a variable that must never be prematurely frozen. Doing so will lead to failure of the product at the show or in the marketplace. Making sure constraints are respected and variables sufficiently investigated is a talent that a good manager must cultivate. The program manager needs to work with upper management to set the product development schedule, such as appropriate deadlines for completion of the four phases. Doing so will make sure that the team has the time to explore the variables and meet the constraints.

In balancing the interaction between upper management and the team, the manager must shield the team from distractions, providing an environment that promotes focused work on the project at hand. Distractions with constant peripheral meetings break the concentration of the team members. Further, the team manager must prevent upper management from interfering with the iNPD process, especially when upper management does not understand the issues. Bruce Claxton from Motorola managed to shelter the team from interference during the development of the Talkabout. Dave Smith, a consultant for Crown Equipment Corporation, set up a skunkworks away from the corporate setting to promote integration in the team during the development of the Wave. One way to shield the team from distractions is to prevent them to begin with. Problems in terms of time pressure, budget cuts and restrictions, and personnel cuts, as well as other unanticipated problems that arise outside the focus on the product, should be the responsibility of the manager. Let the team members focus on the project at hand.

Be Unbiased

Most managers have a core discipline that they consider theirs. When managing an integrated team, having a discipline bias can be threatening to team performance. Very often a discipline-specific focus can lead to a perception that the manager's domain is considered superior to other fields. iNPD managers must learn to see the program through the eyes of different disciplines. They must learn to respect the commitment and value that an integrated team has. One way to resolve this is to create management teams from key disciplines. While this may not seem cost effective in that extra personnel are required, it can be a very successful model in the long run.

Although team members will collaborate with each other across disciplines, they must bring their own discipline knowledge to the process. Integration means joining *together* different knowledge, ideas, and approaches. Managers must be sensitive to the wisdom of disciplines through team members, allowing each perspective a voice appropriate for the discussion or problem of focus. The Part Differentiation Matrix, mentioned earlier, can help a manager frame out the approaches to different aspects of the product.

Empower and Support the Team

▮ While a dictatorial style can succeed in the short term, the long-term stress on the team is enormous.

It is appropriate to make the analogy that managing an iNPD team is similar to other creative fields in sports and entertainment, such as a coach, orchestra conductor, and movie director and producer. There are two main approaches to management: dictatorial or benevolent. The dictatorial approach — where fear, power, and intimidation are used for strict control and direction and violations of control are dealt with quickly — cannot work in a creative environment. For example, despite a successful winning record, college basketball coach Bobby Knight was dismissed from Indiana University because his intimidating style of coaching was seen as excessive. While a dictatorial style can succeed in the short term, the long-term stress on the team is enormous. In contrast, Duke coach Mike Krzyzewski focuses on trust, communication, and pride, as discussed in his book *Leading with the Heart.*[9] Similarly, at the professional level, Phil Jackson has developed a coaching technique in his tenures with the Chicago Bulls and Los Angeles Lakers that takes the most talented and controversial individuals in professional basketball and motivates them to be part of an integrated team. Jackson empowers his players to play because *they* think it will work. Michael Jordan was a great basketball player in his first year. Phil Jackson helped him to become the best team player. Dennis Rodman was an extreme personality seemingly on the edge at all times. Jackson helped him focus on the game while on the court. In Los Angeles he has worked equally successfully with the individual talents of Koby Bryant and Shaq. Jackson can build a team of complementary talents and get them to play together at the highest level. It was not that he had the best players in each position but that he had the right player to complement the rest of the team.

An orchestra conductor also manages an integrated team of musicians. Getting the string, woodwind, brass, and percussion sections to play in harmony is as challenging as any team or group. Each part of an orchestra is very similar to a different discipline. Directing a movie, TV show, or play is also similar to managing an integrated design team. Directors must work with actors, cameramen, set and costume designers, special effects designers, and film editors. This diverse group of people must be brought together to produce a seamless piece of entertainment, often dealing with very large egos. All of the cost constraints and timelines that product programs face, film producers and orchestra conductors also face. The director and conductor are right in the middle of all of it.

The more understanding of the user-centered iNPD process, and the more experience in its application, the better will be the manager's ability to efficiently guide the process. Each time through the process the manager should perform a self-assessment that leads to feedback used to modify future approaches, actions, and the process itself. We have perfected our own joint approach to management of design teams through experience, evaluation of our and the team's performance, and continued iteration.

Let the Team Become the Experts

By the end of the second phase of understanding the opportunity, a team should know more than any manager about that particular program. A manager must learn to question the assumptions and ask for proof or clarification without telling the team what to do. The manager must learn to argue for the customer as well as the company and the team. It is important to help a team recognize why a "good" solution may not be the most appropriate for the program.

At times the manager has insight from years of experience that can assist the team. More often the manager finds that the team is lacking expertise in a certain support area. In that case it is the manager's job to establish help through a support network. Such a network can be built up throughout a company or, for smaller companies, outside the company structure.

Recognize the Personality and Needs of the Team

▌ Criticism without purpose or direction is not productive.

Teams have very different personalities. They work together in a variety of ways. The best high-performance teams require very little maintenance. Some teams are that way from the start. All teams should reach this level by the end of the second phase. We have seen all types of team dynamics as discussed earlier. The manager must recognize and manage the overall team personality. The team must function as a whole. It tends to develop its own group personality but the team is still built of individuals. Individuals have their own needs from recognition of their own effort to help in overcoming personality differences. The manager must also recognize individual needs and nuances and work with the individuals and team to create a positive iNPD environment. It is important that criticism is constructive and productive.

Use of an Interests-Based Management Approach

The members of a product development team are a vital resource to the future of a company. They are a set of creative individuals with the knowledge needed to develop the future capability of a company. They are as important to a company's success as a set of actors is to a movie, musicians to an orchestra, or athletes to a team. With the shortage of talent at this level and the need for new products and services, employees know their services are a precious commodity. Fostering their sense of self worth and commitment to a project and a company is an important part of managing. People inherently want to do well and be part of a process that they feel integral to. A hidden part of the role of a manager is helping to foster a positive relationship between the employee and company. Given that long-term loyalty by employers and employees is not the guarantee that it was in the middle of the 20th century, the manager is the short-term representative of the company for optimizing loyalty and commitment for the duration that someone is working for a particular firm. One of the most rewarding experiences for a manager is to take a group that is perceived as mediocre and help transform them to become a high-performance team.

This current business atmosphere requires a management style rooted primarily in interests, and at times rights, and requires a thoughtful use of power only as a last resort. Managers must help teams reach decisions using the customer's interest and at times disciplines' rights. Only when teams are hopelessly deadlocked should management power come into play. Managers need to empower the team with the ability to make decisions and every use of power is a potential threat to the team's morale. As teams become experts, a manager must trust the insight of the team because they will normally surpass the knowledge of the manager. Managers need to let that happen. Managing today has more to do with responsibility than power. Building trust and clear communication with a team is more important than forcing them to take directions the team does not develop on its own. The approach of balancing interests, rights, and power can work in a Burger King as well as the auto industry. Although you may be able to use an approach that relies more on power in the fast food industry where pay, morale, and dedication are low and turnover is high, when you are managing a team with the range of fields involved in the product development process, the power approach will have detrimental effects. While people may work hard for a manager who uses power, they will never work creatively. While a use of power may help teams make deadlines and hit cost targets, it will not help teams achieve a breakthrough that has insight and produces true product value to the customer. Only through the use of an appropriate balance of an interests, rights, and power approach can managers hope to move the products produced by their teams to the Upper Right.

We are not saying that power plays no role in the process. Dr. Peter Johnson, CEO of Bioinformatics, has said that doctors are educated to be Athenian and Spartan. They are usually Athenian when working with others. They use a diplomatic approach to problem solving — when a surgeon is operating he or she needs to have a good team atmosphere. There are times, however, when emergencies arise and decisions must be made quickly. Doctors in this type of life-saving situation must become Spartans and make quick, decisive decisions. There are times when management must step in and recharge, redirect, and reprimand a team. Knowing when to shift from Athenian to Spartan is part of the art of managing. The Spartan approach should be done in a non-threatening way and the relationship of trust between managers and teams should allow for direct and clear exchange that re-energizes the teams.

Visionaries and Champions

While day-to-day managing is critical, it is important to recognize the role that vision plays in developing successful products. Coupled with vision is the role of being a champion for a product program. Sometimes it seems that companies feel that they can just plug in the numbers and use methods in a distant and detached way and the process will take care of itself. At other times, companies fail to recognize the role that key people have played in keeping a dream alive and maintaining an atmosphere that fosters excellence. The methods and ideas we describe in this book are important for any new product program. However, the greater the vision is at the top, the easier the process will flow. The greater the ability for top management to infuse the rest of the company with that vision, the better all projects will run. In contrast, failure to champion the insights of a team will take the best process and push it dangerously off course.

Very often product programs hit go/no-go decision gates or places where major assumptions are challenged. In the course of doing research for this book, we have come to understand how important it is to have a visionary who acts as a champion when these major events occur. A visionary has a broad sense of the mission and goals of the program and trusts the people charged to carry it out. The team is infused with a sense of commitment and enthusiasm. When the team clicks, the visionary knows it. At key design points, the visionary manager can support the team and allow it to overcome a challenge by keeping core ideas intact. Conversely, a visionary can also critique a team successfully and offer suggestions because the team trusts his or her motives.

At Crown, Dave Smith felt he had a champion in Tom Bidwell, Executive Vice President. Bidwell was the executive who hired Smith and Dean Richardson to redesign Crown's lift equipment several decades earlier. He knew that factory workers were like any other consumers. They would appreciate lift equipment that worked, looked, and felt like products at home. Dave Smith, acting as a consultant under Bidwell, developed a shared vision and helped Crown to develop one of the best product lines in the lift truck industry. Bidwell championed the development of the Wave from the top and supported Smith's skunkworks approach to develop the initial concept. The same situation was true for the development of the Talkabout at Motorola, the Miata at Mazda, the Aeron chair at Herman Miller, the VW Beetle, the PT Cruiser, and many other Upper Right products discussed in this book.

Summary: The Empowered Team

■ As the product development process is user-centered, so is team management people-centered.

Managing interdisciplinary teams is hard but rewarding. It takes patience, adaptability, and flexibility. Managers must understand people as well as disciplines. They must be willing to learn new ideas and trust in the team's ability to get the job done. As the product development process is user-centered, so is team management people-centered. Learning to be a team manager takes time. The teachings and methods of this book, coupled with experience gained from trial and error, are the best tools for taking on this exciting challenge. The reward is a team of individuals that come together and produce a successful product or service that no one discipline could have ever produced alone.

iNPD Team Integration Effectiveness

This chapter began with a goal of converting members of independent disciplines (Figure 6.1) into an integrated team as shown in Figure 6.2. Four major elements were presented to assist in this integration:

■ The need to overcome perceptual gaps between team members of different disciplines,

■ Ways to optimize team functionality including negotiation strategies that focus on users' interests,

■ The allocation of parts of a product in the Part Differentiation Matrix based on lifestyle impact and complexity in order to understand where true integration is necessary and when different disciplines will take the lead in the development process, and

■ Management strategies that empower the team to function independently as appropriate through the development process and that respect individual disciplines.

As shown in Figure 6.16, each of these elements works collectively to enable an effective iNPD process. Effectively addressing these components results in a high-performing team that enjoys the process and is poised to develop a breakthrough product.

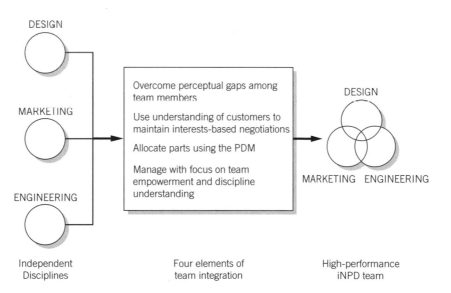

DESIGN

MARKETING

ENGINEERING

Overcome perceptual gaps among team members

Use understanding of customers to maintain interests-based negotiations

Allocate parts using the PDM

Manage with focus on team empowerment and discipline understanding

DESIGN

MARKETING   ENGINEERING

Independent
Disciplines

Four elements of
team integration

High-performance
iNPD team

Figure 6.16   Four elements to effective iNPD team integration.

Although this may seem ideal, our experience is that this model works. Teams that integrate quickly and fundamentally consistently excel in the product development process, producing great products that meet or exceed cost and time constraints and performance and quality specifications. In order for the process to work, however, the team needs to understand the interests of the user as a basis for critical decisions. The next chapter focuses on techniques to develop a common shared understanding of a target user.

Summary Points

- ❑ Perceptual gaps between team members from diverse functions exist and must be overcome.

- ❑ An effective use of interests-based negotiation is critical to the long-term success of a team; power is a last resort that should only be used sparingly by management.

- ❑ The user's interests should drive critical decision-making.

- ❑ The Part Differentiation Matrix helps teams understand where parts integration is critical and when engineering or design should take the lead.

- ❑ iNPD team members must respect all other disciplines that participate in the team and appreciate each contribution to the overall process.

- ❑ iNPD teams should be managed through empowerment and support, recognizing that all disciplines have an equal voice in the overall process.

- ❑ High-performing teams enjoy the process, improve their potential of success, and carry their positive experience to other programs.

References

1. Cagan, J., C.M. Vogel, and L.R. Weingart, "Understanding Perceptual Gaps in Integrated Product Development Teams," *Proceedings of the 2001 ASME Design Engineering Technical Conferences: Design Theory and Methodology Conference*, DETC2001/DTM-21681, September 9–12, Pittsburgh, PA, 2001.

2. Weingart, L.R., C.J.S. Houser, J. Cagan, and C.M. Vogel, "Functional Diversity and Conflict in Cross-Functional Product Development Teams: Considering Perceptual Gaps and Task Characteristics," in: *The 13th Annual Meeting of the International Association for Conflict Management*, St. Louis, MO, June, 2000.

3. Weingart, L.R., and K.A. Jehn, "Manage Intra-team Conflict Through Collaboration," in E.A. Locke (ed.), *The Blackwell Handbook of Principles of Organizational Behavior*, Blackwell, Oxford, UK, 2000, pp. 226–238.

4. Ury, W.L., J.M. Brett, and S.B. Goldberg, *Getting Disputes Resolved: Designing Systems to Cut the Costs of Conflict*, Jossey-Bass, San Francisco, 1988.

5. Katzenbach, J.R., and D.K. Smith, *Wisdom of Teams: Creating the High Performance Organization*, Harper Perennial, New York, 1994.

6. Covey, S.R., *Seven Habits of Highly Effective People*, Fireside, 1990.

7. Kao, J., *Jamming: The Art and Discipline of Business Creativity*, HarperBusiness, New York, 1997.

8. Csikszentmihalyi, M., *Flow: The Psychology of Optimal Experience*, Harper Collins, New York, 1991.

9. Krzyzewski, M., *Leading with the Heart: Coach K's Successful Strategies for Basketball, Business, and Life*, Warner Business Books, New York, 2000.

Chapter Seven

Understanding the User's Needs, Wants, and Desires

In order to create a breakthrough product, your company must know who your customer is and how to place that knowledge in the perspective of the market that your product competes in. This chapter provides techniques to help you balance qualitative methods for understanding needs, wants, and desires with more quantitative approaches for assessing issues of usability. Traditional methods of ergonomics research are complemented by a range of other techniques, which include new product ethnography, scenario development, and lifestyle reference. The results of this research provide insights that characterize potential customers in the target market and serve as a basis for testing the validity of product concepts.

Overview: Usability and Desirability

According to the Human Factors Ergonomics Society (HFES), the discipline of human factors focuses on the "discovery and exchange of knowledge concerning the characteristics of human beings that are applicable to the design of systems and devices of all kinds."[1] What is often thought of as a focused approach in biomechanics and anthropometrics is actually a much broader understanding of who and what a person is. As you will learn in this section, there are many other members of the product development team, beyond human factors specialists, who are interested in the characteristics of human beings and their relationship to systems and devices.

The HFES evolved from the systems analysis conducted by the military during WWII. The three main types of research were anthropometrics, interpreting and managing complex information, and systems analysis in the deployment of troops and equipment. The systems analysis varied in scale and complexity, ranging from the large-scale systems planning used in preparing the invasion of Normandy to the understanding of how to best place and equip personnel from an aptitude and size point of view. The D-Day invasion is one of the most complex events of the 20th century. It required a scale of logistical organization of men and material that was unknown prior to the beginning of the war. At a smaller scale, the range of equipment and military assignments meant understanding how to organize, train, and assign military personnel to make the most of their aptitude and body type. Soldiers had to be trained quickly and effectively to use

175

and maintain the vast array of war technology developed during WWII. There were size limitations for pilots, submariners, and tank drivers. The development of complex new equipment required finding the best personnel with the right training for navigators, cryptographers, code breakers, radar and sonar operators, and bomber pilots and crew.

After the war, as post-war companies and the products they produced grew in size, scope, and complexity, many of the systems analysts found opportunities in the commercial sector. While this post-war focus gave rise to the formation of HFES in 1957, the early origins of human factors can be traced back to the development of mass production and the need to improve efficiency in production. As the nature of work shifted away from craft production and agrarian labor, new concepts for working in factories evolved. The Ford assembly line and Taylor's theories of efficiency[2] started to have an effect on the planning of the nature of work and education, and even in home economics, where women were instructed to organize and plan their homes around modern principles of domestic management. At the end of the 20th century, there is a much broader concept of human factors emerging. This new version is in response to the recognized need for a deeper insight into customers' patterns of behavior. It is starting to involve qualitative research methods and to explore emotional as well as cognitive issues in human factors. The HFES has a variety of technical groups, including aging, cognitive engineering and decision making, environmental design, individual differences, industrial ergonomics, medical systems and rehab, macroergonomics, safety, and visual performance. Currently, however, most research in the discipline of human factors focuses on usability, not on desire.

▌ A successful brand creates a Gestalt image in the market formed from a variety of factors, which include the look and features of the product, the name, the advertising, the price, and the perceived value to the customer.

There are a number of new trends that are beginning to change the way companies attempt to know their customers and their needs, wants, and desires. Many companies are using ethnography as a research tool in early stages of product development. Ethnographic techniques are qualitative processes that take methods from cultural anthropology and apply them to the field of product research. These techniques are proving to be valuable in early phases of marketing and in helping product teams develop the actionable insights they need to translate into the style and features that people are looking for. A second reason this is changing is the result of the new focus on brand management. As discussed in Chapter 4, many companies realize that giving a product a strong brand identity is a clear competitive advantage. The book *Marketing Aesthetics* by Schmitt and Simonson[3] describes the value of a visual identity system and how all aspects of a product must communicate clearly and consistently with customers. A successful brand creates a Gestalt image in the market formed from a variety of factors, which include the look and features of the product, the name, the advertising, the price, and the perceived value to the customer. By taking a broader view of what it means to factor the characterization of humans, this new category of human factors explores how a company's core values can connect with the lifestyle goals of its customers. Harley-Davidson has created one of the most powerful brand identities in the world, which merges the logo, core product (motorcycle), and complementary lifestyle products (clothing and gear) with the way their customers want to live their lives. Even the noise a Harley makes is part of the brand. Another reason the study of human factors is changing is as a result of the emergence of interaction design. Interaction design is a new area in human factors research and is based on human–computer interaction (HCI). This group recognizes that there is a need to create more humane interactive products that cross hardware and software boundaries. It is also clear that quantitative research is not enough to solve these problems alone. Ethnographic research has become a part of HCI research so that researchers can better understand how people use and need computing in work and play (and how computers are integrating work and play).

While the human factors discipline is comprised primarily of professionals and faculty from the fields of systems engineering, physiology, and cognitive psychology, both the origins and current manifestations of the field are far broader. For nearly a century, advertising, marketing, industrial design, communication design, architecture, and the entertainment industry have all used a variation of human factors to help to define the parameters and evaluate the success of their products. Although these other fields may have lacked the formal research and forum for dissemination of their methods through academic journals, recently their methods for abstracting behavioral models and likes and dislikes of their customers have found important relevance in industry and research. The newer view of human factors by those in the field reaches out to this view of what it means to characterize and interface with the human. A human factors/ergonomics conference held in Singapore in the Summer of 2001 used the term "Affective Human Factors" as the theme. The conference was endorsed by the International Ergonomics Society and was an attempt to bridge the two schools of thought about usability and desirability. The work of interaction designer Pat Jordan[4] deals with this new area human factors, which has not been otherwise covered extensively in the literature. His book delves more directly into issues that Don Norman introduced several years ago.[5]

Because of new research and diagnostic apparatus in kinesiology and biomechanics, it is now possible to follow the mechanics of swing in sports, record the pressure of each finger on a keyboard or track the eye movements of someone in a purchasing environment looking at competitive products. It is even possible to know what parts of the brain are involved in making a decision or observation.

The SET Factors have changed, the pace of industry has accelerated, and yet markets have become "demassified." Product development has moved from a period of mass manufacture and consumption to a period that can be defined not only as mass customization but also as mass *customer-zation*. Mass customer-zation is the act of

■ Too often
companies try
to customize
before knowing
the true needs
of their
customers.

attempting to understand the needs, wants, and desires of ever smaller and rapidly changing markets. Mass customization is the product that results from that understanding. Too often companies try to customize before knowing the true needs of their customers. Every category of products now demands the use of a variety of research methods to gain insight into the way people live and work and what their desires are. The Pontiac Aztec is an example of attempting to capture the X generation with a car customized to their every need. Yet it failed to hit the market the way the Nissan Xterra did several years before because, while it incorporated style and technology, it did not properly respond to the Value Opportunity attributes of pinpointing time and sense of place. As we have discussed in the earlier case study on Crown Equipment, even in fields as seemingly conservative as manufacturers of lift equipment, the ability to add a sense of pleasure and pride in the design can be a major factor in determining success. The Crown Wave meets all the safety and anthropometric requirements for lift equipment. However, the style and name also help it to be viewed as enjoyable to use and create a positive incentive for people to come to work. The enjoyment factor is another type of broader view of human factors. We describe a number of methods in this chapter for helping you to understand your customer. While the method of task analysis is a more commonly accepted method used by human factors experts, scenario development is not. Scenarios are as essential as any other facet of early product development. The scenario gives a product development team a common and concrete vision of who the customer is. It takes the generic term "customer" and translates it into a person (or persons) with a name and personality attributes and places him or her in the context of where the product will be used.

In characterizing the inherent difference in philosophy and approach between the two main categories of consumer research, the quantitative systems analysts tend to be searching for errors in existing approaches and the potential for injury in the use of products and environments. The process focuses on physiology and cognitive processes. The use of these methods can identify areas that must be addressed to reduce fatigue, stress, and injury, or reduce the number of steps needed to perform an operation. The qualitative methods tend to identify emotional and expressive aspects of customers' expectations and focus on the potential of what a product could be. Both types of analysis are needed. The best products produce an effect that is usually not anticipated by customers. They instantly fill a need no one knew they had. No one predicted that car buyers were interested in buying a two-seat retro convertible with rear wheel drive. Not even Mazda realized how big the market was when they introduced the Miata. No one anticipated the success of a peeler with an attractive, ergonomic handle made out of black rubber with fins under a new brand named OXO. Those factors were not measured directly but instead were sensed by "reading" the SET Factors. Then, using form development and ergonomic research working in tandem through conceptualization cycles and refinement, the final design was developed and launched.

The challenge is in mediating these two seemingly opposite approaches to understanding human behavior. While a successful product must reduce the likelihood of injury and misuse, it must simultaneously make a person feel that the product enhances their experience. The PT Cruiser is an example of how human factors research has been used in the design of the interior, while at the same time the exterior look and feel of the vehicle is pure emotion. The interior design is the result of human factors analysis that maximizes the interior space of the vehicle, thus making it comfortable, safe, and flexible through seating that allows reconfiguration for optimum storage. The design of the interior is also visually designed to complement the exterior look and feel without compromising usability. The exterior look and feel provides a highly emotional response that customers see as either highly desirable or not. This type of response is a qualitative response that is just as important for Chrysler as the interior safety. The design of the deployment of an airbag is critical to the safety of a driver in an accident. Failure to design this with the proper ergonomics analysis can result in the death of a driver. The steering wheel itself is something the driver uses every day. The look and feel of the steering wheel is a combination of visual appeal, cognitive understanding of controls, and understanding how the hand interacts with a circular form with a round cross section. The driver looks at the steering wheel and uses it every time he or she drives the car; its design is critical to the driving experience. The airbag only deploys in an emergency and it is hoped that the driver will never need it. Both of these design features are critical to the success of the product. The look and feel of the steering wheel is important from the point of purchase through the lifetime of the vehicle; it is a long-term product detail. The airbag is not. But if the airbag fails in an accident, everyone who owns a version of the car will feel unsafe and it could affect others when shopping for a new car. The airbag requires research and testing rigor and manufacturing standards that are greater in some respects than the design of the steering wheel. The steering wheel is in the primary lifestyle impact upper right cell of the PDM discussed in Chapter 6, while the airbag is in the secondary lifestyle impact lower right cell. However, both are important to the overall success of the product.

In all the products we have reviewed, there is a balance between the type of human factors that is the result of research and testing and the kind of research that creates insights that lead to the proper balance and expression of product form and features. Companies involved in new product development must try to merge the thinking between these two seemingly disparate approaches to understanding human behavior.

An Integrated Approach to a User-Driven Process

It is critical that each discipline be involved in user research. Fundamental to the success of a product is a positive user experience. When all is said and done, a consumer will use the vegetable peeler, drive the SUV, or drink the cup of coffee. The product enables the user to do something he or she either couldn't otherwise do, or couldn't do as well or as easily. The product also enables a fantasy of what could be. The interaction of the product with the user and the quality of the resulting activity summarize the overall user experience. If the experience is good, people will buy your product, recommend your product, and use your product. If it is poor, the consumer will be let down, frustrated, and negative. The goal is to understand how to create a product that facilitates a positive user experience.

As shown in Figure 7.1 (inner loop), surrounding the user experience is the user's expectation of interacting with the product. This expectation has three features: First is the look and feel — does the product affect the user's lifestyle and image appropriately or improve the aesthetic or psychological experience. Next is the performance — does the product function as anticipated and does the overall interaction with the technology enhance the overall experience. Third is what we defined in Chapter 3 as *psycheconometrics*, the psychological spending profile of a niche market — does the product offer the value people perceive is worth paying for. The goal is to understand these expectations and translate them into product features.

The expectation of what the experience will be is realized by the attributes of the product (Figure 7.1, middle loop). The way that the look and feel of a product is perceived by the user is through the sensory factors — the visual, tactile, auditory, olfactory, and gustatory aesthetics. The performance of a product is a direct result of the features incorporated into the product. The psycheconometric element is accomplished by focus on a target market.

These attributes become the product and are manifested through style (creating sensory factors), technology (enabling features), and the price and brand strategy (describing cost preferences of the product and a brand appropriate for the target market) as shown in Figure 7.1, outside loop. As shown in the figure, these manifestations map directly into design, engineering, and marketing (and finance). Each discipline, then, directly affects the user's experience with the product and each is required to contribute to the development of the product.

Understanding the expectations of the user experience gives each discipline a direction to pursue in developing the product. The goal in developing a breakthrough product, then, is to understand the user's expectations. We now turn to tools and methods for understanding the user.

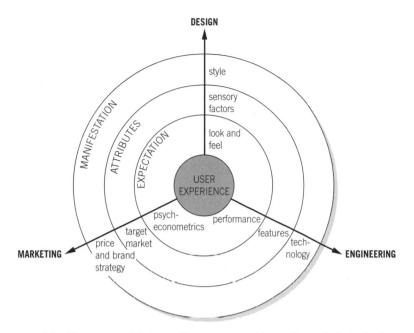

DESIGN

style

sensory
factors

look and
feel

MANIFESTATION

ATTRIBUTES

EXPECTATION

USER
EXPERIENCE

psych-
econometrics

performance

target
market

features

price
and brand
strategy

tech-
nology

MARKETING

ENGINEERING

Figure 7.1   User-centered design — the user's expectation sets up attributes that are manifested through the disciplines.

Scenario Development (Part I)

Recall that the SET Factors are a scan of the Social trends (S), Economic forces (E), and Technological advances (T) in society. The goal is to recognize the need for a product to influence the lifestyle of a group in society, in other words, a product opportunity. Once that opportunity is identified, the first step in qualitative research is to create a scenario, or story, about a typical user in the targeted activity, and how the lack of a product makes their activity harder or less fulfilling.

The initial scenario is short (maybe a paragraph or two in length) and covers the basic elements of the opportunity. These elements include the who, what, why, how, and when of a situation. In other words, *who* is the target customer, *what* is their need, *why* do they have that need, *how* is the task currently accomplished, and *when* does this happen?

For example, a scenario that eventually led to a product concept and a patent application for the product by Ford Motor Company was:

> Ron is an independent contractor. He typically works alone or with a crew of one or two. When Ron arrives at the work site in the morning, he drops off his larger equipment as close to the work area as possible. Setting up a work area typically

means carrying sawhorses and boards as well as large ladders and tools. Most of the equipment is heavy and many trips to a destination far from the truck can be time- and energy-intensive.

If Ron can work near his truck, he often uses the tailgate as a cutting or work surface, even for eating lunch. Ron's truck has side-mounted toolboxes that he installed and both a ladder rack and towing hitch that were installed professionally. This means that Ron has no free space within his truck bed and that his tools often have to be put on the ground during unloading, which is damaging to both the tools and Ron's back.

This scenario identifies:

Who: Ron, a contractor;

What: Need for flexible workspace associated with his truck;

Why: No room in typically loaded truck; makeshift solutions are not satisfactory; current approach is bad on the back and tiring;

How: Equipment carried and put together on the spot, or tailgate used as makeshift table;

When: Throughout the workday.

We still don't know a lot about Ron's needs and the details of his activities. We also don't know a lot about the solution to his dilemma. But we do know that there is a wonderful opportunity here to create a product to meet Ron's needs. We also know, from our SET Factors and informal discussions with contractors, that Ron is not alone, that many contractors have these same problems every day.[T1]

The project surrounding Ron and his needs, wants, and desires will be used throughout this chapter as an example to illustrate several of the methods of user-based research. Chapter 9 will revisit Ron and this project and see how this scenario eventually led to a superb and innovative after-market product for trucks. This product, being patented by Ford Motor Company, resulted from a 17-week part-time effort by a team of novice engineers, designers, and a marketing person who followed the user-centered iNPD process laid out in this book.

As discussed in Chapters 1 and 3, the SET Factors and Value Opportunities will change over time. If the product meets a wider range of needs, wants, and desires, then it will stay in the Upper Right for a longer time. The scenario can help to create a more robust Upper Right product, one that is not sensitive to slight variations in the SET Factors and resulting VOs. Once the core scenario is stated, then it should be considered under different environments. For Ron, how would the scenario change if the consumer base became more "green" (i.e., environmentally aware)? How would increased fuel costs affect Ron's business? Or how will Ron's need for workspace change as his truck becomes networked and becomes his sole office? Such context variation will help the team think in a broader context about the product opportunity.

A scenario is a powerful tool to keep the development process focused. Although the scenario may get more refined, it is critical at each step along the way to revisit the scenario and make sure that the evolving product meets the who-what-why-how-when of the scenario. If at any time the product deviates from this description, then the design team must decide if the purpose of the product has changed (with evidence from further qualitative research) or else rethink the solution to get back on track with the scenario.

Once an initial scenario is completed, the next task for the team is to seek to understand in detail the activities, needs, and preferences of someone like the person or people in the scenario.

New Product Ethnography

▌ Ethnography can help to determine the qualities that products should possess.

During the second half of the 20th century, companies involved in new product development looked to the social sciences for information about ergonomics and attitudes of consumers. Most recently, techniques used in the field of anthropology have been employed to aid in the preliminary stages of new product development through the use of ethnographic methods. Traditional ethnography is the art and science of describing a group or culture. It is a form of cultural anthropology using fieldwork to observe the group and derive patterns of behavior, belief, and activity. Fetterman[6] provides a clear overview of traditional ethnography. The new form of ethnography used in product development is a blend of these traditional methods with new emerging technology for observing, recording, and analyzing social situations.[7] New product ethnography, however, is more than just applied anthropology. The most important element of this new form is that it is not merely descriptive but also predictive. This new branch of ethnography has emerged into a powerful new area for predicting consumer preferences for product features, form, material and color, and patterns of use and purchase. In other words, ethnography can help to determine the qualities that products should possess. Wilcox[8] sums up the motivation for including ethnography in the design process: "We should be concerned about the study of culture for one central reason: It is the primary determinant of what people want to buy and how they like it."

Ethnography techniques have emerged as a research tool for both marketing and human factors. In marketing research, ethnography can be used to identify and understand emerging trends. In human factors research, these same techniques can be used to better understand people's patterns of use and preferences when developing the criteria for products. The use of ethnographic methods is critical in the early phases of product development because they provide deeper insights than broad statistical surveys. Existing databases compiled by market research can complement and help direct this type of research. Broad surveys and focus groups, however, are more useful downstream when there is a basic understanding of the user. You need to know what questions to ask to make a focus group or survey useful; ethnography helps you find out what questions are relevant.

New product ethnography provides four benefits to the product development process. The first is an in-depth understanding of a small representative sample of the intended market. Again, the goal in the early stages of the process is *not* to obtain statistically significant, general information about product features. Rather it is to understand indepth the needs, wants, and desires of a market segment. Ethnography provides insight into all of these and is a keyhole to understanding the everyday *behavior* of the customer.

The second benefit of ethnography is a focus on the consumer's lifestyle, experiences, and patterns of use. These insights allow the team to identify the features of a product that will make it sell. But beyond features, these insights help define the essence of the product — the look, feel, function, and purpose of the product. Ethnographic insights are the difference in defining the gap between the functional generic vegetable peeler and the GoodGrips line, the walkie-talkie and the Talkabout, and the coffeeshop and Starbucks. These insights can help car companies understand why some people prefer a basic pickup truck while others prefer an SUV.

The turnaround time between identifying the need for a product and seeing the product on the market is anywhere from six months to four years. There are huge financial commitments that must be made from cost of design and engineering to manufacturing equipment, labor, marketing and sales. Given the significant amount of money and resources at stake, it is critical that the product designed today will be successful one to three years down the road. How can a company commit its resources to a guess as to what a consumer will want to purchase in the future? Ethnography is a key to making the right decisions by removing the guesswork. So the third benefit of ethnography is predicting major shifts in consumer needs. By seeking out the essence of how people think about the world around them, what is coming into their focal point, and what is leaving, then the product development team can gain insights into what needs, wants, and desires people will shift to in the near future.

Rather than just focusing on the product itself, the team must understand the levels of detail surrounding the product. How will people use the product and in what situations? What other products will people use in conjunction with this one? What activities, besides the one of focus, does the customer like to participate in? What difficulties does the customer have in the current experience? These difficulties go beyond the details of a task analysis. They exist in the storage, access, and maintenance of the product; in the environments where current products fail; and in the type of environments in which people live, work, and play. Understanding the essence of the lifestyle and patterns of use of the user is like peeling away an artichoke — the heart is at the bottom but each leaf has meat to enjoy and contributes to the overall experience of eating an artichoke, or designing a product.

The fourth benefit for new product ethnography is the ability to monitor dynamic markets. What people like today they will probably not like tomorrow; what people liked yesterday they will like again soon. Why is rock climbing in vogue after so many years? Why do GenXers like to skydive and bungie jump? Why are the PT Cruiser and Beetle so popular when their styles have been "out" for so long? When will DVDs overtake VHS as the forum of choice for movies (probably by the time this book is printed)? Why did the style and ease of use of the iMac succeed when consumers had been obsessed with faster processing speed and more features? Ethnography can help the team see changes in the marketplace before they occur by observing the frustrations and enthusiasm of customers to aspects of technology, style, and activity.

The techniques of ethnography useful in product design include:[9]

- Observation — Taking a birds-eye view of a situation allows the ethnographer to obtain a (somewhat) unobtrusive understanding of the context and particular activities surrounding a product opportunity. Observation methods include the ethnographer physically being at an event or using video and sound recording for later analysis. One product ethnography firm pays people to keep a camera in their living room for a week! The videos are then analyzed, section-by-section, looking for interesting insights into behaviors. The result of the observation is often interpreted by the ethnographer in conjunction with data from interviews and visual stories using state-of-the-art video editing and organizing software.

- Interviews — Within the context of use in which people encounter the product or general opportunity under consideration, interviews provide insights into the way individuals think about, understand, and relate to their behavior in relationship to that part of their lifestyle. Stories about situations and objects are desired in order to understand the context within which a product would function. Here the interviews go much deeper than just the details of the product into the general lifestyle of the user and overall target experience. The emergence of the Web and Internet research tools have opened up this medium as an interview option.

■ Visual stories — Visual stories are data produced by the target users (the research subjects) themselves. They are narratives that provide insight into typical activities surrounding a particular lifestyle. Visual stories are created by participants via disposable cameras and diaries/journals where people record what they think is important in a defined setting. This setting may be the activity of focus, the highlights of a day, or even photos of their favorite fashion or colors.

The goal of each approach is to contribute to an overall understanding of the issues surrounding a potential product opportunity and lifestyle issue. The result is insight that leads directly to an understanding of the Value Opportunities for the product. From the resulting patterns of behavior, a model emerges that indicates the flow of activities, behaviors, attitudes, or emotions surrounding the product opportunity.

Consider the opportunity of organizing and storing medicines in the household for families. A team using ethnography to understand this opportunity visited several families in their homes and applied the ethnographic methods of observation and in-depth interviews. After analyzing the data, they derived a model of behaviors of medicine use shown in Figure 7.2. In the model, the following loop is followed:

Needing medicine — someone gets sick and tries to find a remedy to make them feel better. This could involve getting a prescription from a doctor and learning about the medicine from the doctor.

Remembering to get the medicine is required to move to the next step.

Getting the medicine — obtaining medicine from a pharmacy, herbalist, or anyplace else. This may involve further education from the dispenser.

Managing the medicine — integration of the medicine into people's lives by creating or adopting routines.

Remembering to take the medicine is required to move to the next step.

Taking the medicine — consumption of medicine, possibly with other requirements such as with food.

Recording that medicine was taken is sometimes done or desired. The process returns to "Needing medicine."

No product is defined or suggested, but at every arrow or box in the model, clear opportunities for products exist.[T2]

As a different example, the team that focused on Ron and other contractors discovered many relevant lifestyle issues through observation and in-depth interviews. In

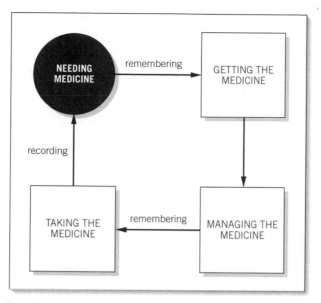

Figure 7.2 Behavioral model of medicine taking and storage in the home derived from ethnographic research.

terms of their trucks, all contractors had some sort of accessories on their trucks. Few had a cap, many had ladder racks, few had behind-cab toolboxes, and most had side-mounted toolboxes. These observations showed that this market is willing to spend money to buy accessories for their truck if they are useful and help them work. The wide range of accessories and set-ups on the trucks indicated that the team was going to have to design a product that does not interfere with the present configuration of the contractors' trucks.

All of the people interviewed had a make-shift workspace that they themselves made at the site. This usually consisted of two sawhorses and a board to make a table. About a third of the people interviewed said that they used worktables that they bought in addition to the one they made. These tables were usually foldable tables that came with a tool and were only used with that one tool (i.e., a circular saw and the factory-made, collapsible table that it attached to). Half of the people interviewed used the tailgate as a workspace. The activities at the tailgate include setting up a brake and bending material, cutting material, using it as a workbench, using it as a sawhorse for the worktable, and sitting and eating lunch.

The information gathered from the interviews led to a list of additional concerns that had to be addressed when developing the product:

- How much space does it take up?

- Where does it live on/in the truck?

- Can it have its own power source?

- Can it be removable?

Using Ethnography to Understand Customers at Polaroid

There are several Fortune 500 companies already using ethnography as a source for understanding their customers. Companies have used the results of ethnographic research to understand the customer in broad general terms and in a more targeted way to understand how to develop specific products. This section presents a case study that illustrates how ethnography helped Polaroid better understand their customers. Polaroid hired E-Lab, a consumer research consulting firm that was recently purchased by Sapient, to carry on this research. In this study, E-Lab used the methods outlined in the previous section to better understand how consumers feel about the experience of photography in general and instant imaging in particular. The results of their research helped Polaroid verify the appropriateness of some of its current projects as well as identify some new product and service opportunities. These new opportunities strongly connected with the brand identity of Polaroid in the market, demonstrating that insightful user research strengthens the relationship of a company's brand strategy with the products they produce.

In this study, E-Lab used visual stories, observation, and shadowing, along with in-depth lifestyle interviews and reference, to better understand how people integrate photography, especially instant photography, into their lives. This included 28 detailed two-to-three hour interviews and tours within people's homes — observing photo displays and understanding how people take pictures, display and store them, and how they exchange photos with others. One aspect of note was what photos people value and why. E-lab's research team also observed several participants during photo-taking events with an emphasis on how people compare instant pictures to 35mm images. Visual stories were also taken by participants to capture what and when they used their own photo equipment in the course of a week. Finally, field observations in several localities documented tourists at zoos and other tourist sites using cameras.

The result of this effort was a clearer understanding of why people take photos, namely to record and give form to personal experiences. Photos allow people to exchange information about themselves to others and to maintain and strengthen those relationships over distance and time. People take images of many everyday activities and special events, leading to an understanding of what technologies people need for different activities. The more people are able to successfully integrate photos into their lives, the more likely they are to take even more images, thus promoting the idea of ease of use for not only taking, but working with and storing images. A gap was found between what people desired and what products actually gave them. This gap defined areas (POGs) where new products could be developed.

The ethnographic researchers integrated the observations into a model of the photographic process proprietary to Polaroid. The model differentiates between taking and using photos. In general, photo companies have successfully focused on the process of taking photos. However, products to support the process of how people use photos were less explored. Both 35mm and instant photography relied on an exchange process that took place through printing the picture. With Polaroid's cameras, this happened instantaneously and bypassed the more traditional delay of an independent processing medium. Digital photography allows for an array of new opportunities to directly exchange, display, manipulate, and store images.

This research provided a new and fresh look at the photographic market and helped to indicate Polaroid's specific role in it. As stated earlier, the study validated some of the directions Polaroid was already going. For example, the Olympus C211 camera was a partnership between Olympus and Polaroid where a digital image could be instantaneously printed with Polaroid's digital printing technology. According to the E-lab study, digital offered more flexibility that consumers want but lacked the ability to easily get hard prints. This combination in the C211, already under development before the E-Lab study but confirmed by it, was exactly what consumers indicated they wanted.

The research also influenced future projects at Polaroid. By concurrently re-examining Polaroid's customers' needs, wants, and desires (through the ethnography study) and Polaroid's approach to brand, the company was able to think more broadly about the current and future state of the photography product world as they move into the digital age. Polaroid sees itself as the "Apple Computer of the camera world" — they take a different approach to photography than all of the other camera companies and always have. They were "differentiated at birth." Thus they found it easy to think differently about how they were to address digital photography.

New products will eventually emerge as a result of this new way of thinking about the photographic product space and as a result of the ethnographic research. This ethnography study helped Polaroid further understand that for people to take more pictures, the camera must be readily accessible in their ongoing world. An example of this is a digital camera concept that mimics the cordless phone by residing in a living environment, charging in a cradle (as shown in Figure 7.3). By always being in the living area

Figure 7.3   Polaroid concept model. (Reprinted with permission of Polaroid Corporation.)

■ A deep
qualitative
understanding
of the customer
can lead to an
innovative new
product concept.

and always charged, it is always available for spontaneous photography, a unique characteristic of Polaroid. And rather than having to place the photos in albums, the camera, when not being used to take pictures, constantly displays the pictures in its memory on its viewing screen, behaving as a live picture frame. In context of the behavioral model of the photographic process developed from the ethnographic research, the camera supports taking a picture and jumping immediately to using it in the picture frame mode. This case study shows how a deep qualitative understanding of the customer, through ethnographic research, can lead to an innovative new product concept positioned in the Upper Right.

Lifestyle Reference

Why do so many products for some target markets have the same look and feel, even though they are made by different companies? Clearly companies try to copy successful and current styles. Some companies are leaders and some are followers. It is best to be a leader, but that can only happen if the new styles that you introduce anticipate and meet the expectations of the market. New styles and trends start in industries where style changes each year or even season, as in the fashion industry. At the same time, music, film, and sports are indications of the current emotional and stylistic trends. The cartoons of Disney have clearly influenced the cartoon-like products Michael Graves has designed for Target. The Bengal is a new sports car designed by Buick to capture the spirit and style of its primary spokesman, Tiger Woods. New products in one industry or product line are influenced by products from other lines. The wrap-around design of the clear plastic cover for the Black & Decker SnakeLight discussed in Chapter 8 was inspired by the contemporary wrap-around headlights in cars. Finally, although a company wants to be the leader, it is critical that it doesn't miss an opportunity identified by a competitor or related market.

A method that integrates these factors is *lifestyle reference*, namely reference to other products, styles and activities from the target market segment. The goal of lifestyle reference is an understanding of what people buy, the context of how people use products, what people value, and what people define as their expectation of quality. The idea is to identify and surround yourself with a snapshot of the customer's life, to immerse yourself into the world of the user. General Motors blasts the music of the target customer and creates areas filled with products being used by the target generation in their concept studios. Ford has huge picture boards with a variety of images including product photos. The idea is that the music, colors, styles, and looks each give the designers a feel for who the customer is and what he or she wants in a product.

The ability to capture a lifestyle reference is really quite simple. We recommend beginning by purchasing magazines targeting your market segment. For example, magazines for an older, upper class economic group might include *Gourmet*, *Architectural Digest*, *Golf*, and travel magazines, while X-Generation magazines might include magazines about mountain biking, snowboarding, *Spin* magazine, *Gear* magazine, and *Wired*. From the magazines, create a collage of the key lifestyle images and typical products. The collage can be organized by subject, color, or randomly put together to give an interpreted snapshot of the user. An example collage is shown in Figure 7.4 that represents issues surrounding the task of shaving the head for the X-Generation crowd. Figure 1.4 showed the HeadBlade, a product to meet just that opportunity.

From the magazines, identify products from feature stories or advertisements. Purchase these products or borrow and use them. Photos indicate a first look, but touching and

(a)   (b)

Figure 7.4   Lifestyle reference collage of X-Generation head shaving (b is close-up of part of collage in a).

■ If the team
tries to reach
too broad a
market with a
given product,
at least initially,
then the prod-
uct may not
gain enough
buy-in from any
one group to
succeed.

using a product gives you a sense for the current use of materials, accents, and touch and feel of the products.

Identify music and films popular with the target group. The sense and emotional tenor from the music or the tone of imagery from a movie translates into product style.

Of course some products can be trans-generational. In that case, a mix of reference materials is necessary. Be careful, however. As product opportunities stem from the SET Factors, they are also targeted to a specific group of users. If the team tries to reach too broad a market with a given product, at least initially, then the product may not gain enough buy-in from any one group to succeed.

Ergonomics: Interaction, Task Analysis, and Anthropometrics

Interaction

Ergonomics refers to the dynamic movement of people and their interaction with both static and dynamic man made products and environments. A product has two primary and interrelated levels of interaction. Human beings experience the world through cognitive perception and physical contact. The two modes work in a dynamic cycle that produces the world we experience. Both levels of interaction must be accounted for when designing how customers navigate the use of the product. When a consumer looks at a product, it must be consistent with cognitive models that he or she has already developed. If the product is perceived as cognitively dissonant (inconsistent with former patterns), it will be difficult to use and often rejected. Computer screens are a good example of cognitive dissonance. The use of menus and function keys only add to the confusion. When many older consumers (above 60) look at a screen, it is usually unfamiliar to them and they only see one layer of the information. In contrast, a book or magazine has a front cover and table of contents, and both can be quickly scanned. The entire product is visible and parts are instantly accessible by physically thumbing through. The logical order used is linear. While the Web is a very useful resource, it is not deemed as usable by many people who are confused by the interface currently required to gain Web access. And, once on the Web, people are often confused by the complexity of a particular website. A product interface must account for a variety of users that vary in language, age, ability, gender, education, and cultural norms. In the medical field, a product may be used by a sixty-year-old doctor, a twenty-five-year-old nurse, and a thirty-year-old medical technician who is a recent immigrant and who can barely speak English (or other local tongue). The chance for error with a product that has multiple users is very high. It is a challenge to develop one interface that all these potential users will find easy to navigate and in the medical profession an error can easily be fatal. That same product may be sold in several countries around the world. Does a multinational product have to be redesigned for each country or should the product team try to use or develop terms and symbols that are internationally understood? Just think of the liability riding on that decision.

When people interact physically with a product, there is also the issue of physical comfort and ease of operation. A product can be uncomfortable by causing pain on contact or through awkward positioning or extension of the body or any part of the body. A sports car is usually very uncomfortable for tall or overweight people because the interior comfort and space is often compromised for aerodynamics. Food is often packaged in sealed containers that are difficult to open. Reaching an ATM machine from a car window is often a very uncomfortable activity. Office chairs are now designed to provide a stable mobile base, support the lumbar section of the spine, and adjust to different types of tasks. They have a curved front edge that helps to promote blood flow to the legs and prevents the numbing effect (falling asleep, pins and needles) that can occur when seated for too long.

It is important to understand the physical interaction of the product in use. One of the common problems with products that are tech driven is that they are often brought to market before ergonomic issues are identified. If engineers and programmers determine the cognitive and physical interface, they will often design it for themselves and not for the general public. They will under-design and create a product that is too complex for the average person to use. Industrial designers can also put form ahead of usability, creating products that look beautiful but are difficult to use. The former issue is described in Moore's book, *Crossing the Chasm.* Products designed using an engineering technology-driven approach will be attractive to lead users and early adopters who look for the latest versions of products. But this approach will not transfer to the larger consumer segments because the followers of lead users demand a simpler and friendlier interaction with a product. While Moore clearly describes the problem for high-tech products, he does not give the whole solution. The method in this book, using ethnographic customer-centered research and integrating design, engineering, and marketing, will give a product a much higher chance of success in the larger market. This scenario is clearly illustrated in the Iomega case study presented in Chapter 4, where a high-tech product failed in the mass market until an appropriate interface and identity were established. If ergonomic problems are not predicted and integrated into the product early, they are not easy to account for later and will invariably have an effect on the style of the product. Just adding in physical product features or warning labels will compromise the look and trust of the consumer.

Products must be easy to understand cognitively and comfortable to use physically.

Discomfort can be immediate or develop over time. Industrial and office labor has highlighted the problem of repetitive stress injury. By reducing the number of activities in a work task to improve efficiency, companies often create situations where workers will fall victim to an array of injuries that occur when the same action is repeated non stop for days, months, or years. Carpal Tunnel Syndrome is the best known example of repetitive stress injury and can appear in the computer industry or the factory. Scanners in supermarkets were causing a high incidence of Carpal Tunnel until the scanners where redesigned to be handheld. These new ergonomically correct scanners allow cashiers to hold the product and scanner. It reduces the number of repeat attempts and prevents the need to continually use the same motion — dragging items over the static glass window. It is now common to have a masseuse come into computer intensive environments to release the tensions in the neck, shoulder, and arms of people who work at keyboards most of the day. The Wave is a product designed as a response to back injury in the workplace due to lifting and climbing. Products must be easy to understand cognitively and comfortable to use physically.

Task Analysis

The goal of task analysis is to break down the current approach to solving the problem in a step-by-step manner. The result is a flow chart of each step that constitutes an activity. It may be as broad as the major steps in the day of a construction worker, an analysis of each motion that a person goes through to pick up or put down an item, or motions that the body goes through to climb or descend stairs.

If the goal is to improve the situation for a person who has physical challenges, then how does that person's process differ from those without physical challenges? Here the task analysis is performed for both types of people and the differences compared. Of course one may question if the process is ideal for even the "normal" person. For example, consider the design of the OXO GoodGrips. The original focus was to provide a vegetable peeler for a person with arthritis. How, then, does an arthritic person use a generic metal peeler? How does a person without arthritis use the peeler? What actions are the same and what are different? What actions cause pain for the arthritic person and what adjustments does he or she go through to compensate for the pain? Further, consider the non-arthritic person. How effective is the action of peeling with a generic peeler? Are there any aspects of the process that are uncomfortable? This type of analysis led, eventually, to the GoodGrips peeler. The large grip, the improved tactile feel, and the quality of the blade all addressed the needs of the arthritic individual and, it turned out, even the non-arthritic user as well. A task analysis of the GoodGrips shows a significant difference in the way a person with arthritis uses the GoodGrips versus its metal predecessor.

Because of the level of detailed analysis required for a task analysis, most often the activity is first video-taped and the video is used to break down the task. Usually several people are each videotaped and their processes analyzed together. The task sequence is written down step by step. If different people perform parts of the task differently, then branches in the sequence occur to show the different options. If the sequences converge again, then the points of convergence are shown. The approach is general and must be adapted to your own needs and context. The challenges in this process are to look carefully at each step and develop the ability to separate important steps from more trivial elements in the task. Someone who is not trained to look carefully at situations can often miss essential issues. Having a number of people with different perspectives reviewing the tape is ideal. Different disciplines are sensitive to different issues.

Once the task breakdown is completed, the resulting flow chart or step sequences are analyzed to indicate what is good or ineffective about the process. Also, how does one process differ from another in number of steps, number of alternatives, and number of places of difficulty? The goal in developing any product is to either reduce the number of steps in the task or make the steps more effective and easier to accomplish. A task analysis comparison of the prior state and the new state affected by your product can verify the effectiveness of the product. The comparison can also be an effective means of proving to the company, investors, or user the value of the product. The goal is to use task analysis to help create an understanding of the current user experience in a given situation and to help identify where a product can best improve that experience.

Consider an opportunity to create an automated door opener/lock for the home. One aspect of the research is to understand how people negotiate unlocking and opening a door in the current state and how a product that addresses the opportunity might improve the experience. A task analysis of a person carrying packages attempting to unlock and open a door is shown in Figure 7.5(a). Twelve distinct steps are found in the process. Figure 7.5(b) shows a task analysis of the same person using an automated door opener — the desired process is reduced to 5 distinct steps. Such an analysis clearly articulates the benefits from such a system and the requirements for the product (it must unlock and open the door without further intervention).[T3]

Another use of task analysis is to help organize and model process information. Consider the opportunity to clean all of the nooks and crannies in the kitchen like the grooves inside Tupperware lids, holes in cheese graters, or blades of egg beaters. An analysis of over 30 such objects led one team to a form representation of the majority

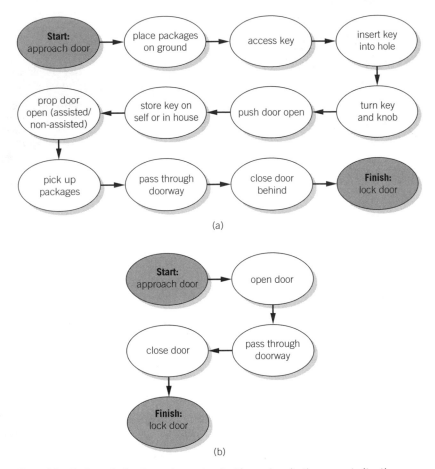

Figure 7.5 Task analysis of opening and unlocking a door in the current situation without (a) and in the desired situation with (b) an automated opener.

of such nooks and crannies (shown in Figure 7.6). Such a summary of the types of slots and holes that need to be cleaned keeps the process generalized to all applications rather than fixated on a specific example.[T4]

Finally, a task analysis of Ron the contractor in the scenario above showed a significant number of activities centralized around the beginning and end of the workday. Contractors typically work in small or solo teams. Additionally, two or more trips to and from the supply store and the site are often needed before work can begin. Organizing, loading, and unloading small- to medium-sized objects in, out, and around the truck bed emerged as a primary task for this user group. Another key task is the need to remove the workspace and set it up closer to the work being done when it is not possible to locate the truck close enough. Tasks in this situation would include cutting, planning, and elevating supplies.

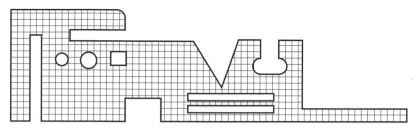

Figure 7.6   A representation of nooks and crannies found in the kitchen.

Anthropometrics

During WWII, issues of man-machine relationships became critical. Given the size of armies and the mass production developed to equip them, it became critical to design equipment to be usable by the largest range of soldiers and to understand the limitations of use. It was an early version of what would evolve into mass marketing during the 1950s. Boots, uniforms, and bunks were designed for the average soldier, what would become known as the 50th percentile. Other military equipment had size limitations and taller soldiers were usually banned from certain assignments. For instance, pilot cockpits, tank driver compartments, and submarines are examples of the type of equipment that were designed for function only and thus limited the height and weight of the soldiers that could work comfortably in those spaces. After the war, the information from this field was then applied to manufacture of industrial and farm equipment and office work environments.

A seminal book in this area is the *The Measure of Man and Woman: Human Factors in Design*, by Henry Dreyfuss.[10] The book is the third version of a publication developed by the design firm Henry Dreyfuss and Associates and originally published in 1959 and titled *Measure of Man and Woman*. Henry Dreyfuss was a pioneer in the use of ergonomics for seating and work environments. While the original version relied heavily on data gathered by the military, the newest version represents decades of research gleaned from the work of the firm in a variety of product programs which include farm equipment, transportation, office environments, seating, phones, and cameras. This expanded version includes information that responded to ADA requirements. It is perhaps the best introductory book and collection of data on the market. The current version has excellent anthropometrics charts (e.g., Figure 7.7) that range from infants to seniors. It covers the ergonomics of living and working environments for fully abled people and those with disabilities.

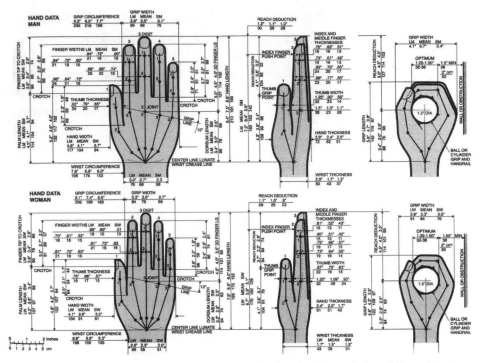

Figure 7.7 Example Dreyfuss anthropometric chart. (Reprinted with permission of Henry Dreyfuss Associates.)

The team focusing on space for contractors to work on used the Dreyfuss charts to determine what anthropometric constraints their design would need to take into consideration. The data covers 95 percent of the population ranging from the first percentile female to the 99th percentile male:

- Table height will range from 32" to 36".

- As the height decreases, the easier it becomes to lift heavy objects. This translates to a height of 6"–8" below the user's elbow.

- Table depth can range from 18" to 36", allowing the user to reach across the work surface and access shelves above the workspace.

- Table length is dictated by the ability of the user to handle and potentially carry the work surface, no more that 6 feet, allowing for use on different-length trucks.

The use of anthropometric analysis in product development is complemented with a detailed understanding of biomechanics. Including nuances down to the level of muscle activation lends insights that lead to the successful design of products. The ergonomic pipette designed by VistaLab Technologies and Frogdesign, discussed in Chapter 3, resulted from a detailed ergonomic analysis of physical motion of the body in conjunction with a task analysis of the steps required to use a pipette. A snapshot of that analysis is shown in Figure 7.8. As shown in Figure 7.9, in the development of the Aeron chair (presented in Chapter 8), designer Bill Stumpf performed a detailed study of the variation in shapes and sizes of body types, a biometric task required to truly understand the bounds and range of interactions with the product.

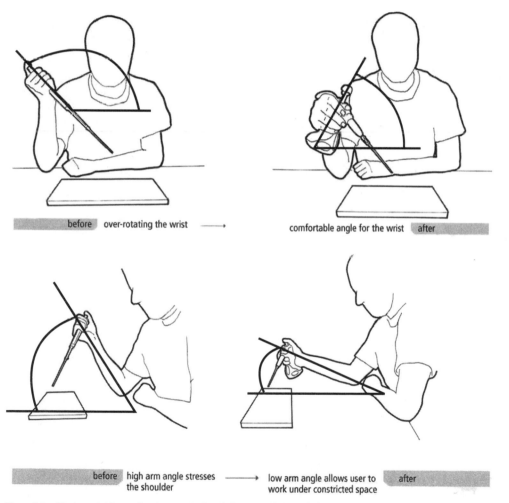

before   over-rotating the wrist   ⟶

comfortable angle for the wrist   after

before   high arm angle stresses   ⟶   low arm angle allows user to   after
              the shoulder   work under constricted space

Figure 7.8 Task and biomechanics analysis of the use of the original and new pipette for VistaLab. (Reprinted with permission of Frogdesign and VistaLab Technologies.)

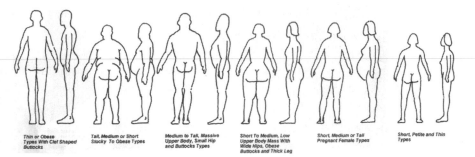

Figure 7.9 Illustration of the variation in body types of people who might sit in the Aeron Chair. (Reprinted with permission of Stumpf Weber Associates.)

The AT&T Dreyfuss Phone

An excellent example of the evolution of human factors understanding is the evolution of the telephone. The first attempt by AT&T to blend style and technology was in the phone shown in Figure 7.10, designed using the firm of Henry Dreyfuss as consultants. Dreyfuss conducted their own human factors research and form development and worked with the engineering systems group in AT&T. The phone housed the latest communication technology in a product that was the result of thorough research in the encoding and decoding of sound. The receiver and mouthpiece were set in a hand-held product that was the result of the best average distance an ear and mouthpiece needed to be separated around the face. The Dreyfuss firm conducted research and determined the best overall fit that would accommodate the broadest range of customers — the type of analysis used during WWII and known as designing for the 50th percentile. This meant designing for the largest part of a population within a normal bell curve distribution (shown Figure 7.11). The handle was designed with a cross section that made it easy to hold. The development of a dial in the design reflected a change in the technological factor of making phone calls: automated switching systems that allowed callers to phone directly. There was no longer a need to contact an operator to make phone calls. People could just dial a set of numbers to reach another person. The dial was placed at an angle to make it more comfortable to see and dial and was set on a base that was heavy enough to provide stability to dial with one hand. The base needed to surround the core technology required to send and receive calls, which was too large and heavy to be put in the handset.

The shift from a heavy two-piece product designed for a mass market to a one-product-fits-all approach has led to the evolution of a vast array of communication products. Today, Nokia, a small company in Finland, is one of the most successful producers of mass communication products. Nokia uses the latest concepts in mass customization. They also need to design phones with a set of interaction symbols to compliment the original dial mode. Their use of postponement allows them to match the latest style trends with the latest technology. The evolution from the original Dreyfuss phone for AT&T to the contemporary designs of Nokia reflects the changes in the field of user research in new product development.

Figure 7.10   Model 302 phone for AT&T by Henry Dreyfuss, 1937. (Reprinted with permission of Henry Dreyfuss Associates.)

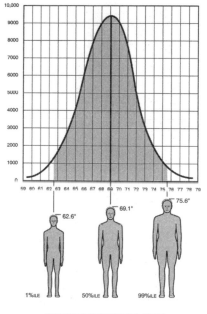

FREQUENCY DISTRIBUTION CURVE

Figure 7.11   Bell-shaped distribution showing the 50th percentile used by Dreyfuss. (Reprinted with permission of Henry Dreyfuss Associates.)

Scenario Development (Part II)

Earlier we explained the use of scenarios in the product development process. The initial scenario helps the team understand the user profile enough to find target users for ethnographic study and task analysis, and to follow up on lifestyle reference and human factors analyses. The scenario is a reference point for the entire product development process. The result of the qualitative research, then, can and should augment the original scenario, fleshing out details and context for the use of the product. The scenario for Ron was revised after observation, interviews, task analysis, and lifestyle reference, and now includes more detail and a better articulation of the issues involved, as presented in the sidebar.

Final Scenario for Phase II

Ron is an independent contractor. He accepts jobs ranging from siding and roof repair to interior/exterior renovation and restoration. He has a wife and three kids and a nice house in a suburb. His wife is a homemaker and helps him manage his business by taking phone calls and helping him with the books.

Ron typically works alone or with a crew of one or two. His jobs often require large quantities of building supplies, like siding or roof shingles, not to mention a variety of tools. While he can hold most of his smaller tools in the side toolboxes, his larger tools like the break, miter saw, compressor, and saw horses fill the bed of his F-150 such that not even a small amount of building supplies will fit. This means that he has to make two or more trips to and from the site before work begins every morning.

When Ron arrives at the work site in the morning, he drops off his larger equipment as close to the work area as possible. This sometimes means that he has to put tools on the ground in a pile next to the truck and pick them up off the ground later. Next, he drives to the supply warehouse and loads the building materials for the day. Then he returns to the site and sets up a work area next to the building. Setting up a work area typically means carrying saw horses and boards to work on, as well as large ladders and tools. Most of the equipment is heavy. Many trips to a destination far from the truck can be time and energy intensive.

If Ron can work near his truck, he often uses the tailgate as a cutting surface, for assembly, tool cleaning and maintenance, reading drawings, or even eating lunch. He has noticed, however, that because his toolboxes block the sides of the truck, he has no access to the bed if he uses the tailgate for these things. He also has noticed that his back gets sore when he works over the tailgate too long because it is lower than his workbench. He also worries about accidentally cutting into the tailgate and damaging his saw blades. So, even though it is convenient to work on the tailgate, he tries not to make it a habit.

Ron's truck has side-mounted toolboxes that he installed. He also has a ladder rack and towing hitch that were installed professionally. Ron stores his smaller tools in the side-mounted toolboxes. He has noticed that as he is digging for a specific tool he has no convenient place to put other tools to get them out of the way except on top of the boxes. The top of the box is over his head, however, and doing that has caused him to hurt his shoulder in the past. So, he sometimes sets the heavier tools on the ground, but this can make them dirty and cause his bad back to act up as he tries to pick them up. These inconveniences, like other things, are just part of having a truck, at least in his mind.

After a hard day of putting up siding, he puts the tools in the back of the truck. The first thing he does is put the ladders on because he has to stand in the bed of the truck to move them up onto the rack and secure them. Then he loads the tools and excess materials. Sometimes a tool or piece of equipment arrives at the truck out of order and has to be placed on the ground before being loaded into the truck. This means that it might get mud or dirt in it and that Ron has to bend down to pick it up before loading it.

We now have a deeper understanding of Ron's home life, the extent of his business, the types of supplies he carries, the truck he owns, how he uses the tailgate and the difficulties in doing so, and ergonomic issues in loading and unloading his truck. The scenario still has no focus on a particular product or its features, but it clearly indicates what the difficulties are and what opportunities exist for products to improve Ron's daily activities.

Broadening the Focus

Other Stakeholders

Our focus has been on the user. Fundamentally the end customer is the one who will use the product and, generally, will pay for the product. Of course there are multitudes of people that interact with the product during the development process. Within a company, warehouse and distribution, sales, and facilities management all interact with the product. At times these seemingly secondary functions can have a major effect on the development process. For example, if a new car cannot fit on specially designed vehicle transport trailers, then the company might need to spend money and time to redesign trailers. Similarly, shipping of many products is a significant added cost. Truck sizes are standard and so a slight increase in a box size might significantly reduce the number of products that can ship in a given truck. As another example, the lifecycle costs of the product, often not a focus in the design process, might have huge financial effects on the company. As discussed in the sidebar of Chapter 3, European companies are given some responsibility for the disposal costs of products. By taking into account the disassembly and disposal costs of a product during its development, the overall cost effects can be reduced.

Outside the company are distributors and point-of-sale issues such as the packaging size, the look of the packaging, and the means of displaying the product. Many times, especially in the medical industry, support individuals (nurses, family, etc.) need to operate the product in addition to, or even instead of, the targeted user. In terms of purchasing, there are many situations where the end user does not make the decision to purchase the product. A major aspect of this issue is the approach to sales of the product.

Installation and service of a product is critical. Otis Elevator not only needs to be concerned with the use of their products by people entering a building but also the interface with the building's construction methods, the people who install it, service it, and inspect it.

In general, all stakeholders should be identified and prioritized, and their needs, wants, and desires understood early. If secondary stakeholders are significant, then their input should be directly included in the process, possibly by inclusion of a representative from that area on the team. Otherwise, the team should at least understand the requirements and desires from these other downstream disciplines to reduce redesign efforts that hinder the development process timetable, cause added frustration to the team, and, often, reduce the overall effectiveness and quality of the product.

Identifying Users in Non-Consumer Products: Designing Parts Within Products

The focus of this book is on consumer-oriented products and services. The ideas and methods introduced in the book, however, are applicable as well to products within products. OEM parts and core technologies, the parts found in the lower cells of the Part Differentiation Matrix, often function within a product but are never touched, seen, or otherwise directly managed by the user. Many times these parts are designed and produced by suppliers independent of the end user of the product in which they will be used. A generic part like a bolt or other fastener, an air conditioning unit in a vehicle, a turbine in a jet engine, and a chip in a computer are all technology- or manufacturing-oriented parts that are never touched by the user of the heating system in a home, the air conditioner in the car, the airplane that is flown, or the PDA that organizes a person's busy day.

However, users are very much an integral part of the design of these parts. The user here is not the end consumer but the person who will assemble the parts into products. These parts are technology-oriented and the word *style* may not be as relevant here. Instead the words *interface* or *interaction design* may be more appropriate in that the parts must be designed to be used or interacted with. The notion of value here may focus on the quality, core technology, and ergonomics VOs, although creating a part's corporate identity or aesthetic attribute may differentiate an OEM part from that of other suppliers in the field (as is done by Intel).

■ Every part, no matter how simple or small, has a user.

Within this context, all of the methods in this book are relevant to the design of these types of products. The Positioning Map and Value Opportunity Analysis can help differentiate one product from the rest. Ethnography serves an important role in helping the design team understand in what context their parts are used within the larger product, and how the parts are handled and manipulated. Recognizing that usability is an important attribute in the development of the product and that part context and ergonomics, at least, must be included with manufacturing in the part development team is a critical step toward creating successful parts. Every part, no matter how simple or small, has a user and must be designed with the needs, wants, and desires of the user in mind to create successful, differentiating products.

Product Definition

Ethnography and lifestyle reference together define the characteristics of the product that the team will design. Task analysis and human factors give details on the mechanics of use of the product. An understanding of the needs of the key secondary stakeholders broadens the context of the product requirements.

This analysis provides an understanding of what the target customer needs, wants, and desires in a product and, further, what the customer *expects* and *values*. The research offers a basis to define the Value Opportunities (VOs) of the product and perform a Value Opportunity Analysis (VOA) of the product relative to the competition.

The VOA in conjunction with the qualitative user research provides actionable insights into the POG, insights that lead to a differentiating definition of the product.

What will it do? What is the basic function of the product and what qualities in performance will the product have?

Who will buy it? Who is the target market?

What will be its rough dimensions? Rough sizes and even rough 3D block models give the product some physical context in relation to competing or alternative products for the target group.

What styling features will it have? What types of lines, corners, material qualities, and embellishments will it have?

What are the major competitors? Specify competing products or alternative products that the market spends money on. Motorola had no competition in equivalent products when developing the Talkabout. Instead their competition was a set of rollerblades and a Walkman of comparable prices and interest to the target market.

What functional features should it have? In addition to style, what performance qualities and capabilities does the target market expect?

What are the psychological descriptors or *semantics* of the product? Product semantics is an interesting phenomenon. A product should be designed in such a way that users describe it in an anticipated way, using words of choice by the design team. These descriptors come from the styling of the product within the context of other products used by the market. For example, a sports car should be called "fast," and "exciting," a minivan "safe" and "practical," the GoodGrips "contemporary" and "comfortable," and the iMac "friendly" and "cool."

What is its context? Where will the product be used and where will it be stored? What other products must it be compatible with? How often will it be used?

In our training sessions with companies, we teach teams how to understand the user, sometimes through just a half-day exercise. We provide a product opportunity statement, the history of similar products, an ethnographic interview of several potential users, a human factors/ergonomics analysis, and a series of appropriate magazines. From this information, teams are able to create a scenario capturing the product's use, establish a lifestyle reference of the target customer, build a Value Opportunity profile and compare it to the competition through a VOA, describe the characteristics and features of the product including rough dimensions, attributes, and visualization of use; and develop product solution concepts that meet each criteria specified by the team.

Summarizing the product to be developed to assist Ron the contractor, the opportunity is a workspace that would be mounted to the side of the pickup truck for use by contractors and others in the building trades. Having the workspace on the outside of the bed would leave more space inside the truck bed itself for loading building materials. The table could be used on the side of the truck or could be taken off and used closer to the job site. Some of the tasks that could be performed on the table while it is attached to the truck are cutting, assembling, material and tool prep work, and paperwork. The table could also serve as a type of loading platform. Tools and materials could be placed on the table before being loaded into the bed of the truck. In this way, the table could serve as a stage for organizing items prior to putting them in the truck bed.

Semantics of durability, ease of use, and versatility are the three main factors that would drive the design of the product. The target market is makers who are involved in the building trades as a part of a small (one- to four-man) residential contracting company. This market should expand to all makers in contracting businesses once the product is established in the market.

Chapter 9 will show how this team used their product definition from their user research to develop an exciting new product. Other case studies in Chapters 8 and 9 will further illustrate how a fundamental understanding of who the user is and what drives successful product development.

Visualizing Ideas and Concepts Early and Often

As the product development process evolves, the team must constantly research who the user is and what he or she desires. The research in this chapter helps in creating a model of the user's characteristics and behavior. As the process moves into Phases III and IV, product concepts and forms are created based initially on this model. Research continues, as these products are constantly tested against the target user group and refined. All of this information must be processed by the team so that all team members have a shared understanding of the user and the product concept. This shared understanding is critical if they are to communicate the product to people outside of the team as well.

Whether it is a case of dealing with inter- or intra-team communication, visualizing early and often is essential to develop that shared understanding. Keeping a record of the evolution of the ideas is also important and requires a visual representation to do so. The important thing is that ideas are represented in a clear way that everyone sees. While quality programs have promoted the use of communication though written ideas, they have not stressed the use of visualizing concepts of products in two and three dimensions.

Already we have seen clear visual representations of tasks, behavior, and lifestyle reference. Visualization continues to be critical as the process unfolds. There are a host of ways to visualize ideas that are efficient and essential to testing ideas and making improvements. Even developing information on a whiteboard, large pads, or using Post It Notes are some of the many methods. Once ideas have been developed in simple ways, they can be transferred into computer images with software that is easily shared between design and engineering. Many design firms have employees that fill the gap between engineering and design. These computer technicians can help to translate computer-aided design images into engineering files for technical development and manufacture.

■ Early in the process, it is important to start to visualize the product and then to run the representation through a number of evaluations.

Early in the process, it is important to start to visualize the product and then to run the representation through a number of evaluations. There are two basic directions for representation: drawing or three-dimensional models. Designers have the ability to develop a range of visual representations as early in the process as a set of constraints can be determined. This type of anticipatory imaging has become essential to the product process. While designers in the past often gave preliminary ideas to engineers to develop and had little say in the final detail and manufacture, in the case of the breakthrough products we have analyzed this was not the case. The shift in the use of visualization is based on the fact that concepts must go through cycles of review and refinement. In the best cases, designers work with engineering, marketing, and manufacturing from beginning to end to constantly modify and reconfigure the product as it evolves. Visualization in the early phases is often simple and allows for customer and stakeholder input. As the process evolves, the two-dimensional and three-dimensional representation become more detailed and focused.

Early drawings may be made by hand and may even be cartoon-like. This stage is accompanied by the development of lifestyle boards. For example, Figures 9.6 and 9.7 in Chapter 9 show cartoons discussing the evolution of the SET Factors for the redesign of the Mazda Miata. These cartoons helped the team understand how their work was targeted toward a unified set of design goals. Figure 7.12 shows studio renderings of the Miata. These sketches helped management understand what the product would look like and the team understand how their parts would integrate into a theme. Some ethnographic researchers actually use a technique where they let people build or draw their own prototypes. As they do, researchers work with potential customers and ask questions about their decisions and choices. A company that is developing a new layout for a truck dashboard could invite truck drivers to a concept development session and give them pieces that represent components and ask them to lay out the dashboard themselves. The truck drivers could give interesting potential solutions. What they also provide is the reasons why they want to change and what problems they are having with existing versions. Designers can develop a variety of alternative drawings that can be used in focus groups to promote discussion and direct teams to the next level of refinement. Early drawings of products start the dialogue between design, engineering, and manufacturing. This establishes the tension between the external configuration and the internal components. Current software allows designers to work in traditional free-hand methods and quickly convert to computer-based imaging software to enhance images in three-dimensions. Some companies tend to rely on computer-generated images but quick, free-hand sketches still have value.

Rapid prototyping is a term that is used to refer to the variety of computer-aided methods used to make three-dimensional models of products. Stereolithography, NC milling, and wax deposition are some of the primary processes usually used. There is another type of

Figure 7.12 Studio renderings of the Mazda Miata. (Reprinted with permission of Mazda.)

modeling that works well in the early phases. This process is often referred to as *desktop modeling*. Using a variety of inexpensive materials that are easy to cut with hand tools, designers can produce quick and inexpensive representations of products. These 3D models can be used with drawings to give team members and customers an idea of the potential directions that are being considered. The advantage is that early in the process the team has a physical concept that can be touched and "used." The less time and economic commitment a team makes to imaging and modeling, the easier it is to make changes. As concepts become clearer, the use of more expensive computer-driven processes is an excellent way to refine a product idea. Larger companies, like Motorola, have full capability for this in house. They can quickly go from rough prototypes to wax deposition then to stereolithography. They can even produce short-run functional prototypes. This capability allowed them to shorten the product cycle time in the development of the original Talkabout and all subsequent versions. In the early phases of the DynaVox DynaMyte, simple block models made out of lead-weighted blocks of wood were used to test the size and interface of the product (shown in Figure 5.4). Figure 7.13 shows the evolution of a wearable computer based on research at Carnegie Mellon University. The sequence from urethane blocks to sterolithography prototypes or breadboard prototypes shows the advantage of creating rough prototypes early. The main point is that producing a series of prototypes is important; however, the way you do it should be based on time, budget, and availability to

(a)

(b)

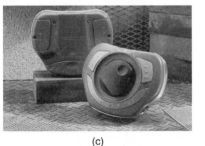

(c)

Figure 7.13 Evolution of a wearable computer through various iterations of prototypes; a) form prototypes; b) breadboard prototypes; c) final "VuMan 3" developed at Carnegie Mellon University. (Reprinted with permission of Dan Siewiorek, John Stivoric, and Chris Kasabach.)

processes. You can do some effective modeling early without a major time expenditure or costly investment.

Whenever possible, it is always more effective to have information visible and sketches and/or models present when discussing issues. The more cycles of concept testing and refinement you have the better. In our research for an automotive company, we were able to attend a meeting of representatives of internal team members and suppliers. Their goal was to attempt to resolve design problems with the door of a vehicle. The meeting was an excellent example of the value of visualization. The meeting started with several sub-groups discussing door subsystems. Each group had a limited representation of the door based on their own focus. There were clay models of the interior trim, full-size technical plots of the door component layout, wiring diagrams, and actual internal sheet metal of the structural carryover. As the day progressed, the groups started to merge when they realized how interconnected the door was. Soon groups started to bring the different types of representation of the door together. They needed to see the clay models to determine where the interior details were to connect with the location of internal systems. Even though they had all seen computer images and had been working on CAD systems to develop internal components, this was the first time that these groups were in the same room at the same time with multiple full-scale representations of the product. This meeting enabled the internal groups and external suppliers to work out problems that had been unresolved for months. Everyone was finally on the same page.

Creating shared understanding is more challenging than it seems. Visualization of information and concepts is one way to overcome perceptual gaps within a team. Visualization in the form of two-dimensional images and three-dimensional models is essential for marketing, engineering, and design to get feedback from customers. Later versions of full working prototypes can be used to refine elements of products. The process must move from simple and suggestive representation to refined, highly detailed representations. This method allows teams to stay in an improvisational framework and react and refine rather than get down to details too early.

Summary Points

❏ The user's experience is the driver in the development of breakthrough products.

❏ Qualitative research on user desire, including new product ethnography, is necessary to gain an in depth understanding of the user.

❏ Methods that analyze usability and desirability that work together to develop that understanding are: scenario development, new product ethnography, ergonomics (interaction, task analysis, and anthropometrics), and lifestyle reference.

- ❏ Human factors as a field is growing beyond physical interaction analysis to begin to include issues of desirability.

- ❏ A successful product will balance usability and safety with desirability and fantasy.

- ❏ Visualizing concepts early and often helps the product evolve consistently through the team, management, and potential customers.

References

1. Human Factors Ergonomics Society web site: www.hfes.org, initiated 1995.

2. Taylor, F.W., *The Principles of Scientific Management*, W.W. Norton & Co., New York, 1967 (originally 1911).

3. Schmitt, B.H., and A. Simonson, *Marketing Aesthetics: The Strategic Management of Brands, Identity and Image*, The Free Press, New York, 1997.

4. Jordan, P., *Designing Pleasurable Products: An Introduction to the New Human Factors*, Taylor & Francis, London, 2000.

5. Norman, D.A., *The Design of Everyday Things*, New York, Doubleday, 1990.

6. Fetterman, D.M., *Ethnography Step by Step*, Sage Publications, Newbury Park, 1989.

7. Cain, J., "Experienced-Based Design: Toward a Science of Artful Business Innovation," *Design Management Journal*, Vol. 9, No. 4, pp. 10–16, 1999.

8. Wilcox, S.B., "A Tool for Design Research," *Innovation*, IDSA, Summer, pp. 10–11, 1996.

9. Robinson, R., and J. Nims, "Insight into what Really Matters," *Innovation*, IDSA, Summer, pp. 18–21, 1996.

10. Dreyfuss, H., *The Measure of Man and Woman: Human Factors in Design*, Watson-Guptill Publications, New York, 1993.

Research Acknowledgements

Credit for user research in this chapter to understand opportunities:

T1 This scenario and other reference to this product opportunity were created by designers Josh Guyot, Mark A. Ehrhardt, and Emily Gustavsen, engineers Scott Froom and Richard Bohman, and market researcher Dan Darnell.

T2 This ethnographic research was done by designers Freddy Anzures, Matthew Modell, and April Starr, engineers Cormac Eubanks and Kristo Kreichbaum, and market researcher Eric Hoffman.

T3 This task analysis was done by engineers Noah Brinton, Jay Chu, and Alper Ozturk, designers Robert Suarez and Sanjay Vora, and market researcher Eric Close.

T4 This task analysis was done by market researchers Mark Brownlee, Paul Cinquegrane, and Alex Cook, engineers Stacey Gabor, Thang Ngo, and Jenny Williams, and designers Francine Gemperle and Peter Sellar.

Part Three

Further Evidence

Chapter 8   Case Studies: The Power of the Upper Right

Chapter 9   Automotive Design: Product Differentiation
through User-Centered iNPD

Chapter Eight

Case Studies:
The Power of the Upper Right

In Chapters 8 and 9, we present case studies of products and companies that have successfully Moved to the Upper Right. The examples in this chapter, ranging from baseball parks to office chairs, epitomize the ideas and methods discussed in this book and serve as benchmarks for any company that wants to create breakthrough products.

Overview of Case Studies

This section summarizes the nine case studies presented in this chapter.

- We begin with America's favorite pasttime, seeing how the new breed of baseball stadiums position themselves clearly in the Upper Right.

- Next the Black & Decker SnakeLight focuses again on consumer products responding to a new POG in a somewhat saturated arena. The Positioning Map and VOA show how this high-valued product redefined the competitive positioning of the industry to the Upper Right. The SnakeLight development also illustrates how supplier partnering can lead to effective innovation.

- The Marathon industrial carpet cleaner highlights how turnkey consulting firms can provide the solution for new designs for small companies. This design by HLB also illustrates how highly integrated design teams can produce decidedly creative solutions.

- The next case study also highlights a partnering between a company (DynaVox Systems) and a design consulting firm (Daedalus Excel) to create a socially important product (maximizing the social impact VO). The design of the DynaMyte Augmentative Communicator required an integrated team that included members from the company and the design firm and that incorporated secondary stakeholders into the design process.

215

- Kodak's single use cameras were redesigned from "throw aways" to "reusables," maximizing the environmental impact VO and also saving this great idea for a product from itself being "thrown away" due to the outcry over its negative effect on the environment.

- The next case study examines how UPS has maintained its brand, services, and products as a leader in a competitive and rapidly changing service industry.

- The Aeron chair revolutionized office seating and redefined use of materials and hierarchy of features in the workplace. It also illustrates the growing aware-ness of ergonomics in product development, emphasizing that particular Value Opportunity.

- The iMac is an excellent example of design pushing material performance. This case study illustrates how VOs move a product from the high tech Lower Right to the value-oriented Upper Right.

- Finally, the Freeplay Radio responds to a critical social need for underdevel-oped countries in Africa. It highlights the social impact VO. The case study illustrates how design for people in emerging nations can still be effective and found in the Upper Right. The product was so successful that it is finding appli-cation across the globe in a variety of uses.

Baseball Moving to the Upper Right

The design of new baseball parks is an example of how professional sports reacts to trends and also helps to create them. Every major city has built, or is proposing to build, a new baseball stadium. The interesting thing is that all of the new stadiums are designed to look like the oldest professional baseball parks, Fenway Park in Boston and Wrigley Field in Chicago. The nostalgia trend has hit every facet of society and ball-parks have become a primary symbol of the phenomena. The difference is the new fields look like the classic ballparks, however, they have a new infrastructure and array of amenities that are state of the art. New ballparks provide a variety of experiences that complement the game on the field. Sky boxes bring in a new revenue stream that has allowed the owners to build more intimate parks that seat 30–40,000, rather than 60–70,000. In turn, the small, intimate fields are attracting more fans back to watching baseball live. Averaging 25–30,000 in the park is better than the unsteady attendance that is the typical pattern in many larger, multi-use parks. Baseball owners are respond-ing to and helping to fuel the nostalgia trend.

The opening of the new home of the Pittsburgh Pirates, PNC Park, mirrors the current trend in the industry. Consider the Positioning Map for baseball parks shown in Figure 8.1. The

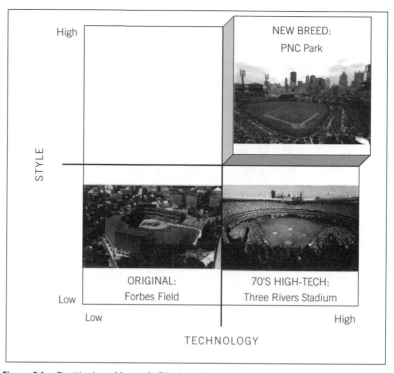

Figure 8.1 Positioning Map of Pittsburgh's baseball stadiums. (Park images reprinted with permission of Pittsburgh Post-Gazette; photo of Three Rivers Stadium by John Beale; photo of PNC Park by Fong.)

Lower Left shows the original park, Forbes Field, which closed in 1970. Fans loved and still love these old parks (at least the two remaining: Wrigley and Fenway), but their outdated facilities, lack of amenities, structural posts blocking the field of view, and limited capacity (and thus limited revenue streams), motivated a new stream of parks in the '60s and '70s. There were a number of parks built in the period, including Three Rivers Stadium in Pittsburgh (shown in the Lower Right in Figure 8.1), Cinergy Field in Cincinnati, Busch Stadium in St. Louis, and domed versions such as the Houston Astrodome and the Super Dome in New Orleans. All these stadiums were developed as multi-use facilities for baseball and football with re-configurable seating. These parks, clearly in the Lower Right, followed society's trend of pushing efficiency, creating parks never well tuned for either sport. They also introduced artificial turf, which altered the play of the game and resulted in a series of new and devastating sports injuries (turf toe, concussions, turf burn, and torn ACLs). These structures were technical wonders, especially the domed versions, however, they took something away from the game.

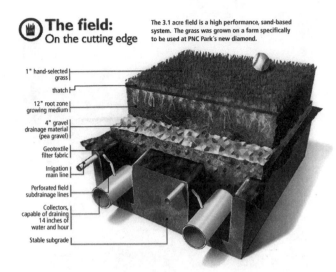

The field: On the cutting edge

The 3.1 acre field is a high performance, sand-based system. The grass was grown on a farm specifically to be used at PNC Park's new diamond.

1" hand-selected grass
thatch
12" root zone growing medium
4" gravel drainage material (pea gravel)
Geotextile filter fabric
Irrigation main line
Perforated field subdrainage lines
Collectors, capable of draining 14 inches of water and hour
Stable subgrade

Figure 8.2 Illustration of the high technology playing field in PNC Park. (Reprinted with permission of Pittsburgh Post-Gazette; graphic by Dan Marsula and James Hilston.)

■ The Upper Right has power!

The new breed of parks for the turn of the century, such as PNC Park (and others like Camden Yard in Baltimore, Jacob's Field in Cleveland, and Comerica Park in Detroit), bring back the intimacy and nostalgia of the early parks with all of the modern infrastructure and amenities of the latest theme parks. The new parks are all returning to the use of real grass, reversing the trend toward using Astroturf. The high technology is often hidden from the fans, such as the high-performance, sand-based grass in PNC Park, which includes a drainage system that can process 14 inches of water per hour (Figure 8.2). These parks, found in the Upper Right (with PNC Park shown in Figure 8.1), merge style and features while adding value back to the game for the fans. Amenities include baby changing facilities, a variety of edible fare that includes sushi, and luxury suites with individual HVAC control. With the new parks is an understanding that the experience of going to a game is as important as the game itself. The Pirates hired Disney to train the ushers and other greeters at the park. For many of the smaller-market teams, these parks are the last hope to keep baseball from being monopolized by the big guns in the larger cities. In cities such as Cleveland, attendance has skyrocketed in the new Jacob's Field, providing revenue for the Indians to once again become competitors. The Upper Right has power!

Black & Decker SnakeLight™

The SnakeLight case study illustrates the development of a new product in a thought-to-be saturated industry, demonstrates the evolution of product definition based on early research, exemplifies issues of brand identity, and shows an effective partnering with a supplier. It is also an example of balancing the use of quantitative and qualitative market research to understand customer needs. Finally, this case study reveals how an iNPD team can be managed effectively. The team overcame perceptual gaps and was empowered to improvise as needed.

There are a few problems with traditional flashlights: they require a person to dedicate one hand to holding the light; if they are set down it is difficult to direct the light where needed; they have a limited directed beam; and they require a stable surface when set down. A designer at Black & Decker was renovating his home and was frustrated by the fact that he needed a good, portable, independent hands-free task light to work in the areas of his home. He decided that a flashlight should be designed to solve this problem and proposed this idea to Black & Decker.

This individual insight was connected to a new SET trend. Fixing up or adding to people's homes had become a national obsession in the early '90s. New home improvement stores, particularly superstores like Home Depot, were popping up all across the United States. People were buying tools and materials at an unprecedented rate. Many people knowingly and unknowingly were looking for the product that Black & Decker decided to develop. The POG for this product was the gap between the limits of existing flashlights and the need to have the hands free and to have flexible task lighting for projects around the house. The POG would eventually extend to other new active lifestyle experiences. The first hurdle the team faced was overcoming the concerns of the financial arm of the company. Finance was dubious that such a novel product concept could turn a profit in a competitive market where Black & Decker was not even a player. The objections could have jeopardized the future of the project. Fortunately, the president stepped in and overruled the objection and the project was given the green light. This show of support from the top helped to protect the program and proved to a be visionary decision.

The original product strategy for the Black & Decker SnakeLight was to develop a hands-free rechargeable task light that was flexible and could wrap around objects and the human body to aid people in performing activities working around the home. The first name given for the product internal to the company was the "Flexilight," and the design was to build off the company's line of rechargeable products. The technical challenge was to develop a flexible core that could wrap around 1-inch pipe and that could be bent and unbent thousands of times without failing. The team's early internal concepts failed to meet these performance specs for the proposed flexible core. A team member noticed a flexible hose on a milling machine that delivered oil to the milled surface. That became the point of departure for solving the flexible core. Lockwood Products, Inc., was willing to meet the performance specs at the cost that Black & Decker was willing to pay and was chosen over a competitor as the external supplier. This presented two challenges for the companies. The first was performance: Lockwood had to agree to make a flexible core that worked and housed wires in its core of interlocking beads and that functioned in more demanding-use environments than the flexible core on a milling machine. The second issue was the need to integrate Lockwood's manufacturing technology into Black & Decker's manufacturing process. This was the only way that Black & Decker could hit their projected manufacturing rate and cost.

Lockwood delivered a flexible core that met the performance criteria. The core worked by including a collar into each bead that would prevent it from over-rotating in its socket. This bead could withstand over 60 lbs. of force before the connection broke. The plastic material of the core was impregnated with Teflon to offset the friction caused by the high-tolerance fit between the bead and socket. The joint was tight enough to prevent the core from moving once in position, while the Teflon created a smooth surface that allowed the core to bend and twist with force. The Teflon also prevented the creaking and cracking noises that would have otherwise resulted in the surface tension on the plastic used for the core. Lockwood then worked with Black & Decker to develop a hollow core to allow the wires to pass through from the light in the head to the batteries in the tail. This process was then seamlessly integrated into the manufacturing and assembly line process.

Another early development came when the team realized that creating a product for the existing line of rechargeable products was a much smaller market than the market for alkaline battery-powered task lights. At the time, Black & Decker did not have any alkaline battery-powered products. The size of the market and the projected share and profits, however, convinced the company to commit to this direction. What had started as a commitment to a flexible light to add to the company's existing line of rechargeable products had developed into a battery-powered flashlight and a need to partner with a supplier to provide the flexible core. Both of these directions were the result of letting the product concept follow its own course of development and allowing discovery in the early phase to redirect the product development path. Had these insights not been made early, they would have been extremely expensive to engineer into the product once major decisions had been made downstream. With the change of direction, the product had to be sold as feasible within the company and eventually to the retailers that would carry the product. Imagine asking a company to support the development of a $30 flashlight when the standard was a tenth that amount, and then convincing retailers that customers would buy it. In Sam Farber's case with OXO and the GoodGrips, he owned the company. His gamble on a $7 peeler was up to him. In both cases, the insight into the customer's perception of value proved correct as both products were successful at the projected price points.

The next major decision facing the team was the relationship among the three elements of the product: the light, battery pack, and flexible core. Engineering supported putting the battery directly behind the light and to let the flexible core extend off the back like a tail. The designers and marketing argued for a separation of the light and the batteries at the end connected by the flexible core. The engineering solution reduced the cost by having one instead of two housings. It also reduced the potential for problems in running the wire through the flexible core to connect the head and tail. The wire could fail after repeated twists and bends. The solution proposed by marketing and design was more expensive, however it created a visual and physical counterbalance relationship that would help the product wrap around things and stand on its base. The decision was made to go with the separate head and tail with a flexible core as a connector.

Deciding on the quality and throw of the light cast by the product was an additional challenge. In order to compete with task lights and to use a small 7-cent bulb, a large, specially designed reflector had to be developed to cast a wide even light at a range of two to three feet. The decision was made that the head would have to be wider than the diameter of the flexible core, scratching the original ideas for a continuous tube. This created the form that would lead to the perceived snake-like appearance. It also meant that Black & Decker would have to hire a specialist to design the reflector. They found a designer who developed the reflectors for professional sport stadiums, a different scale but the same type of problem, since stadium lights have to throw a large, even light over a long distance. By coincidence, the reflective pattern looks a lot like snakeskin.

The team needed to solve a number of other technical and styling problems. The transition between the hard plastic housings and the flexible core necessitated a transitional neck to prevent both the neoprene cover and the core from disengaging from the head. The slanted angle that formed the opening for the battery storage unit required a release that slid back rather than a threaded cap, which was the standard on most flashlights. There were three required modes of operation: wrapped around things, sitting by itself on its own base, and held in one hand as a traditional flashlight. The latter mode meant that the tail would have to connect or dock with the head to make it a comfortable product to hold in the hand. This required a mechanism for the two to lock together easily and also disengage easily. Each of these technical challenges affected the look of the product, requiring a tight collaboration between the engineers and designers. Figure 8.3 shows the final product and Figure 8.4 shows the high value style and technology details of the SnakeLight design.

The last detail was the final name for the product. As stated earlier, the project had started under the name Flexilight. As the product form evolved, the name SnakeLight was suggested. The name did not get favorable scores in focus groups. People felt the

Figure 8.3 Black & Decker Snakelight. (Reprinted with permission of Black & Decker.)

name was too negative and aggressive. The support for keeping the name came from the David Stone, the President of Black & Decker. The name SnakeLight was chosen and it became the primary brand identifier over the use of the company name itself. This decision was a clear example of a corporate head with vision willing to take the risk and make the decision against the grain. The name, it seemed, was a logical extension of the development of the product. At times, one needs to reinterpret what a negative response from a consumer means. As it turned out, the name and product shape created a brand identity that worked in conjunction with advertising and public relations to make this product an instant success. It is doubtful that a tubular product named Flexilight would have been anywhere near as marketable.

The product was supported with a high-budget ad campaign that cost $14M the first year and $10M the second. One of the television advertisements, "Wanderer," won best ad for 1994. The advertising campaign was complemented by the free press and publicity the product received. It won a number of awards and was a great product to talk and write about because it had both innovation and personality. Even David Letterman said he would buy one for his mother. The first Christmas the product sold out. By Father's Day in 1995, the company was ready for anticipated sales and was not disappointed. The next Christmas

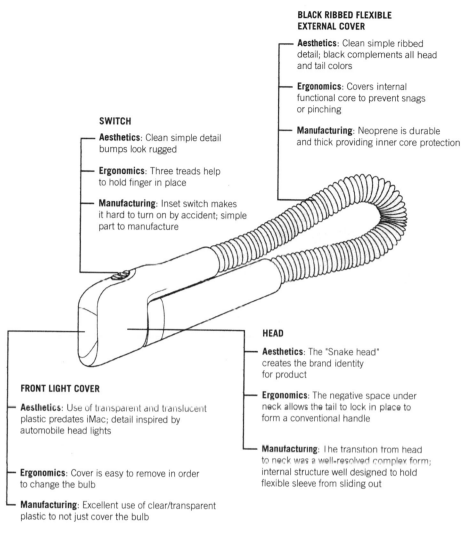

BLACK RIBBED FLEXIBLE EXTERNAL COVER

Aesthetics: Clean simple ribbed detail; black complements all head and tail colors

Ergonomics: Covers internal functional core to prevent snags or pinching

Manufacturing: Neoprene is durable and thick providing inner core protection

SWITCH

Aesthetics: Clean simple detail bumps look rugged

Ergonomics: Three treads help to hold finger in place

Manufacturing: Inset switch makes it hard to turn on by accident; simple part to manufacture

HEAD

Aesthetics: The "Snake head" creates the brand identity for product

Ergonomics: The negative space under neck allows the tail to lock in place to form a conventional handle

Manufacturing: The transition from head to neck was a well-resolved complex form; internal structure well designed to hold flexible sleeve from sliding out

FRONT LIGHT COVER

Aesthetics: Use of transparent and translucent plastic predates iMac; detail inspired by automobile head lights

Ergonomics: Cover is easy to remove in order to change the bulb

Manufacturing: Excellent use of clear/transparent plastic to not just cover the bulb

Figure 8.4   Product details of Snakelight showing integration of style and technology.

and Father's Day, sales continued to climb. When it was clear that the product was a success, Black & Decker was able to double the manufacturing capability to respond. The integration of the manufacture of the flexible core into their own process allowed Black & Decker to increase the output without having to depend on the capability of a supplier. Black & Decker had projected a demand of 200,000 units; the actual demand turned out to be over 600,000. It would take them 18 months to catch up with demand. The first two years' sales were roughly $150M /year; the original projection had been $57M.

The Positioning Map of the SnakeLight (Figure 8.5) shows the generic and basic flashlights in the Lower Left. The Lower Right holds the tech-driven versions such as the hand-cranked flashlight produced in Russia, as shown in Figure 8.5, and the Freeplay product. Unlike the Freeplay radio discussed in Chapter 8, for hard-to-access tasks, the flashlight version would have limited application. The hand-cranked product has a very poor ratio of hand power-to-light generation and can never be hands free. For hands-free task lighting, the SnakeLight is positioned alone in the Upper Right, even after half a decade. It is readily apparent when looking at the Value Opportunity charts (Figure 8.6) for this product why it was worth the extra cost to consumers in the early phases of the product's sales cycle. The VOA is in comparison to a Lower Left, generic flashlight, demonstrating how the strong emotion, ergonomics, aesthetics, identity, and quality surpass the generic counterpart, bringing the flashlight into the high-value Upper Right. The consumer use of the light was extended beyond the original target market. It was used by children for walking or riding bicycles and used for everyday lighting as well as task and emergency lighting. The success of the portable, hands-free flexibility of the SnakeLight was extended to the semi-professional line of DeWalt products with the design of "rugged" work lights that used the DeWalt power tool battery pack, and to products outside of Black & Decker through Lockwood's agreement with the company (the flexible core became the basis for Teledyne WaterPik's flexible shower head).

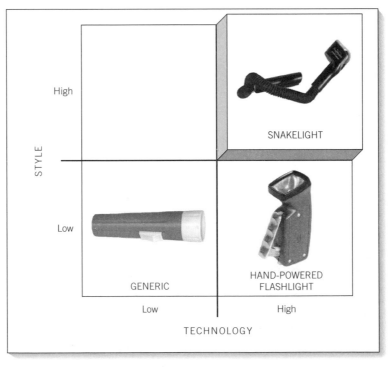

Figure 8.5 Positioning Map for Snakelight.

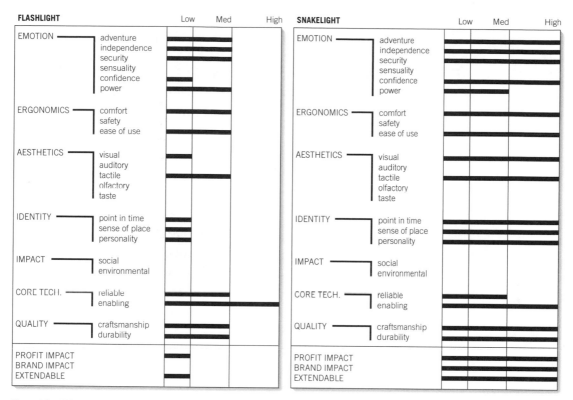

Figure 8.6 VOA of SnakeLight versus generic flashlight.

The second year of sales marked the beginning of the rip-offs. The competitors came in at lower price points and failed to develop products that maintained the quality of the SnakeLight. In particular, the competition compromised on the flexible core. None of the competitors improved the product and most changes were cosmetic and often were actually worse on purpose to avoid infringement rather than improve on the product capabilities. One competitor ran the wires outside of the flexible core, claiming that approach did not infringe on the core developed for the SnakeLight. It made the wires vulnerable to being twisted and breaking. For those customers looking for a bargain who bought the cheap versions, the lack of quality undermined the high-performance standards created by the SnakeLight. Black & Decker aggressively and successfully defended its utility and design patents and trade dress against 16 imitations (nine of which were taken to court), requiring all of the competitors to remove their rip-off products from the market. This is an excellent case of utility and design patents used in combination to effectively defend intellectual property. The company actually made a profit from the damages won from these cases.

An external review of the project commissioned by Black & Decker points to the successful management and function of the team as a key factor in the program's success. The study noted that Program Manager James Raskin demonstrated many of the ideal attributes of an iNPD manager highlighted in Chapter 6. He empowered the team and provided guidance without micro-managing. He let them use the company's product development process as a set of guidelines rather than strict limitations. Although trained as an engineer, he respected and communicated effectively with all team members. Finally, he promoted an atmosphere that allowed the team to improvise and develop the characteristics of a high-performance team discussed in books by Kao[1] and Katzenbach and Smith.[2] Figure 8.7 shows the evolution of the product by the team in response to emerging understanding about the product opportunity.

The Black & Decker SnakeLight is a classic case of recognizing a Product Opportunity Gap by responding to a SET trend and fulfilling a true need in the marketplace. While the study mentioned above cited a number of positive factors, there are a few more that are important to point out. In an interview with James Raskin, he felt a major factor was the combination of quantitative and qualitative research. This research was conducted early in the project and helped to convince upper management of the viability of the program. The Conjoint analysis conducted by an external research group established the set of features and economic potential of a flexible flashlight. The team from within Black & Decker conducted its own internal qualitative research to better understand the needs of potential customers in context. This helped to shape the function and style of the product and to educate all the team members on user needs. A second factor is the successful partnering with a supplier. Many companies have the goal of creating a strategic partnership with a supplier where both stand to benefit from an equal investment in the future of a product. Few companies have had the success that Lockwood and Black & Decker enjoyed. Third is the successful use of design and utility patents in combination to protect the investment and maintain market dominance for an extended period of time; four years of success is a significant achievement in a competitive market. Fourth is the ability to extend the core success of the product to other products produced by Black & Decker and DeWalt, allowing the company to gain even greater returns on their original, significant investment in product research, development, and advertising.

The SnakeLight demonstrates the power of the point-in-time VO. At the time this book went to press, the SnakeLight was on the downward slope of the bell curve of the product life cycle. Black & Decker still owns and protects their intellectual property for the flexible task light and has extended the concept to other products and the process to other product programs. The sales have lowered but stayed stable. The company is not attempting to redesign the product and is in a holding pattern. While the successful litigation eliminated the influx of cheaper imitations and prolonged its market success, it

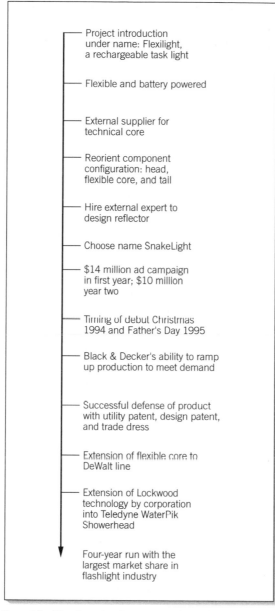

Project introduction under name: Flexilight, a rechargeable task light

Flexible and battery powered

External supplier for technical core

Reorient component configuration: head, flexible core, and tail

Hire external expert to design reflector

Choose name SnakeLight

$14 million ad campaign in first year; $10 million year two

Timing of debut Christmas 1994 and Father's Day 1995

Black & Decker's ability to ramp up production to meet demand

Successful defense of product with utility patent, design patent, and trade dress

Extension of flexible core to DeWalt line

Extension of Lockwood technology by corporation into Teledyne WaterPik Showerhead

Four-year run with the largest market share in flashlight industry

Figure 8.7 Timeline showing the evolution of the product in response to new understanding of the product opportunity.

could not withstand the eventual market saturation. The copies also undermined the price point in the market. This demonstrates that even the most successful products cannot maintain their market share in the Upper Right without the injection of new useful, usable, and desirable characteristics that refresh the product, as discussed in Chapter 2. This product broke all sales projections and the market was substantially larger than originally predicted. The high-performing iNPD team and core supplier were complemented by equally successful support from advertising, PR, packaging, legal, and vision from the top. The SnakeLight brand actually helped the company brand. The innovation and quality of the product had a positive effect on customers' perception of the existing products and the products that were introduced after the SnakeLight.

Marathon Carpet Cleaner Designed by Herbst Lazar Bell (HLB)

In this next study, a consulting firm develops an entire product: a commercial carpet cleaning machine. Previous products in this market were bulky, cumbersome to use, and lacked any serious styling. Recognizing that the product was outdated from both a human factor and manufacturing standpoint, HLB didn't just slightly improve the existing product but rather re-designed the way the product was used, serviced, manufactured, and worked. The firm actually changed the base technology for carpet cleaning. The result changed the product dynamics in the market and led to new designs for other Breuer/Tornado Corp. products.

An example of a company hiring a consulting firm to do a turnkey product development program, HLB provided all of the product development support in-house to conceive, develop, and produce the new product for market. Design firms range from small one- or two-person offices to large product development consultancies that can fully support all aspects of strategic planning, product development, and corporate identity. Herbst Lazar Bell in Chicago is one such firm. It integrates industrial design (its original core competency) with engineering and business planning to provide a full product development capability. They have won numerous awards in a number of product categories and helped to produce a variety of products that have been highly successful in the marketplace.

The SET Factors in this case called for a radical redesign of a product, not a slight improvement. The importance of maintaining a clean healthy work environment, OSHA standards, servicing and maintaining products, and branding all played a role in the forces that caused Breuer to significantly change their product. Carpets are great for dampening sound and providing an inexpensive solution to covering floors in commercial settings. They are harder to keep clean, however, than other hard-surface alternatives. Commercially available carpet cleaners looked like Zambonis used to smooth out ice skating rinks. The machines were large and cumbersome. As clean water was sucked from one bin then dumped as dirty water into another, the center of gravity shifted, causing stress on the user's body, especially the back. Back strain in the workplace is a significant factor in health insurance costs and the turnover of labor in custodial jobs. The bulk also led to bad sight lines for the user, adding stress to the job and potentially causing dangerous situations when the machine was in use.

These large, bulky machines were made of sheet metal and had no style or brand equity. Who needed it to clean commercial carpets? Industrial businesses such as Breuer's that previously never thought of creating a strong brand identity were now realizing its potential. The result was an opportunity to take a vanilla product and make it stand out in the market. The first and foremost problem was the large, bulky product. The use of sheet metal has significant limitations in the range of shapes and the perceived quality of a product. Sheet metal panels are no longer seen as an acceptable solution for a product that needs to be opened and closed daily for routine service.

All of this led to a POG for a new carpet cleaner that would be more ergonomic in use, more effectively clean carpets, and that would be built of new materials that would decrease the weight of the product and allow greater range of shapes, which could lead to a stronger brand recognition at trade shows and in daily use. The gap was the space between existing ergonomically inefficient Zamboni-like carpet cleaners and a product that could respond effectively to the new demands and opportunities for quality of the work environment, the task of cleaning, and the ability to promote a clear innovative brand in the market. HLB developed a product that responded to the POG and the entire product program was accomplished within one calendar year.

■ The success of the product came from insightful innovation that emerged from the collaborative efforts of the engineers and designers.

The development of the Marathon took an integrated team from HLB of three engineers, three industrial designers, and one marketing/finance person. The success of the product came from an insightful innovation that emerged from the collaborative effort of the engineers and designers. The two cleaning compartments, with one filling while the other empties (shown in Figure 8.8(a)), leads to two major shortcomings: a shifting center of gravity and wasted space. If there were a way to remove the empty space, the machine could be smaller. If the center of gravity didn't shift, the machine would be easier to use. The team came up with the idea of a single displacement bladder system, negating the need for containers. With the bladder collapsed against the wall, the clean water fills the container. As the clean water is taken from the container on one side of the bladder, the dirty water fills the container on the other side of the bladder. As one side empties, the bladder shifts within the container until it is compressed against the other wall. The result is that the water fills a constant volume with the clean and dirty separated (as shown in Figure 8.8(b)).

The result of the bladder system is a compression of space, allowing for a constant low center of gravity, a smaller unit, and the ability to mold the product from polymer rather than needing to make it with sheet metal. The rotationally molded unit has a single

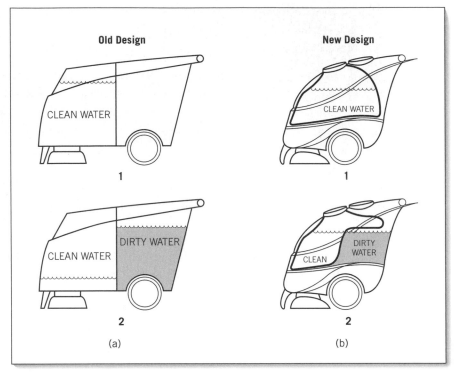

Figure 8.8 (a) old system for carpet cleaning and (b) new bladder system from HLB. (Reprinted with permission of Herbst Lazar Bell.)

hinge, making maintenance easy and the product less expensive to manufacture (the product actually cost 15 percent less than the company's own target). The molded approach enabled the designers to create a Ferrari-styled personality instead of the antiquated Zamboni-like shape of the predecessor (shown in Figure 8.9).

In the development of the Marathon, the team used an ethnographic approach of user shadowing and interviewing to understand the needs, wants, and desires of the users. The product was developed on CAD, with foam models NC machined. A single alpha prototype was generated, followed by only four rotationally molded, short-run beta prototypes. To reduce prototyping costs and time, performance was analyzed through finite element methods.

The patented product has had ten times the expected sales. It has won several awards, including the 1996 Appliance Manufacturers Excellence in Design award for industrial appliances and Best of Category in equipment for *ID Magazine's* Design Review. The product was so successful, Breuer Tornado hired HLB to redesign its larger model, the Pheonix.

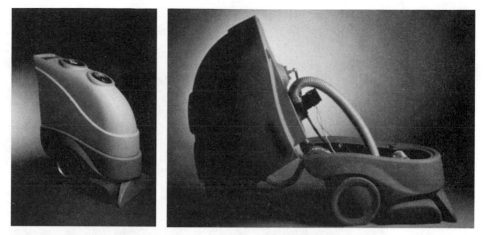

Figure 8.9 Marathon cleaner (closed and open). (Reprinted with permission of Herbst Lazar Bell.)

DynaMyte Augmentative Communicator by DynaVox Systems and Daedalus Excel Product Development

This next case study is a wonderful example of a small company partnering with a small design firm. Although DynaVox Systems had around 40 employees, it had no industrial designers or mechanical engineers on its staff. They turned instead to Daedalus Excel to fulfill their design and mechanical engineering needs.

Gary Kiliany and Tilden Bennett of DynaVox are entrepreneurs in the true sense of the word. They create markets and look toward products that go beyond the state of the art. Their company develops and markets augmentative communicators — computers that synthesize speech for people who are unable to speak. They had developed the first augmentative communicators to use dynamic, touch-screen-driven displays. The latest version of the product, the DynaVox 2 (shown in Figure 8.10), was appropriate for use mounted to a wheelchair, but its large size made it cumbersome for handheld use. Because of the success of their dynamic-display touch screen products, the company had climbed to the number two position in the market. To increase sales and leapfrog to the number one slot, DynaVox had to Move to the Upper Right — they had to differentiate their product from those of the competition and their own DynaVox 2 through added value.

The SET Factors indicated that a significantly new design was feasible and desired by the market. As a result of increased social awareness, people were willing to spend money to improve quality of life for everyone, regardless of ability. One particular focus was on devices to help those with disabilities to overcome their limitations to participate in a

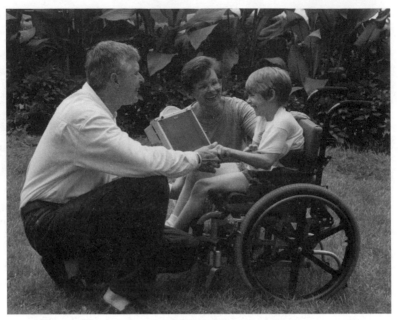

Figure 8.10 DynaVox 2 (the previous model from DynaVox). (Reprinted with permission of DynaVox Systems LLC.)

richer life with more respect for what they can contribute. The advances in computing power allowed for smaller and smarter products. Finally, insurance companies, government, and individual families with the financial resources all provided sources for funds that targeted devices for the disabled. Gary Kiliany and Tilden Bennett were well aware of all of these factors as they looked to create a device for those that could not speak that improved ease of use and capabilities. Another issue was whether the device could be made portable enough for those users who were ambulatory. This was a goal that, whether or not it could be achieved, would push the product toward a smaller size. The range of potential users included children and adults with a range of disabilities that prevented speech.

Daedalus Excel is a small design consulting firm in Pittsburgh (at the time having only five employees, although they've more than doubled in size since then) that had had a fair amount of experience in the design of medical- and health-oriented products. Matt Beale, the president of the firm, led the design effort for DynaVox. In beginning the project, the two initial tasks were to understand how to differentiate this new product from the market (i.e., what were the Value Opportunities) and how to form an appropriate team.

The VOA (Figure 8.11) shows where Daedalus and DynaVox saw the market as compared to where they wanted to go in the Upper Right. The current DynaVox had its strength in its ability to give the users a sense of independence and even adventure, but

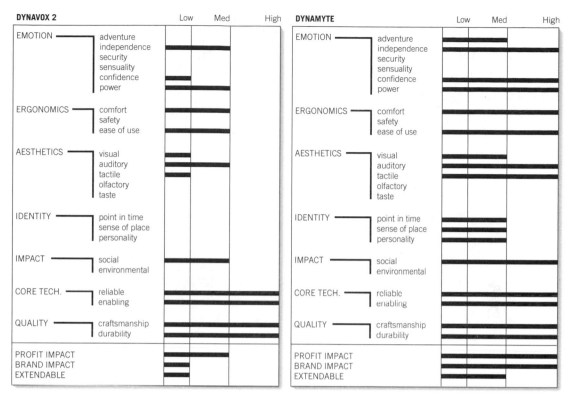

Figure 8.11   VOA of DynaMyte versus previous DynaVox 2.

it was limited to those in wheelchairs. The emotion VOs were the same but there was opportunity to make them stronger by making an ambulatory device. The DynaVox had focused on technology alone, and, since technology alone is not enough, there was a huge opportunity to improve product identity VOs as well as the visual and tactile aesthetic VOs. The DynaVox had strength in the social impact VO, but even here, due to the heavy and cumbersome design with its limited use, there was an opportunity to improve on that VO. In addition, because of this cumbersome, bulky design, the new product could also improve on the comfort and ease of use ergonomics VOs. The last question was what effect a new design could have on the quality and core technology VOs. The technology could be made smaller, but with the smaller size comes other limitations such as the size of speakers. Further, an ambulatory device would take more abuse than one permanently attached to a wheelchair.

With a clear insight into where the product could be improved, and an understanding of open questions on technology, the team could be formed. DynaVox contributed five people: Bennett (the president), Kiliany (Head of R&D), a manufacturing engineering, an electrical engineer, and a speech pathologist. The speech pathologist represented the customer and had access to potential users through her clinics. The inclusion of the speech pathologist illustrates the need for a secondary stakeholder to be integral to the design process. Deadalus contributed three industrial designers and a mechanical engineer.

Kiliany and the speech pathologist had significant experience working with the user group. The team as a whole, however, needed to gain that experience. The group met with parents of children with challenges and spent time observing these children. Through the process, numerous scenarios were developed surrounding the potential use of the device by users that included children with cerebral palsy, adults with mental retardation, children with learning disabilities, and users with a variety of ambulatory capabilities. It became clear to Beale that meeting the needs of the wide variety of ambulatory users was the core challenge.

Based on the evolving understanding of the user, the team went through numerous iterations between prototypes (starting with lead-weighted wooden blocks shown in Figure 4.2 and progressing to more refined prototypes) and user feedback. The goal was to find a single solution for all their scenarios and provide adaptability, such as through software cards, for those areas that required diverse features. The team looked at comparable technologies such as the Apple Newton to get a sense of possible size and weight specifications. As the design evolved, the team needed to tightly integrate the electronics with a form most appropriate for the user group. The shape drove the design to maintain usability and Beale, the industrial designer, found himself working jointly with the electrical engineer on the placement of electronic components and the shaping of circuit boards.

The Part Differentiation Matrix (shown in Figure 8.12) helps explain the intricacies of the design of the product. The upper right cell houses all of the parts except the OEM batteries which are in the lower left, and symbol illustrations which are in the upper left cell, and the screen which is in the lower right cell. Even the design of the foldout legs required an integrated effort between engineering and design. The screen was specified by, and required integration between, the two disciplines, but was purchased from available parts from a supplier and thus its complexity more than its lifestyle impact design places it in the lower right cell.

The form was critical. Kids needed to find the unit "cool" and adults needed it to be competent and professional. The team succeeded in their development of the DynaMyte (Figure 8.13). Joel, an 11-year-old with Down's Syndrome, became an early adopter for the product. His older brother (who did not have the disability) thought the device was cool and liked to play with it. A leading figure in speech pathology called the DynaMyte "the Porsche of augmentative communicators." The product became the most popular communication device of its kind, helping push DynaVox to number one in sales in the

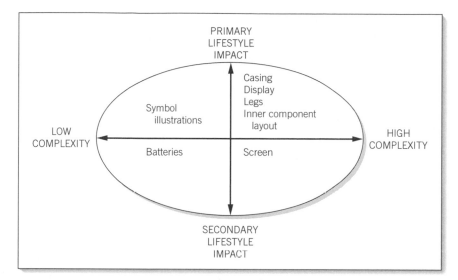

Figure 8.12   PDM of DynaMyte.

Figure 8.13   DynaMyte designed by Daedalus Excel. (Reprinted with permission of Daedalus Excel; photos by Larry Rippel.)

product area. When the product was introduced, DynaVox showed record sales for the month and then continued showing increased sales for the company until it was purchased by Sunrise Medical, one of the top medical supply companies in the country.

The development process dealt with product tensions between size, technology, and style. In the end, the small size required a decrease in auditory aesthetic quality, though the sound quality was still acceptable to the customer given all of the other benefits. In addition, the small size and realities of abuse due to ambulatory use (the product is at times thrown across the room), required additional costs to manufacture and initial limits on reliability. These problems, however, were later addressed in future versions of the product as technology advanced.

The product took seven months from inception to production. Four months were spent on design and three on tooling. The four-month design time brought the team through Phases II, III, and IV in our user-centered iNPD process. The effective and efficient design process owes much of its success to the integration of the team, the user-driven focus, and, of course, the design team's talent. The product was awarded the 1998 Silver Industrial Design Excellence Award in the medical products area from the Industrial Designers Society of America and *BusinessWeek*.

This case study illustrates a further benefit for small businesses of a user-centered iNPD process and a Move to the Upper Right. A major reason DynaVox was bought out by the much larger Sunrise Medical was the success of the DynaMyte. Owners of many small companies look for such an exit strategy. Such an outcome is most likely to occur from a successful, targeted product in the marketplace. Products in the Upper Right have those qualities.

Kodak Single-Use Camera

This case study highlights the advantage of the environmental impact VO for products in the Upper Right. In the 1980s, prior to the introduction of the single-use camera, photography of events was limited by the necessity of having a camera with you. If you forgot your camera, you missed an opportunity. If you found yourself at an unanticipated event without a camera, then you missed another opportunity. The SET Factors in an on-the-go world moving into the information age highlighted the need to record on the fly experiences through photography. As well, fast-food packaging, disposable diapers, and disposable razors led to a society unaware of the effects on the environment of "use and throw" products.

Kodak understood those factors and in 1987 introduced the single-use camera to meet the needs of customers who wanted an inexpensive camera to take pictures that would have otherwise been missed at various occasions. The first camera was called the "Kodak Fling," highlighting its disposable feature — use it and throw it away. However, society was already experiencing a backlash against products that hurt the environment. Soon environmental groups and customers were protesting the sale of the cameras due to their negative effects on the environment. Kodak itself now says that the original throw-away was an "environmental ugly duckling"; yet at the same time the camera was a hit in its intended market.

Kodak found itself in the same position many other companies are in. They had three choices: take it off the market, ignore the protests, or address the concerns. The company chose the third option and in 1990–1991, through a highly integrated effort, totally redesigned the camera to facilitate recycling and reuse of parts.

Since the only way to get the film in the cameras developed is to bring it to a photo finisher, Kodak had a unique opportunity to control the lifecycle of the camera. Once the film is removed, the camera itself is sent to vendors to be processed. The camera is designed with minimal variability in materials, and includes recyclable materials wherever possible. All major parts are marked as to their material composition to ease recycling. Although snap fasteners were used to reduce manufacturing time, the number of parts, and variety of materials, the disassembly process at times causes the snaps to break. The vendor disassembles the camera and inspects the main polystyrene body. If the mainframe is in good shape it is marked to indicate the number of times it was used and sent back to Kodak for reuse. If the part is defective or has been used more than 10 times, it is ground up and recycled. Whenever possible, functions are integrated into a single part to reduce the number of parts used, which also improves tolerance quality. The circuit boards are also tested and, if still functioning well, marked and used up to seven times before being disposed of.

Several parts are only used once to maintain Kodak's high standards as a dependable product. The outer package, made from recycled materials, is again recycled. The lenses are used only once to maintain clarity and then ground and recycled. The batteries too are only used once to guarantee that the flash will function each time. The worn batteries are either used within Kodak for internal pagers or donated to various charitable organizations.

■ By moving the camera's environmental effectiveness from non-existent to high, Kodak has improved its brand equity and overall sales.

By weight 77 to 86 percent of the single-use camera is now recycled or reused. Over 400 million cameras have been recycled rather than thrown in a dump (representing 71 million pounds of waste diverted from landfills). Kodak has an Upper Right product (Figure 8.14) that maps high in many of the VOs. The only significant difference in value between the re-introduced model and the original Fling is the environmental impact VO. By moving its effectiveness from non-existent to high, the company has improved its corporate brand equity, its product brand equity, and overall sales. Recent injections of innovation include improved lens materials and production, which challenge the photo quality of reloadable cameras.

Figure 8.14 Kodak Single-Use Max Camera. (Reprinted with permission of the Eastman Kodak Company.)

Service Industry: UPS Moves Beyond the Package Delivery Industry

Since the founding of UPS in 1907 by Jim Casey with just $100 in financing, the company has grown today to be a $30 billion corporation. What is often thought of as a package delivery company has transformed into a global service provider of information, financing, and delivery of goods. After going public, the company was named the "1999 Company of the Year" by *Forbes Magazine*, which stated, "UPS used to be a trucking company with technology. Now it's a technology company with trucks."[3] This case study explores the positioning and product opportunities in the service industry of package and letter delivery, highlighting the positioning of UPS through brand and how they are looking to future directions through the PDM and SET Factors.

UPS has developed the most recognized brand in the package delivery business and overall one of the most recognized brands of the '90s. Their shield, color brown, and drivers are core to their brand and, along with their vehicles and employee loyalty, have made them one of the most successful companies of the second half of the 20th century. UPS has targeted and achieved attributes of reliability, trust, quality, and attention to detail. Customers send their packages around the world with confidence, knowing that they will arrive on time and intact.

It is interesting to note the history of their logo. The shield goes back to the '30s, but the current rendition (Figure 8.15) was developed by Paul Rand in 1962. In 1993, UPS gave a facelift to their vehicles, adding in the globe, the web address, phone number, and the words "world wide," but the core shield and color remained untouched. The

Figure 8.15 UPS shield. (Reprinted with permission of UPS.)

core color and shield have power and value, promoting customer loyalty. So while other companies tweak and evolve their logos, UPS has stayed with theirs for over 40 years.

The identity system is applied with a consistency that graces a plethora of products, which include packages, drop-off boxes, store fronts, interiors and counters, uniforms, trucks, containers, and aircraft. This is complemented by an automated delivery system that is backed by an equally consistent set of digital products that process and track deliveries. These products include software and hardware products that range from a large central database and mainframes to small personal computers and software that allow customers to track their own packages.

UPS saw a POG in the evolving global economy. Companies spread across the globe required the ability to exchange goods quickly. Their development of a global infrastructure allowed them to develop their own new business in global commerce. Today the company is in constant evolution as it anticipates the effects and needs of the global economy.

UPS has become an "enabler of global commerce." Their goal is to play a role in the supply chain over the life cycle of a product from the sourcing of raw materials through manufacturing of the product, to delivery of the product, and, finally, after-market repair, replacement, and disposal of the product. To accomplish this vision, the company has broadened its focus to the movement and control of goods, information (that accompanies those goods), and funds that enable the transaction of the goods. UPS recognized that in addition to an infrastructure to support the transport of goods, their infrastructure supported the transport of information. UPS spends over $1B each year in the development and maintenance of information technology to support their services. Their package tracking system rivals that of any competitor. They know where a package is at any time and, through an electronic signature, when the package is delivered. UPS knows the buyer and seller and possesses information about their shipping methods and product inventory. Knowledge is power, and in this case, this knowledge gives UPS the power to provide additional services to the customer. For example, financial transactions between buyer and seller are triggered once a package is delivered. The electronic delivery signature coupled with a growing financial arm to the company allows UPS to commence financial transactions between the buyer's and seller's banks.

UPS, then, has grown to be not only a package delivery service company, but an information company. By contributing to the production of a product and tracking that product over its life cycle, the company has successfully identified numerous POGs. For example, they may not own the ocean liner that transports the goods across the ocean, but they can control the information about the inventory on the ocean liner. They might also use their capital arm to fund the inventory and support the transactions with the inventory. They can also control the information that moves the goods across customs and then transport the goods from there. As another example, the Internet has created E-commerce. Not only did UPS sense this POG early and establish itself as a core service to transport goods purchased over the Internet, but they also provide services to support the infrastructure to enable commerce over the Web.

To establish and maintain their reputation as an information company, UPS's challenge has been to move their brand at the speed of the company, while maintaining brand loyalty. The company wants customers to associate their brand with the attributes of speed, express delivery, innovation, technology, and global reach, in addition to their established attributes of reliability, trust, quality, and attention to detail. In this competitive industry, the company must constantly anticipate new challenges from the competition. For instance, UPS has been delivering overnight packages since 1954, but with the integration of overnight transportation into the speed of business in the '90s, overnight delivery became a critical service and the new cost of doing business. As other companies got into the market, UPS took advantage of their infrastructure and evolving technical expertise to remain the leader in overnight delivery today, delivering more packages overnight today than any competitor. The challenge is for the company to counteract advertising and branding messages from other companies, like FedEx, and to maintain the consumer's perception of possessing the speed and technology to be the best overnight delivery company.

As mentioned earlier in the book, product companies and service companies overlap. This is certainly the case with UPS. The product that UPS produces is an increase in the speed in which companies can do business. They manufacture/process deliveries, their manufacturing starts with accepting information in envelopes or packages (raw material) from one point and distributing it to another point. The process in between is a delivery factory/ central processing unit that collects and redistributes information. It encodes from the pickup customer and decodes to the delivery customer with each package as if it were a byte of information. UPS measures its success by its percentage of on-time deliveries the way companies measure the manufacturing quality of their products. The UPS on-time delivery rate is the 6σ of the service industry. Behind the package that someone receives is an array of people and products that are required to deliver that package.

The PDM serves not only to understand where UPS must focus its effort, but also to see where the focus on information comes from. The PDM for UPS is shown in Figure 8.16. In the lower left cell are the packaging materials used by customers, speced out by UPS but readily manufactured to order by many vendors. The lower right cell holds UPS's 160,000 vans, tractors, and trailers, each built to UPS specification, and the planes and buildings that process their packages. The upper left cell includes the brand and logo design. The upper right cell, as always, shows critical components to UPS's business. Located there are the technology to process the packages en route; the tracking system; the information technology to process tracking, delivery, and financial information; and the information itself. The information must be included there because it is the resource that allows UPS to deliver its services. Thus it becomes clear that information is core to UPS's growth, which explains why UPS has become an information company.

UPS has extensive and ongoing user research. They take three complementary paths: First is what they call a Customer Satisfaction Index, an ongoing, in-depth analysis based on an extensive questionnaire sent to several thousand customers on a quarterly basis. Second is their Dialog Program, a constant (24/7) program where customers are phoned and asked about one or two issues for feedback on their delivery. Finally, UPS uses small focus

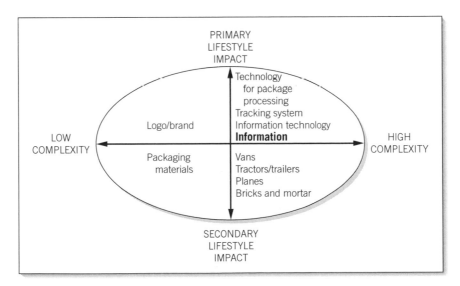

Figure 8.16 PDM for UPS.

groups that target specific markets and geographic locations. It would be interesting to see how the ethnographic methods of Chapter 7 might further benefit this successful company.

UPS is a company in the Upper Right. They clearly add value and merge technological innovation with brand equity. The VO chart shows the service product high in the security and comfort emotional VO, the visual aesthetic VO, the product identity VOs, and of course enabling and reliable core technology VOs. The company also addresses important social impact VOs by supporting communications across the globe. Between overnight delivery, domestic package delivery, and global delivery, UPS transports seven percent of the U.S. gross domestic product every day. As the company targets new areas and finds emerging competitors with different services, the package and information delivery service promises to be an exciting arena in the 21st century.

Herman Miller Aeron Chair

The Herman Miller Aeron Chair (Figure 8.17) is a major departure from competing solutions to office seating. While it was a significant change, it was quickly accepted as

Figure 8.17 Aeron chair. (Reprinted with permission of Stumpf Weber Associates.)

an appropriate solution to the needs of current office workers. What did design consultants Bill Stumpf and Don Chadwick see that no one else did and why was Herman Miller willing to gamble on such an untested seating concept? Herman Miller's gamble paid off, as the design responded to a series of SET Factors that created the opportunity filled by the Aeron. This case study provides a glimpse into the process and insights behind the Aeron Chair, arguably the most successful task seating designed in the last decade. The Aeron chair is a product that integrates ergonomics, aesthetics, material and manufacturing innovation, and mechanical invention.

The Social factors (S) that Aeron responded to were based on the changing nature of work in the digital office. These changes included the increase in repetitive stress experienced by office workers from the constant use of computers, the need to dynamically change from individual task work to interacting with co-workers, the recognition that the range of men and women using task seating required more significant variation than existing seating, and new research findings. These studies identified new areas of stress on the body from the effects of spending long periods of time seated in the same position. They looked at issues of body temperature, blood circulation, and spinal compression. Next, the light and open aesthetic of the time had not been applied to seating design. Finally, office seating had been traditionally used as a way to denote the class structure of the office. The Aeron chair shifts the emphasis from hierarchy to comfort. Everyone has the same basic design and differences are based on size not on rank. This is a major statement and reflects the changing nature of the way people work in offices. It supports the idea of a horizontal business organization.

The economic issues that drove the design were the costs associated with the kinds of illness and reduced performance that results from the prolonged effects of repetitive office work. Keeping employees healthy and functioning at full capability is a major challenge in business today. Replacing key personnel, or dealing with employees constantly missing work, have a major effect on companies in two ways. The first is the reduction of work output and the loss of continuity of performance. It has become clear that keeping employees and helping them function at their fullest is more profitable and stable for companies than constantly replacing and retraining new people. The second issue is the insurance cost that is required to cover employees who develop the range of occupational illnesses caused by the stress of office work. Carpal Tunnel Syndrome and neck, shoulder, back, and circulatory problems are all the result of what takes place when someone is forced to sit in the same position for hours involved in highly repetitive movements.

There are a number of technological breakthroughs in this product. However, the main new innovation is the synthetic weave developed for the back and seat pan. The ability to achieve the performance demands of a breathable interface between the body and the chair gave the product its unique ergonomics and aesthetics. The success of the chair lay in the ability to identify a supplier who was willing and able to meet the demanding performance requirements of a mesh seating surface for a work environment. This is another example of a successful partnering of a product manufacturer with a material supplier. The engineering mechanisms are also extremely well designed. They give the person seated in the chair the ability to easily shift position for different tasks or just change to allow for a shift in posture. The controls for everyday changes are easy to find and operate, making them useful and usable. Many chairs allow for adjustments, but the fact that you have to get out the chair to do so makes it less likely that you will change the settings.

Bill Stumpf and Don Chadwick worked with marketing, the ergonomic research group, and engineers at Herman Miller to design a chair that redefined the office chair in the '90s and caused all other companies to respond to its success. The project began as a potential seat design to replace the existing recliners used by seniors. This led to an early emphasis on ergonomic research of anthropometrics, which reviewed body type, the ergonomics of sitting for extended time periods, and the issues related to sitting down and getting out of a chair. As the project shifted to task seating, it retained its strong ergonomic base and shifted to the dynamics of the current office environment. The SET Factors were clear to the team. In the U.S. and around the world the current work environment has become far more diverse. Companies needed to accommodate a greater range of body types. Everyone, regardless of status, has become involved in two types of office work. The team designated them as Socio-Technic Work and Social Work. Everyone was involved in both types and had to shift several times during the day from one type of work to the other. Socio-Technic work involves working at a screen either alone or with one or two others. Social Work involves meetings with others in larger groups around tables and usually involves sitting and standing (see Figure 8.18). The chair was also designed to reduce the incidence of spinal compression. It allowed kinesthetic motion, rotation of the back, and stretching of the spine. Armrests were designed to be adjustable in height and rotation to allow for elbow support, which thus achieves optimal ergonomic positioning to reduce the incidence of Carpal Tunnel Syndrome.

The team developed an "outside in" approach rather than the traditional "inside out" approach. This meant that the team would account for a variety of body types. Traditional ergonomics tends to support the center of the bell curve distribution of size and weight, people clustered around the 50th percentile. Chairs have historically been designed to have one size with adjustable features that attempted to respond to the needs of all users. Clearly, however, people of various shapes and sizes use chairs (see

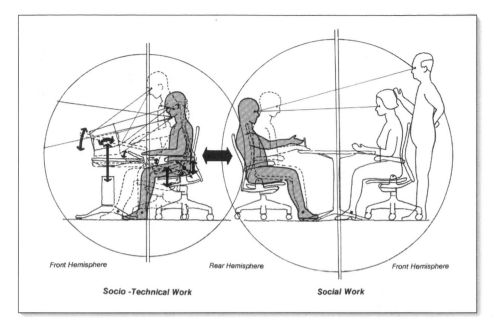

Figure 8.18 Socio-Technic and Social Work illustration. (Reprinted with permission of Stumpf Weber Associates.)

the variety in Figure 7.9). The result of this analysis led the team to propose three different sized chairs. While each would be adjustable they would respond to the full range of customers from the 2.5 percentile female to the 97.5 percentile males.

The team relied on new research studies that identified issues related to long-term seating in weight distribution and heat transfer. This led to the proposal for a breathable seating surface (a pellicle) design that would allow people to maintain an even heat distribution in the front and back. Other research revealed that most materials used to distribute weight in the seat and back will fail over time. New synthetic weaves like DuPont's Dymetrol had the ability to remain neutral longer than synthetic foams. The frame that holds the mesh is designed to create a smooth transition from the open mesh to the solid frame. This allows the mesh and frame to work together to support the body and prevents pressure forming on the back or legs.

The team also recognized that work required a variety of seating options. The chair needed a new type of adjustment capability with controls that would be easy to learn and alter.

The final element was the aesthetics of the chair. The functional elements of the chair, frame, and pellicle surface gave the product a distinct aesthetic departure from the competition; however, it also had elements of past designs. The designers sought to integrate past, present, and future ideas (shown in Figure 8.19). The designers chose to look to the past for inspiration in the work of Charles and Ray Eames' biomorphic designs and "economy of means." They were inspired by the lyric quality of the designs of George Nelson and the simplicity of the Thonet chairs. The chair

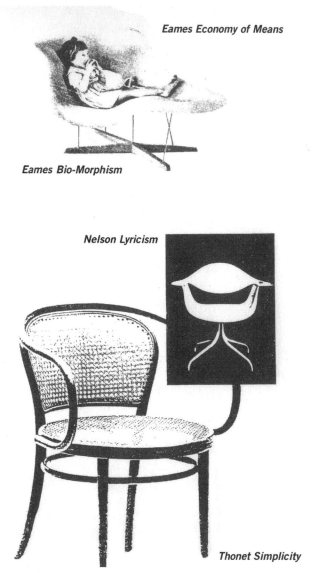

Figure 8.19 Design references that influenced the aesthetics of the Aeron chair. (Reprinted with permission of Stumpf Weber Associates.)

frame and mesh in synthetic materials created a new aesthetic, which took on an elegant, skeletal quality in dark gray. The arms and mechanism became equal to the frame and seat. The chair looks light and open. The natural finish of the materials created a statement of simplicity and directness in the use of material as well as form. The parts of the chair are not painted or treated with additional finishes and are all coded for recycling. These qualities give it a sense of integrity and environmental responsibility.

There are a number of Value Opportunities that Aeron achieved, which allowed it to become a major competitor in the office seating market. Clearly all of the ergonomics VOs are the driving focus of the design. Emotionally, the Aeron gives people a sense of security and safety from a health standpoint. Office workers feel they are sitting in a chair that is designed to fit their body and support them in the variety of tasks they must perform. This sense of security inspires a confidence that they can perform tasks with less chance of injury and reduced potential for the long-term negative effects that many office workers face. Manufacturing and mechanical innovations highlight the quality and core technology VOs. The attention to recycling concerns and the ease of adjustment between individual and group work score high on both environment and social impact VOs.

The chair creates an aesthetic that combines traditional and modern seating elements with a post-modern visual refinement. The chair has a skeletal quality and looks light and easy to move. The skeletal frame in combination with the adjustment mechanisms under the seat give a robotic-like appearance of a motorized chair that could operate on its own. The feel of the materials provides the right tactile cues. The frame, mesh, padding on the arms, and plastic controls are designed to give a sense of comfort and subtle texture that provides the right friction for short-term interaction or long-term comfort.

The Aeron chair has a unique brand identity that is the result of hitting all three factors with a high degree of success. It is the type of design that no one would have predicted and yet when it debuted everyone responded to in a positive way. It anticipated the shift away from the need to make people feel important by rank to the need to make them feel comfortable by design. The chair fits with a range of other products that are also successful in other fields. The open airy look of the Aeron is perfectly complemented by the translucent iMacs and G4 designs for the desktop. The shift from solid mass to open translucency created a sense of dematerialization of form that is a theme of our time. For instance, it is not the computer, it is the connection the computer affords. Similarly, it is not the chair, it is the chair as an open flexible system that moves with you when you are in it, de-emphasizing the mass of the product in favor of its performance attributes. The Aeron fits equally well in a renovated loft space and in new, action-oriented open office designs. It also looks elegant in combination with high-end offices and meeting rooms. It can dress up and down with one set of materials and a minimal, usually gray, color scheme. The use of a neutral gray color allows the chair to fit into any type of color environment. This is a very effective way to prevent having to produce a variety colors and finishes. There are no leather or cloth options, no patterns to choose from, and only a few solid color choices (with gray being the standard). This willingness to risk such a clear departure from the competition has given Herman Miller a strong brand statement. The aesthetic and technical Gestalt makes it even more successful in the marketplace because of its uniqueness. It is difficult for competitors to copy the chair without looking like they are making a direct rip-off.

The chair has won numerous awards and was recognized by IDSA and *BusinessWeek* in their 2000 Designs of the Decade Awards program. Perhaps one of its best signs of success is that the chair is constantly featured in advertising, movies, and TV as the chair that best creates a statement of contemporary success.

Apple iMac

This Upper Right, high-tech product pushes the limits on manufacturing technology to realize a POG in an industry stuck in the Lower Right quadrant of the Positioning Map. The iMac pushes the state of the art in manufacturing technology. It required a true integration between style and technology and it has also created a new aesthetic in consumer products.

This quote says it all: "For the first 139 days from its debut, an iMac sold at the rate of four a minute, every hour, of every day".[4] The product (Figure 8.20) was an instant success. It created a sensation in the computer industry which had grown weary of tortured gray boxes. It broke with a number of conventions in the industry, for example how many computer companies consult with candy manufacturers to solve manufacturing problems? The shift to translucent covers challenged both methods of manufacture and details of assembly.

The iMac's new look integrated the CPU and monitor as they had been in the original Macintoshes. It also introduced an easy-to-install, simpler system for booting up and getting connected to the Internet. Making it transparent and translucent and introducing the candy colors was a major gamble that worked. The aesthetic mirrored evolving trends in society. It is interesting to see how similar the iMac and Beetle are in look and feel, especially since they both used color in a dynamic way to differentiate themselves. To create the aesthetic, it was necessary to get plastic to flow through large high-pressure injection molds without flow lines — a very difficult task. Before, texture was often used to minimize or hide surface variations. Internal components of computers had not been designed

www.apple.com

iCandy.

Think different.

Figure 8.20 The iMac. (Reprinted with permission of Apple Computer and TBWA Chiat Day.)

to be seen by consumers. Now the goal was to allow for transparent material and to make the internal components visible, making it difficult to use the usual material cover-up techniques.

Apple turned a disadvantage into an advantage. Stereolithography produces translucent parts that are used to produce prototypes in the latter concept phases of product development. When these prototypes are assembled they show the technology inside. Furthermore, early tests of injection molded plastic parts were produced using clear plastic to determine the flow of material in the mold and to make sure it dispersed evenly. Looking at these test runs, designers saw the potential of pushing a test process into a final product application. It is not a stretch to imagine that the idea for the iMac evolved consciously or unconsciously from this trend.

Designers and engineers in several product categories had been reviewing parts and prototypes in translucent and clear states for years — someone finally saw the potential here. There were several challenges to overcome after the initial idea was conceived. The company executives had to be convinced that a clear monitor would be desirable to customers. Engineers responsible for manufacturing had to agree to deliver flawless, clear pieces with a high degree of consistency. Finally the electrical and mechanical engineers had to agree to design the interior to complement and actually form part of the aesthetic of the design. They could no longer produce components based primarily on layout and service without any aesthetic accountability because they were no longer invisible to the customer.

The innovative use of material and internal design challenge was elegantly met in this product. The iMac was a major risk, however it was consistent with the original brand characteristics that made the original Mac a user-friendly product and allowed Apple to dominate the competition in the early personal computer market. Steve Jobs' original vision was successfully interpreted by a team of designers and engineers, who found the right values for this time, which were as powerful as the original Mac was in its debut. There were no clear precedents in the computer industry, however there were trends in other areas that lent credibility to the idea.

First of all, people were tired of the simple and dull gray desktop computers on the market. They were waiting for any kind of change. If you look at an iMac and an Aeron chair, you will see that the two go together. The Aeron chair is light and open with a new mesh seating and back that makes the chair almost translucent. Similar technology had been used in the auto industry to design headlights and taillights, which can blend red, yellow, and clear in the same light. The sizes of headlights on cars have increased and began to resemble the size of computer monitors. Athletic shoes have been designed with a variety of materials, some transparent, others translucent. There have been several toys that have been produced with exposed internal mechanisms and an exterior clear shell. Making technology accessible has always been something that consumers respond to. In the 1930s, designing washers and dryers with windows made them a form of entertainment. More recently, putting a window in the Iomega peripheral products helped to make their products more user friendly.

The iMac design is also consistent with the emerging post-industrial philosophy of dematerialization. In the information era, form and mass have given way to communication and interaction with screen software and the Web. The iMac is a metaphor for the dematerialization of the computer in favor of the GUI (graphic user interface) and the software that drives it. It asks users to look through and not at the computer. While all these factors existed for any company, Apple was the first to see the potential for the application of all these trends to the design of computers and peripherals.

This product could not have been produced without extensive interdisciplinary collaboration and respect. The industrial designers had to work with mechanical and electrical engineers to develop the interior components. Both groups then had to work with manufacturing engineers to create molds and materials for the high-quality color translucent parts, which would complement the computer's interior components and work in harmony to complete a new visual aesthetic for the desktop. The iMac is responsible for resurrecting the company and has inspired products in almost every other industry. Many others have followed the trend of translucency and candy colors, so nicely highlighted by the "iCandy" ad campaign shown in Figure 8.20. As other companies responded to the iMac, Apple was ready with other designs, such as the new towcr G3, which pushed the concept further and left the competition to follow its innovative trail again.

Freeplay Radio

This final case study emphasizes the social impact VO and demonstrates how an Upper Right product for people in developing nations can still lead to high sales and high profits. The Freeplay radio (Figure 8.21) is a hand-powered radio originally developed for emerging nations in Africa. The product is a wonderful example of how Upper Right products are extendable to other lines and products. There are now several versions of the Freeplay products on the market (from radios to flashlights) and thousands of stores, cataloges, and Web sites throughout the world that sell them.

The original Freeplay radio was conceived as a response to a group of life-threatening SET Factors that existed in many emerging nations. The AIDs epidemic was spreading in African countries with high illiteracy, poor communication, and little education. Many of these countries lacked the infrastructure to distribute electrical power. Few people had the money to purchase expensive batteries. So it was nearly impossible to educate and broadcast information to entire villages.

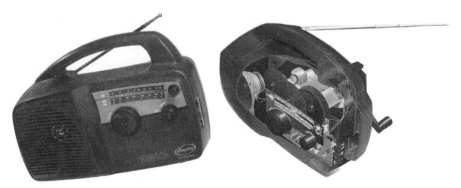

Figure 8.21 The Freeplay Radio: product image and internal schemata. (Reprinted with permission of Freeplay Group.)

Trevor Baylis, a British inventor, realized that a reliable human-powered radio could help to solve this problem. The challenges for Baylis were formidable. He had to find funding for development and manufacture. He had to develop a radio that would be competitive with battery and electric powered radios and would be valued as equivalent. Hand cranking was not as prestigious as electric or battery powered. He received support from a number of people, who were instrumental in helping him to find funding, develop prototypes, and locate the best audience that would find the product the most useful. After failing to attract the attention of British manufacturers, Baylis was interviewed by the BBC World Service, an interview that started the chain of events that led to the creation of the Freeplay radio.

The BBC interview caught the attention of accountant Christopher Staines. Staines provided the economic knowledge for product development and gave Baylis his first contact in South Africa. Staines put him in touch with South African Rory Stear, who had experience working for the UN and who realized that the product could help as many as 600 million people in Africa. Hylton Appelbaum, the director of a charitable foundation in South Africa, saw the interview and suggested that the radio be designed in a way that it could be assembled by people with disabilities. This decision allowed the product to receive the support of many foundations supporting the development of work opportunities for the disabled. A research group at Bristol University in England refined the cranking mechanism to allow it to meet performance criteria that would make it competitive with battery-powered radios. Market research determined the features and style that would be required to make the product appealing and competitive. The product's features were based on feedback from interviews that Baylis and Stear conducted when they took a prototype to rural areas in South Africa.

Results from the interviews determined that the radio had to look robust and that it had to be loud enough to be heard by many people simultaneously. The acceptable ratio of winding to playing time was determined to be 20 seconds of winding resulting in $1/2$ hour of playing time. The early version that played for 14 minutes with a cranking time of 2 minutes was not deemed suitable because it did not really compete against battery-powered radios. The power needed for the higher volume performance resulted in a total reengineering of the winding mechanism. After significant analysis, the right combination of metal and plastic were used to create an efficient and durable mechanism.

The radio had to convey a sense of importance and status. It had to be large and have a durable handle that would allow it to be easy to pick up and move. The result was a strong, simple design with a permanent, rigid handle that gave the radio a sturdy and durable look. The radio was designed to be assembled by factory workers with disabilities. The price was set to be the local equivalent to that of a battery-powered radio plus a year's supply of batteries. After being successfully introduced and produced in South Africa, Nelson Mandela personally thanked Trevor Baylis for his invention.[5]

As has been the case with many of the Upper Right case studies cited in this book, the resulting design was applicable to more markets and the concept could be applied to other products. The radio is now a popular product, which is being purchased for a number of uses throughout the world including survival/emergency kits and camping. It is useful for people in any rural area anywhere in the world. Over 2.5 million units have been sold in the first five years of production. A version with a crank, solar panel, and AC/DC input has been developed. The concept has been extended to a flashlight that uses a crank along with a rechargeable battery option.

▮ Poor consumers in emerging countries have value systems just like the middle and upper classes do in other parts of the world.

This case study highlights a few points. No manufacturer in England saw the potential in this product. Even though the product was extremely useful in its basic technology state, the product still had to be designed to be usable and desirable through additional technology, styling, and a user focus. Poor consumers in emerging countries have value systems just like people in middle and upper classes in other parts of the world. They will respond best to products with appropriate features that fulfill a range of values and do not just simply satisfy a basic need with vanilla style or technology. It is also very clear that an initial idea, no matter how valid, must be improved and supported by a number of other contributors with different types of expertise to make the product a success. Finally, though the product could not be priced at a premium in its initial target market, the Freeplay's Upper Right qualities enabled it to extend to numerous applications, leading to higher overall profits.

Summary Points

❏ There are a broad range of products and services in the Upper Right.

❏ Established Upper Right products and services remain there by injecting new innovations that are considered useful, usable, and desirable.

❏ Each breakthrough new product or service is clearly differentiated from the rest of the field.

References

1. Kao, J., *Jamming: The Art and Discipline of Business Creativity*, HarperBusiness, New York, 1997.

2. Katzenbach, J.R., and D.K. Smith, *Wisdom of Teams: Creating the High Performance Organization*, Harper Perennial, New York, 1994.

3. Barron, K., "Logistics in Brown," *Forbes Magazine*, January 10, 2000, pp. 78–83.

4. "Yum./Apple iMac," *Innovation*, Fall, 1999, p. 76.

5. Maskell, K., "Windup Radio," *Ties Magazine*, March, 1997, pp. 18–24.

Chapter Nine

Automotive Design: Product Differentiation through User-Centered iNPD

The auto industry is one of the most dynamic and exciting examples of the evolution of SET Factors. No other market develops products in an atmosphere where competition is as fierce, the product is as complex, and the challenge of constant refinement and innovation is as great. Through the use of case studies, this chapter is devoted to understanding the design of cars, trucks, and SUVs. The user-centered iNPD process for both vehicle programs and individual parts adds additional support to the arguments made in Chapter 8 and further demonstrates the value of Moving to the Upper Right.

The Dynamic SET Factors of the Auto Industry

■ No industry represents clearer variations in purchasing value than the manufacturers of cars.

No industry epitomizes Friedman's *Golden Strait Jacket*[1] of continual improvement and the challenge introduced in this book to deliver useful, useable, and desirable products better than the automotive industry. At the beginning of a new century, the automobile represents all that is good and bad about the mass-produced products of the last century. The auto industry affects balance of global trade, pollution, fossil fuels depletion, safety standards, insurance standards, unions and workers' compensation, commerce, development of novel manufacturing and assembly technologies, and trend-setting styles. Auto companies are involved in a global competition for ever-demanding and critical consumer markets. Automobiles continue to evolve as the car links to the information age by becoming a mobile communication center. Cars are connected to the fast food industry by becoming a rolling kitchen counter and wet bar. They are now becoming multimedia entertainment centers as well. It is now possible to drive in your own car sitting in a leather seat that is programmed with your comfort settings cruising at 70 miles per hour on a highway in the United States and carry on a conversation with someone in Asia while eating lunch, checking your location and destination on a GPS system, reading your email and, or watching your favorite video (hopefully as a passenger). You can choose from one of several types of power to move your vehicle and there are more choices on the way. No industry represents clearer variations in purchasing value than the manufacturers of cars. One owner can buy a VW Golf while another buys an Audi TT. Both cars are built on the same platform, however they are priced thousands of dollars apart. The Golf is an economy car while the Audi TT is a sporty two-seater. Both owners feel they have a car at an appropriate price that they are equally excited about and value.

The SET Factors driving the design of vehicles are an interesting combination of features and style that include safety, creature comforts, and a sense of power and control combined with environments that create all the features of a family room. Drivers often wear their cars the way teenagers wear t-shirts. It is all about who you are and what you want to project. The styles vary from retro to rugged and from elegant to military. Off road, four-wheel, and all-wheel drive are the themes that many cars are built around today, with sizes ranging from the Lincoln Navigator to the Subaru Outback. The Xterra is designed for the X-generation, while the Cadillac, Lexus, and Mercedes are for the man and woman who have everything. The station wagon gave way to the minivan. The minivan has given way to the SUV. The SUV is now yielding to trucks as the fantasy ride continues. Hybrids of all kinds emerge as companies cross traditional product categories and sport-utility-elegant-off road-compact-luxury are mixed like tropical fruits in a blender to create a stunning array of vehicle hybrids. A stretch Hummer is now available for weddings and no one can define what a PT Cruiser is. The Mercedes SUV is small enough to be a compact station wagon and high enough to see over most cars and the company claims that it is one of the safest SUVs on the road. The features in vehicles are creating a competition for space in dashboards, door panels, and ceilings that are packed with computers, plugs and ports, motors, speakers, wiring, airbags, and individual climate control. Ovens, screens of all kinds, refrigerators, and washing machines are on the way to becoming standard as the war over creature comforts continues.

The design of a vehicle is incredibly complex, exciting, and challenging. There is no user-focused product today that is more technologically complex or highly styled. What other products require 200 designers (or "stylists," as they are called in the trade), engineers (mechanical, electrical, and manufacturing), and business people (marketing and finance) to create a product? Few other products take as much as four years to move from project concept to production. And no other product that consumers regularly buy costs as much on average as many American's earn. The car, van, SUV, and small truck are the ultimate example of positioning through style and technology. Automobile companies are all trying to position themselves in the Upper Right. This chapter is devoted to understanding the role of user-centered iNPD in the design of cars, trucks, and SUVs.

The Design Process and Complexities

The auto industry is an excellent source of examples of good user-centered iNPD. We have worked closely with several such companies applying and developing the methods in this book. But although there are many great cars out there and excellent examples of integrated teams focusing on the customer's needs, many auto programs don't sufficiently follow the principles of determining the SET Factors, POGs, and user-focused qualitative research all in a discipline-integrated fashion as emphasized in this book. The '96 Taurus based its success on the dynamic application of the Ford oval. While the oval was a shape that had become part of a trend, it was overused and did not connect with ergonomics and features in a way that consumers found appealing. While the features and controls in the oval on the dash were well integrated, the interface was unique to that model. It was difficult to learn a new pattern of use. Since most families own two cars, it was annoying to transfer from one console to another. The elements that had made the original Taurus a success were lost and the public rejected the dramatic, contoured reinterpretation.

The AMC Pacer was a unique concept. The company thought that the public was ready for a car with the length of an economy car and the width of a full-sized sedan. They were wrong. The classic of all time was the 1930s aerodynamic Chrysler Airflow — the car that was so well engineered it could withstand rolling down a hillside. But no one in the company realized that customers did not consider that a major reason for purchasing a car. A contemporary example was the debut of the Pontiac Aztek. The early sales were far below GM's projections. The aggressive styling failed to connect with the intended market and received poor reviews from auto critics.[2] However, GM seems to have recovered by using the same platform for the Buick Rendezvous. Applying the Buick brand elements of softer, more sophisticated overall shapes and details, coupled with a strong advertising campaign that includes Tiger Woods, has created a more competitive SUV to bolster the low sales of its Pontiac sibling.

Even beyond these failures, we have seen many opportunities missed in the industry where time was lost arguing over a design feature, features were added for the wrong reasons, and other needs of the target customer were not properly understood. In this section, we summarize the product development process in the typical auto company. This will be followed by illustrations of the Move to the Upper Right in the industry and will focus on examples of good user-centered iNPD within vehicle design. We then revisit the industry design process with an eye toward understanding how the user can be better represented.

In the planning of a new vehicle program, at times a cross-functional team begins the process of identifying the need for new vehicles. However, individual disciplines then pursue individual aspects of the program. Marketing explores the feasibility while the concept studios focus on the generation of new vehicle models. The designers often do not follow through on all phases of ethnography but they do use the technique of lifestyle reference. Some car studios surround themselves with products, colors, and music from a target market. GM has a separate concept studio for each of its brands. One would almost not realize they are in the same company as they move between consecutive studios from Chevy to Cadillac to Saturn.

As the planning team communicates product needs to management and the studio moves the more exciting concepts forward, management selects new vehicle programs to move forward. It is often a visionary at the upper management level that champions a new product program. The company must commit to the production of a car two to four years down the road. As many as 50 concepts are developed to one that is pursued. There is a huge number of concepts that will never see the light of day, but as discussed in Chapter 5, such exploration is necessary to evolve the best concept.

At the point when a design is approved, much of the process does become more integrated again. Product teams are put together with program managers selecting area managers (body, electrical, etc.), and these managers selecting sub-system managers (interior and exterior), and these managers then selecting the engineers (most often) and studio designers to work on the detailed design. Often, only a fraction of the studio personnel — compared to many of the engineers — are working on any vehicle (and we have even observed studio designers assigned to more than one vehicle at the same time). However the team is defined, it is given a concept model or sketch, marketing criteria, and a cost target. Referring to the iNPD process discussed in Chapter 5, this is the result of Phases I and II. In Phase III, the team then moves forth, generating more refined concepts, choosing features, and specifying parts.

■ The better teams working under the least stress often find creative solutions meeting all expectations.

The process is one of iteration and product tension. Initial clays and material choices spec out the design intent of the studio. Initial costing and manufacturing analyses look at the feasibility of the initial designs. There is typically no way to get all of the features that marketing and studio want into the car while meeting the cost and weight targets. So the team begins to look for ways of trading off features, materials, manufacturing processes, and costs. Also, everyone needs to find a location for their component so that it works optimally. The sheer number of components in the car (over 3000, with some of these breaking down into other parts) makes this process one of give and take. The better teams working under the least stress often find creative solutions meeting all expectations. Those teams under the gun find some compromise — often at, or even beyond, the last minute. Numerous clay models of the exterior and interior, coupled with CAD models of every part, evolve into a vehicle that meets the goals of the team and management.

In recent years, the actual, detailed design of specific components or systems and their manufacture is often outsourced to what are called "full service suppliers." Full service suppliers are selected by the auto company as a partner in the design of the vehicle. These suppliers participate in the product development process with the end responsibility of supplying to the manufacturing line a part that integrates into the overall vehicle, meets all quality and finish standards to the vehicle, and meets an agreed-upon cost target. What is so interesting in the selection of the supplier and agreement of a cost target is that all of this happens well before the components or systems are detailed (or at times even sketched). Thus suppliers must commit to a cost and quality level without ever seeing or designing what they will produce. And since the suppliers are not part of the company, they are often not privy to many of the facts that those within the company know about the vehicle. It's an interesting anticipatory game, where the target cost and weight of the vehicle is dependent on the correct assumptions.

At times a team works on a truly new design, but typically the team either refines a current design or, if it is lucky, it follows through on a major design overhaul. Unless the design is new, it will have some level of carryover. In other words, the new vehicle will use the same platform, often with some of the same components or at least same boundaries for the components as a previous model. The less that is revised in the design, the more carryover and the greater the design constraints imposed on the team. At times the design team is restricted to a few changes but must still give the vehicle a new look. Recall the discussion of evolutionary versus revolutionary design in Chapter 2. Most programs are evolutionary and require an understanding of the dynamics of the SET Factors in order to inject useful, usable, and desirable innovation. This is the only way to keep the vehicle at its peak market potential and in the Upper Right.

At least in terms of cross-platform design, these issues arise in all vehicle design. All car companies produce vehicles under different brand names with the same platform. This is true of Lincoln/Mercury and Ford, Chevy and Pontiac, Volkswagen and Audi, and others. In creating the vehicle, there are often many cosmetic and feature differences but the core vehicles are the same. This is necessary due to the overwhelming costs of creating and manufacturing a vehicle (upwards of several billion dollars).

The interesting effects on the design teams are that they are often creating two vehicles that look and feel different with components and parts attaching to the same frame and inner panels.

During the 1990s there was a global consolidation in the auto industry. Companies were merging and acquiring others with the goals of breadth of product line and a presence across the globe. Daimler-Benz bought Chrysler to become Daimler Chrysler. Ford bought Volvo, Jaguar, and a large share of Mazda (among others) to become The Ford Motor Company. As companies become global, they must deal with many issues of cross-culture and cross-regulations. Again, to be cost-effective, platforms become critical. Although companies may push a single model internationally, there is a need to at least modify cosmetic features, and at times go even further in adapting a vehicle for different cultures or different legal requirements such as safety and emissions.

The success of the auto industry is heavily influenced by economic and legislative effects. Will people have sufficient wealth or financial confidence to invest in more expensive vehicles? Clearly a part of the success of SUVs is the excess cash so many Americans had through the economic expansion of the '90s. The design of vehicles is also affected by new legislation. The future requirements for additional fuel efficiency or additional air bags, though not implemented for several years, greatly affects the cost today to build tomorrow's vehicle. And although these changes cost more, people may not be willing to pay more for them, adding pressure on the industry to find ways to deliver more for less.

With all of the money and time on the line, there are many exciting cars out there and many features that surprise and delight us as we drive to work, vacation, the store, or off-road in the mountains. This chapter highlights two aspects of the design process that illustrate techniques from this book: design complexity and its effect on the design process, and approaches to product differentiation. We will then revisit this section and see where improvements and areas of concern result from the user-centered iNPD methodology introduced in this book.

Breaking Down the Process

Chapter 6 introduced the Part Differentiation Matrix (PDM) as a means of breaking down products into components that affect primary, point-of-purchase, versus secondary, long-term, lifestyle impact as well as those of high or low complexity. The PDM actually evolved out of our research with the auto industry. The PDM is an excellent way to analyze the vehicle — a highly complex product with intimate user interactions. Figure 9.1 shows a breakdown of some major components of the vehicle into the four cells of the PDM.

The lower left cell holds the low-complexity, secondary lifestyle impact components such as the tires, fuses, and seat belts. These items are all commodities with multiple OEM suppliers producing them for many auto companies. Cost is a driver but the onus is on the auto company to specify and verify an acceptable level of quality. These parts may not be critical to the design and manufacture of the vehicle or the lifestyle impact on the customer, but their failure can have negative effects on the customer. For example, at the time of the writing of this book the Bridgestone tires on the Ford Explorer are losing their treads and causing fatal accidents. Though the cause of the failure and fault are not yet known, the effects of this OEM part on the performance and customer impression of the vehicle could be significant.

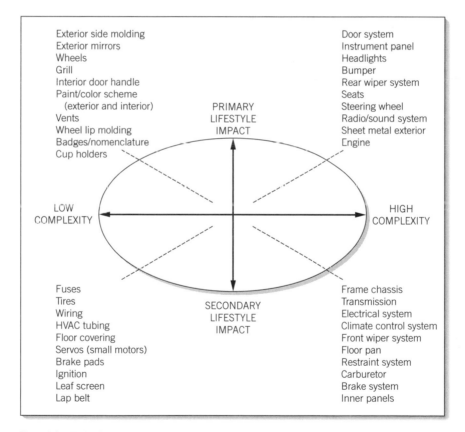

Figure 9.1 PDM for vehicle.

The lower right cell shows the high-complexity but secondary lifestyle impact components. These parts don't interact with the customer directly but are critical to the long-term quality and customer satisfaction of the vehicle. These are the parts that will determine whether a customer will, or more likely will not, return to the company for a future purchase. Included in this cell are the floor pan, inner panels, transmission, and electrical system. There is a basic expectation of the performance of these parts but not emotion or passion in their effects on the vehicle. As discussed in Chapter 6, the engineering part of the team will take the lead in the design of these parts but the studio must have buy-in as they affect the size and style of the vehicle.

The upper cells are the most relevant for this book. The upper left cell represents the low-complexity but primary lifestyle impact parts. These include the exterior side body molding, the grille, the embellishments, and the wheels. The only real technical challenge may be that of manufacturing the part. These parts are tightly connected to brand. They have a strong influence on and are strongly influenced by style and help to sell the car in the showroom. The interesting aspect of this cell, as discussed in Chapter 6, is the different perceptions of the design complexity within this cell between engineering and studio, and is often a source of conflict.

The upper right cell is the critical cell for a user-centered iNPD process. Parts in this cell are highly complex and have primary lifestyle impact, both short- and long-term. The importance of style and technology brings an added complexity into the process. Yet these are the parts that define the vehicle as style, technology, and the user meet in this cell. Parts, typically systems, in this cell include the door system and instrument panel. It is interesting that a part on one type of vehicle may be in the lower right cell while on another it is found in the upper right cell. For example, an engine in a minivan is a lower right cell part while in a sports car or truck the engine becomes an upper right cell part because the performance of the engine is more integral to the statement of what the vehicle is and who the owner is. Engines are designed to respond to perceived needs by marketing the performance features expected by the target market. In other vehicle categories, there is a need to balance engine performance with visual style. A number of years ago the Cadillac Northstar engine won design awards. The goal is to make the engine reflect the brand, particularly for that part visible when the hood is open. These are the parts where all of the methods introduced in this book apply. As such, the next section examines the design of two parts from the upper right cell: the door system and the rear window wiper system.

Door System

In the '50s, the door system was a trivial design task from the point of view of complexity. All that needed to fit into the door was the window crank mechanism, the window, and a lock. Cars (and doors) were large, so that space was never a major issue. Today the door system is amazingly complex. Not only does the system include the window and mechanism and the lock, but typically the motor for the mechanism (rather than the crank), wiring, a speaker or two, lights, vents for air flow, and now even side airbags. In the past, the only real integration concerns were where the crank and arm rest would go. Today each switch, speaker grille, armrest, map pocket, and airbag must integrate into a unified system. At the same time the door is smaller. Thus there is limited real estate in which these parts can be placed. So as one engineer tries to locate her speaker, another is trying to locate his window mechanism in the same spot. As they reach resolution, they change the look of the lines of the door, representing the brand and style used throughout the vehicle. That, of course, is unacceptable to the studio, though the engineers don't always see why. Recall our discussion of platform design earlier in the chapter. Typically, the team has the requirement of certain parts (e.g., window mechanism) remaining the same across platforms while other parts (such as the speaker, and even the choice of a separate bass and tweeter) will change. The flexible components must work within the confines of a fixed inner panel and fixed location of common parts. We have witnessed the design of the door system in several vehicles. Each time it took all parties to sit down at the table together with models of the interior style, the inner panel, prints of proposed layouts, and even actual parts that could be moved. All of these factors served as a forum to negotiate a solution. Again, the user needs to be the voice that pushes the solution to the layout problem.

Rear Wiper System for Lincoln Navigator/Ford Expedition

Even individual components can be highly complex to design. The rear window wiper system on the 2002 Lincoln Navigator/Ford Expedition presented several problems. The motor was located in the door and therefore the blade had to cross the division between the sheet metal bottom of the door and the glass window when the system was turned on or off. This presented a deformation problem and many wipers performed poorly because they were not close enough to the window. The blade had to come to rest on the door and fit in a plastic clip that held it in place. Both the pressure on the glass and the rest position were difficult to achieve because of the challenge of manufacture and assembly. It was difficult to get all the elements involved to fit within the necessary tolerances to clean a window and come to rest in the clip. In addition, the motor was loud. See Figure 9.2.

The Ford team recognized a Product Opportunity Gap to develop a new wiper that did not have to cross over two materials and did not have to come to rest on the lower part of the door. The motor had to be quiet and the design integrated nicely into the style of the vehicle. The team looked at several options and each one presented as many problems as it solved. One solution would have put the motor on the top center of the window and turned the blade upside down. This created several problems. The blade would wipe a wider area on the bottom of the window than on the top, which was against the standard in the industry and could have been rejected by customers. It would also have removed more water in areas where it was not needed and less where it was. The design solved the performance problem of contact on the window but introduced a potentially limited view for the driver. The motor was encased in a box that was visible in the rear view mirror and interrupted the finish of the interior by putting a large black box on the glass. Bringing a wire to a motor on the glass presented other assembly problems. Conduit would have to be placed along the perimeter of the window to hide the wire.

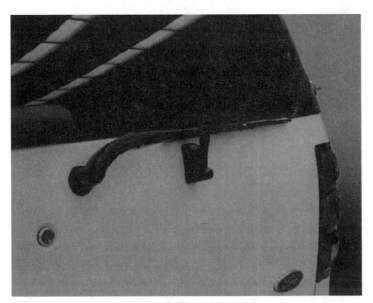

Figure 9.2 Rear wiper on previous model of Ford Expedition. (Reprinted with permission of Ford Motor Company.)

This would create another blight on the finely detailed interior design and, in addition, would add material, parts, and labor charges during installation.

A solution was finally reached that was cost effective, had minimal effects on styling, and utilized a new motor and blade design (Figure 9.3). It was also a solution initially seen as gutsy for the team to take on, charting unexplored territory in a program challenged by cost and weight pressures. The integrated solution responded to all the issues that were factors in determining the success of the new approach. The engineering group found a new supplier that had a bayonet design. This allowed the blade to stay on the glass and the motor to remain in the door. Styling redesigned the window to come down over the glass so the height of the tailgate did not have to change. The new tolerance challenge became the match of the post to the opening in the motor as the window closed. This was seen as achievable both initially and over time. Assembly costs were reduced through part integration — rather than separate handles, latches, and wiper system, the parts were integrated into a single unit. The look and function of the rear window were both improved at a cost that fit within the objectives of the program. Constant customer feedback both drove the team to pursue this solution and confirmed the effectiveness of the effort. In the end, creative problem solving and discipline-integrated discussion led to an innovative, cost-effective, superior solution.

Figure 9.3 Final Upper Right solution of new Expedition. (Reprinted with permission of Ford Motor Company.)

Positioning: Move to the Upper Right

This and the next two sections examine ways that the auto industry uses the user-entered iNPD process to create products that target different user groups and to identify those groups. The complexity of the design of a vehicle, as just discussed, makes one appreciate the enormous commitment necessary to pursue product differentiation. Consumers, however, are demanding and more and more they expect products designed to serve their needs. Companies vying for each customer's business respond through product line creation, feature packages, and customization.

The Move of SUVs

During the last decade, the SUV has become one of the hottest vehicle categories in the auto industry. While once considered a subset of the small truck industry, the category has split from trucks and developed into its own separate area. SUVs now range from smaller "compact models" like the high-cost Lexus or the lower-cost Toyota RAV4 up to the larger options like the Hummer, Ford Excursion, and the newer hybrids combining SUVs and pick-up trucks being sold by Ford and GM. Current SUVs must have the interior comfort of a car, the storage capacity and height of a small truck, and the off-road all-weather features of a four-wheel drive military vehicle. The early evolution of this line of vehicle can be traced back to station wagons, small trucks (1935 GMC Suburban), and the 1940's Willy's Jeep developed for the U.S. military for WWII. In 1946, Jeep introduced the first Jeep Wagon. At the same time Land Rover established itself as one the first off-road vehicles for sport use and was often featured in Safari movies. See the Positioning Map in Figure 9.4.

Inherent in the acronym are the features that separate SUVs from cars and trucks. They are Sport Utility Vehicles. They are not Sport Utility *Cars* or Sport Utility *Trucks*. They are "vehicles" and this generic term puts them in a classification by themselves. The words "sport" and "utility" activate the category. They have to be sporty to capture desires and create a sense of security or adventure and they have to be utilitarian to be useful. SUVs also have to be easy to drive and easy to shift from normal to all-wheel drive. The seating must be easy to adjust to allow for more storage. The early SUVs were awkward-looking. Shifting into four-wheel drive meant getting out of the vehicle and adjusting the wheels and then shifting inside the vehicle as well. Interiors were spartan and inflexible. The utility of the current models is far easier to access; they have become useful and usable. Ford now refers to their SUVs as "Outfitters," a term that lends even more strength to the sport utility theme.

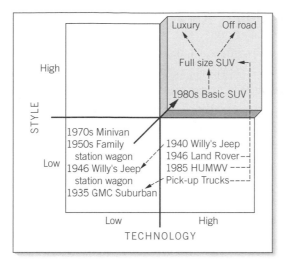

Figure 9.4 Positioning Map of SUVs.

By recognizing the SET Factors, Chrysler, Ford, and GM moved the small truck and Jeep from the Lower Left to the Upper Right. The Jeep Grand Cherokee, Chevy Blazer, and Ford Explorer made the SUV a type of vehicle that started to blend a rugged exterior style with high-tech drive capability, interior style, and features that customers expected in high-end cars. Soon all auto manufacturers started to produce a variety of SUVs. The Subaru Outback, a smaller version of the SUV, capitalized on the Australian craze. The Nissan Xterra was a major hit with the X-generation. Lexus, Mercedes, and BMW developed the high-priced luxury versions for the Y-not?-generation. If you desired luxury and size, then Lincoln, Cadillac, and Land Rover could give you all the size, power, and luxury you could want. A customer no longer had to choose between performance and comfort, or between performance and style.

The evolution of the family vehicle is an excellent example of how SET Factors change over time. Station wagons became the ideal suburban vehicle for post-war families in the '50s and '60s. They held families and their stuff better than a car with a trunk. Families shopped in larger supermarkets and engaged in family events on weekends and often drove on family vacations. The station wagon gave way to the minivan as the primary family vehicle. The minivans were larger, could hold more people, and had more cargo room. The minivan met the growing needs and activities of American families. While vans were roomy and spacious inside, the interior space produced a larger, conservative exterior that made them look like rolling loaves of bread. Vans are boxy because they do not have the engine and hood out as far in front of the vehicle. They do not handle like a car and do not provide a sense of excitement. As the SET Factors shifted, SUVs went from a fringe market to a fast-growing sector of the automotive industry. This type of vehicle had the right combination of technology, features, and style to give people a new dimension for family transportation and satisfy the emerging interest in outdoor X-sport activities for younger drivers. When classified as trucks, SUVs could also be sold as an 8-cylinder vehicle without the fuel restriction imposed on cars. SUVs had the power to carry people and their cargo, and the capability to tow boats and campers. They were also seen as safer than other vehicles. Their height gave drivers better visibility and sense of power and command of the road. The overall size and engine in front made them seem safer in case of accidents and the overall dimensions gave designers a forum to create cutting-edge styles. The four wheel drive aspect of these vehicles gave people a sense of security in all weather conditions and the ability to go off road, whether they intend to or not. During the '90s, as salaries increased in the positive economic period and gas prices stayed relatively stable, mileage was less important than range.

It took over three decades for the Jeep to become a mainline family vehicle. It took half that time for AM General to partner with GM to turn the HUMWV from a military vehicle into a new competitor in the SUV market. AM General delivered their first full order of 55,000 to the U.S. Army in 1985 and moved into the public market in 1991. While Arnold Schwartzenegger and other early adopters purchased the first versions of the commercially available Hummers, it took the combination of the core Hummer technology and the styling of GM to cross the chasm into the larger SUV market. In 1999, AM General negotiated an agreement to partner with GM. The goal was to produce a line of Hummers that would have a more sophisticated style and greater creature comforts while still building on the core of the brand identity established by the minimally-styled, high-tech original. This rapid transformation could not have happened if SUVs were not as hot as they are now. The SET Factors are shifting again. As the economy has slowed and gas prices have risen, a whole new strain of smaller, more fuel-efficient SUVs is being developed. These will allow people to purchase new types of SUVs that are lower in cost to drive. It remains to be seen how long the overall SUV craze will last and how well the automotive industry will adapt to the SET trends and keep this type of vehicle in the mainstream.

The Retro Craze

Why have companies returned to the styles of yesteryear? Retro is in! The Mazda Miata, the VW Beetle, and the Chrysler PT Cruiser are all incredibly successful products. Each has positioned itself in the Upper Right by understanding the SET Factors of the current time — the desire for people to return to what they missed from their past.

Miata: Back to the Future, Take 1   Many people have had a fantasy that they own and drive a two-seat convertible sports car. Carmakers, however, had stopped producing sport coupes. Those that were produced were traditionally unreliable and constantly needed repairs. Enthusiasts (expert users) accepted the challenge and found one of the joys of owning these cars was to spend hours underneath one or have the disposable income to pay someone else to. Car kits had also been available for years that allowed car owners to change the cars into classics. But these fiberglass copies were usually poorly detailed versions of pre-existing cars like the Excalibre. Mazda was the first mass producer of automobiles to see the potential in bringing back the classic two-seat coupe sports car that had been a dream car for most of the century. The Product Opportunity Gap was to recreate the classic look and feel of the sports car while at the same time giving it the performance standards of current vehicles. In short, the car would not need constant servicing and would provide the creature comforts that consumers had grown to expect. Mazda thought they had a market that would buy this car — young to middle-aged men who lived in the southwest and had enough disposable income to own a second car for driving. While Mazda was essentially correct in creating a car for their anticipated niche, they actually underestimated the size of the market in age, geography, and gender!

The retro aesthetic (part of the SET Factors) was prevalent. Look at the trends in city architecture, interiors, and furnishing. The return of ornament in architecture is another major example of this trend toward historical reference. Architects have been renovating buildings for decades as historic preservation groups have halted the wholesale destruction of older buildings. The austere designs of the Modern movement's International Style died officially in 1976 when Philip Johnson designed the AT&T Building in New York. Cities are now being filled with Post-Modern buildings that look like pre-WWII skyscrapers or colonial towers. Interior embellishment has also returned and decorative details from all previous periods are mixed like food in a nouvelle cuisine restaurant. Shaker and Arts and Crafts furnishings and wallpaper have been popular themes for homes. Many work environments in cities are now located in renovated old factories where old architectural details mix with computers and the latest in office furniture systems. Baseball parks now look older than Yankee Stadium as Camden Yards in Baltimore started a national trend. The work of Norman Rockwell has been in the best art galleries in the United States as he is once again hailed as a great artist, after being relegated to the level of a mere illustrator at the height of the Modern era. Coca-Cola brought back the classic bottle, even if it is in plastic. Cars have been the symbol of the future for most of the century. It took several decades for the auto industry to believe that a retro look would actually sell. So when Mazda got the idea for a retro car, the point in time was actually overdue. The tidal wave was already approaching the coast and the Miata caught the wave and started the trend of mass-produced retro vehicles.

The initial design was a competition between two teams — one in the U.S. and one in Japan. After the initial phase, the American team was given the go-ahead to finish the concept. The approach had been to take elements from all previous sports cars and integrate details into a new overall Gestalt that would be viewed as traditional and contemporary at the same time. This approach would become the method used by all other car companies as they started to produce their own "back to the future" vehicles. The concept was realized and the reaction was immediate. When potential customers test drove a prototype, the response was so great that Mazda knew they had a hit before the first Miata rolled off the assembly line. There were a number of other critical decisions made about the features as well. The engineers decided to go with rear-wheel drive to give the sense of being propelled rather than pulled. The muffler was designed to make the right sound — it could have been quieter but that would have taken away from the experience (the auditory aesthetic VO). The convertible roof could be opened or closed by the driver while sitting in the driver's seat. Weight distribution was carefully considered to make sure that the car would handle as required.

■ The Miata became a car that could attract buyers to the higher-priced vehicles in the Mazda line.

At a critical point in its development, the designers and manufacturing engineers disagreed on how the car body panels should be manufactured. The engineers proposed simplifying the design to ensure quality of manufacture. The designers felt the details were essential in maintaining the Gestalt they were after. The support was given to the designers and it proved to be the right way to go. This type of battle goes on in just about every car program and each time a management group is faced with a major fork in the road. Very rarely will a compromise in a body design result in increased sales. When management makes the decision to simplify a design, it is usually to protect cost, not increase value and profit.

Typically, the engineers and designers of cars are not individually recognized. All those that worked on the Miata during its development were mentioned in the book *Miata: Mazda MX-5*,[3] which chronicled the product development process (and sold as an aftermarket product with a part number by Mazda). While the car was reasonably priced, it was designed to be a symbol and a carrot to consumers. The Miata (Figure 9.5) became a car that could attract buyers to the higher-priced vehicles in the Mazda line. The innovative design approach became a rolling advertisement for Mazda and part of an ad series — a little boy stands by the side of the road and says "Zoom, Zoom, Zoom," which then turns into a memorable tune as the entire line of vehicles goes by. The Miata played a strategic role in convincing consumers that Mazda was a company that was Moving to the Upper Right.

Figure 9.5   2001 Mazda Miata. (Reprinted with permission of Mazda.)

The 2001 Miata is an important statement about the dynamics of the SET Factors and the need to inject useful, usable, and desirable innovation into a product to maintain its place in the Upper Right. As the team looked to redesign the car, they recognized that the core attributes of the Miata shown in Figure 9.6 (inspired sensations, affordable, fun, and in sympathy with Nature) must remain as attributes in the next generation. The evolution of the car, however, needed to move from "cute" to "more muscle" (Figure 9.7) in following the trends of sports cars, SUVs, and trucks.

■ A product can have a positive image in one culture and hit the right point in time, while simultaneously having a negative image in another culture and completely miss the mark.

From the VW Beetle to the Audi A6: Back to the Future, Take 2   The VW Beetle development program was similar to Mazda's. However, unlike the Miata, the new Beetle (Figure 9.8) had a clear ancestry that had become part of the American Culture in the '60s and '70s. The POG in this case was how to capture the spirit of the original Beetle and bring it into the present. The Less Flower More Power approach worked and the car became an instant success. As the Baby Boomers were reaching middle age and retirement, it was a perfect time to capture the nostalgia for the '60s and '70s. The contemporary interpretation combined with the friendly and innovative ad campaign made it a popular car for younger markets as well. This car was part of a strategy that brought a resurgence of VW Audi in the United States. The success eventually brought the head of design for VW, J Mays, to the United States to become the head of design at The Ford Motor Company. The VW Beetle styling not

Figure 9.6 Stating four prime customer attributes of the original Miata. (Reprinted with permission of Mazda.)

Figure 9.7 Understanding the impact of the change in SET Factors. (Reprinted with permission of Mazda.)

only borrowed from the original, it also shared design elements with the rest of the VW line and Audi such as the laser cut key, antenna placement, and large back window. The bud vase in the interior of the Beetle was a great touch to add personality and value. The space for the front two passengers is as roomy as any car on the market and ingress and egress is also easy. Side air bags on the seats was the type of detail that made this car a serious option for its class. The VW has one of the highest

Figure 9.8 VW Beetle. (Exterior photo by Larry Rippel. Interior image reprinted with permission of Volkswagen of America, Inc.)

roofiines and least clearance in any car on the market. Its playful dimensions make it fun to drive and a moveable cartoon. It was as if a character from Toy Story was fused with the original beetle (Mr. Potato Head meets the Love Bug). While the new Beetle was priced to be an economy car, it, like the Miata, served as a symbol and moving advertisement and generated a tremendous amount of press about Volkswagen that stimulated sales in all the other categories. The ads were a perfect complement to the look and feel of the line. They helped to reestablish VW as a car for the young, trendy X- and Y-Generation.

The Beetle craze was primarily a U.S. phenomenon. The car is made in Mexico, where the original Beetle is still produced and is the primary car used as a taxi in Mexico City. The new Beetle is not a retro car in Mexico where the SET Factors are completely different. Sales are not great in Europe either. The connection to the original Volks Wagen, the "people's car" pushed by Hitler as the Model T of Germany, has made it less than desirable in Germany. The SET Factors are completely different in the U.S. where the original VW became the first car for many Baby Boomers. It was the car of the flower power generation and was often decorated with a peace symbol. The Beetle and bus were painted and driven everywhere. It even became a movie character when Disney made it the star of *Herbie the Love Bug*. It is interesting and often frustrating to see how a product can become such a positive image in one culture and hit the right point in time, while in another completely miss the mark and maintain a negative connotation that would last for half a century.

The Heart of a Hot Rod and the Soul of a Van: Back to the Future, Take 3   The PT Cruiser (Figure 9.9) is the latest retro winner and it has its own set of factors that contribute to its success. After the success of the low-volume, niche Prowler, Chrysler had the confidence to launch the high-volume PT Cruiser that, like the Beetle and Miata, became an instant success. The PT Cruiser took its identity from the souped-up hot rods that everyone sees in magazines and occasionally tooling down the road. These old cars have been meticulously rebuilt by their owners and painted in bright colors. The body is usually simplified and the engine replaced so that the cars can be raced, though they rarely are. Again this is a fantasy that many car owners have, however, few want to create, or are capable of creating, their own hot rod. If they did, where would they put it? With the PT Cruiser, Chrysler gives you the look of a hot rod with an interior and temperament that makes it a minivan. A fun car you can take seriously. You can now own a hot rod as a primary vehicle… now that is a fantasy!

The Cruiser is a tall wagon, a minivan, and a retro sedan. It's not four-wheel drive, yet it will probably skim some of that market as well. The interior details meticulously connect to the exterior (such as the metallic finish in the console). If you take the back seats out, you can make it into a mini-truck. It looks like one of those old hearses, ambulances, or delivery trucks that were converted into surfing cars. Remember what the characters drove in the movie *Ghostbusters*? Chrysler itself recognizes the draw to the car from a purely fantasy desire. Their web site states: "I want one! Some purchases in life are driven by forces beyond our control, and often our only justification is 'It's so cool.'"

The look of the PT Cruiser was then used as the point of departure for the latest Chrysler Town & Country line of minivans (Figure 9.10). The low front end with the sport grille and the high back gives the van the look of the PT Cruiser's older brother.

Figure 9.9   Chrysler PT Cruiser. (Reprinted with permission of DaimlerChrysler Corp.)

Figure 9.10 Chrysler Town & Country minivan. (Reprinted with permission of DaimlerChrysler Corp.)

In both instances, the cars' exteriors are complemented by a thoroughly designed interior. The influence of the successful retro Cruiser into the more traditional line of vehicles illustrates the power of the point in time Value Opportunity. It also illustrates how a product with a strong identity can influence the design of other members of a product line within a consistent brand strategy.

Positioning: Segmentation through Ethnography for Compact Truck Segmentation

One approach to product differentiation is a new class of vehicles and cross-platform design. Another is to distinguish products through different feature packages. Automakers typically use this approach to offer customers higher-priced features, such as leather seats, electric seats, a roof rack, or a CD stereo system. The feature packaging approach, however, is evolving as a means of responding to the needs of different customer groups. Such segmentation is a far less costly approach than creating an entirely new platform and can enable a product to reach out to a larger group of potential customers. We examine an example of segmentation through feature groups based on ethnographic research in the lucrative and competitive truck market. Besides shedding light on the segmentation process in the industry, this data provided part of the secondary research used to create the products presented in the next section.

Recall in Chapter 7 the Polaroid ethnography study. Here E-Lab conducted an ethnographic study for Ford to identify emerging differentiations in the compact truck market. The goal of the study was to better understand how young adults perceive and use compact pickup trucks to suggest opportunities for product development, feature packages, and positioning strategies. All of the ethnographic methods discussed in Chapter 7 were used. Their research found that for young adults, having a truck was about independence and "truckness" or all of the things that a truck is supposed to do. Owning a small truck allows young people to have their own space and take control of their lives. The truckness translates into five groups, each expressing a different direction: working (called the Junior Hardhats), hauling (the Independents/Dependables), recreation with gear (the Jailbreakers), and recreation without gear (the Cruisers/Off-Roaders). The fifth group buys the truck because it's the thing to do but they have no need for any of the features in the bed (the Why Do I Have a Truck?s)

Next E-Lab mapped the expressive truckness groups onto behavioral axes of what is important to the user (Figure 9.11). The breakdown of work versus play and basic versus modified breaks the space into four quadrants, each mapped one-to-one with the four expressive groups: Cruisers/Off-Roaders use their truck for play, often to show off, and are likely to modify the model they purchase (possibly for personal expression); Junior Hardhats use their truck for work as well as personal use during down time and

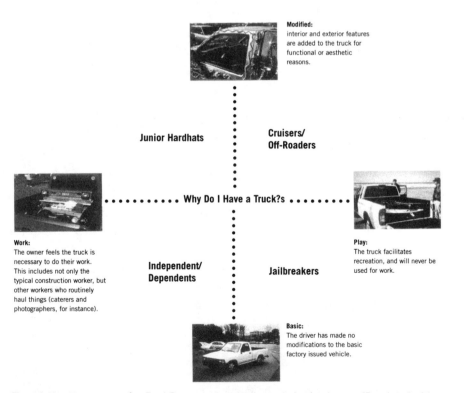

Modified:
interior and exterior features are added to the truck for functional or aesthetic reasons.

Junior Hardhats

Cruisers/ Off-Roaders

Why Do I Have a Truck?s

Work:
The owner feels the truck is necessary to do their work. This includes not only the typical construction worker, but other workers who routinely haul things (caterers and photographers, for instance).

Independent/ Dependents

Jailbreakers

Play:
The truck facilitates recreation, and will never be used for work.

Basic:
The driver has made no modifications to the basic factory issued vehicle.

Figure 9.11 User groups for Ford Ranger segmented over behavioral axes. (Reprinted with permission of Ford Motor Company and Sapient.)

also modify the basic model to suit their work needs; Independents/Dependables use their truck as part of their quest for an independent lifestyle with the cab as their personal space; Jailbreakers use their truck as an escape mechanism on the weekends but also use it to commute during the week; and the Why Do I Have a Truck?s stay in the center, with no behavioral features — they essentially use their truck to commute and rarely use the bed at all.

This breakdown is the result of extensive qualitative research and, though apparently simple, is quite powerful. If these five groups characterize the market segment for young adults, then five-segment truck packages, each addressing the needs and wants of the five groups, would open the truck to the full potential of the market. Features such as storage areas, hauling facilities, and communications devices each suit particular needs of the different groups. Also, aesthetic features (visual, tactile, and auditory) vary based on the lifestyle characteristics of the five groups.

Positioning: After-Market Products for Trucks —
A Case Study of iNPD at Carnegie Mellon University

A large and lucrative market in the industry is in full-size pickup trucks. Although it produces around 1.2 million units per year, the truck industry is recognizing the need to differentiate products among potential markets. As extended cab versions increase seating capacity, more consumers, looking for the added safety, versatility, fantasy, and image, are turning toward pickup trucks. People buy a pickup truck because they need a place for a dog, space for mountain bikes and surfboards, and a vehicle that can haul construction goods (note the SET Factors from the growth of Home Depot and other do-it-yourself stores) and also function as a family car. Auto companies are now looking at ways to push the pickup truck into the Upper Right while satisfying the wants and desires of the broadening market. GM is introducing the Avalanche as a response to customer desires for an adaptable truck bed, where the rear seat of the cab folds down, opening up more space in the bed. Ford has created several niche versions of their F-150, including a Harley version that captures the lifestyle message of the Harley brand; the Lincoln Blackwood, which uses real wood and targets the luxury market; and the King Ranch, with real saddle leather that requires the user to treat it with a leather kit.

After-market accessories are another way to help to differentiate one product from another and are an easy way to customize a product without going through a major redesign or committing to a niche segmentation. Unlike cross-platform design that requires large investment in tooling and requires common features across product lines or product segmentation that requires part changes at the assembly line, after-market products have comparatively minimal investment costs and can be readily tuned to individual product lines. Here we focus on the design of after-market products for the pickup box of a full-size pickup truck. Each of the products described below was created by closely following the user-centered iNPD process. Each of these products is being patented by Ford for use in their F-Series Trucks. Before looking at the products, you might find the context for the design of these products interesting.

Each of these products was designed within a course on integrated New Product Development that we teach each year at Carnegie Mellon University in collaboration with Prof. John Mather from the Graduate School of Industrial Administration. Senior level and graduate students from engineering and design (industrial and communications), and MBA students in our business school work together in integrated teams to create a product concept. In the 17-week course, the students follow the iNPD method laid out in Chapter 5. The students generally do not know each other and come to the course having focused on their own discipline. Teams are mixed, with typically 5–6 students on a team.

Though we have had various themes in the course, recent industrial sponsorship of the course by Ford Motor Company shifted the focus to the design of after-market products for the back of a pickup truck (a Ford F-150). The course helps illustrate the power of this methodology in a confined time-, resource- and experience-frame: the course had 17 weeks duration (including Spring Break!), the teams had minimal prototyping costs (well under $1000), and few of the engineering and design students had any industrial experience except for summer internships, while the MBA students typically had experience outside of marketing/business. The older, more mature MBA students, however, came to the course with a different breadth of experience, each having worked in industry for at least two years. None of the students had any significant experience in the auto industry.

We show you these products for two reasons: First because the large after-market product segment of the auto industry provides an opportunity for new product development. Second, if a bunch of (admittedly smart and talented) students can develop such fantastic products part time with limited cost and resources by following our methodology, you can too!

In following the development of these products note the awareness of the SET Factors, the identification of Value Opportunities, the marketing position as a Move to the Upper Right, the in-depth user research, and the progression from identification of a POG, to understanding the opportunity through ethnographic and lifestyle research, to conceptualization of the design through iteration between prototyping and user feedback, to detailing. In addition to primary user and expert research, all teams had access to the market research presented in the previous section, access to Ford market segmentation, and access the SRI VALs database (see Chapter 5 for a discussion on VALs). All six products produced in this class were patentable ideas; three are being patented by Ford.

SideWinder: Side Worktable[T1]

Chapter 7 presented the scenario of Ron, the contractor, who had the problem of finding the space and equipment both at the truck and the worksite to prepare construction supplies. In particular, the truck was filled with tools and supplies and he had a toolbox and ladder rack on the sides of his truck. The students observed several workers and conducted detailed interviews with 20 other construction workers. In addition, they explored a lifestyle reference analysis, performed an ergonomics analysis, and had access to the VALs database on values and lifestyles. From all of this research, they built up an understanding of Ron and folks like him. By thinking "out of the box" (literally) they realized that an unused part of the truck, and really the best one for their needs, was the side outside the truck rails.

In comparison to the sawhorses-and-boards alternative, the VOs showed great opportunity to add value and create an Upper Right design. In particular, the sawhorses-and-boards approach showed no contribution to any VOs. The potential existed to address the emotion VOs (through independence, security, and confidence), aesthetics (through visual and tactile), identity (personality and sense of place), ergonomics (safety, ease of use, and comfort), core technology (enabling and reliable), and quality (craftsmanship and durability).

They then generated 15 distinct concepts and weighed them (in a Pugh chart) qualitatively against 18 criteria (time, versatility, durability, ease of use, cost, manufacturability, stability, security, safety, mountability, closed profile, implementation of range of motion, prototype, appearance, market size, market versatility, installability, and compatibility with other products) out of which five were weighted more significantly (versatility, durability, ease of use, cost, and compatibility with other products). This resulted in a reduction to five concepts that they took back to their user group for more feedback. They then reduced their designs first to three and then, after further revision, to one. Along the way they refined the features of the product, based on direct and implied feedback from the contractors.

Further refinement led to the "SideWinder" shown in Figure 9.12, targeting the heavy use/heavy utility segment of the F-150. The main innovations were a table that resided on the side of the truck, could be removed and brought to the worksite where it had legs that folded down, and while on the truck folded up and locked during transportation. Since many small contractors use their truck for personal business on the weekends, the

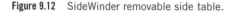

Figure 9.12 SideWinder removable side table.

table and brackets must be removable. They decided to attach the table to the underframe of the vehicle in much the same way as a tow hitch worked; the idea of a tow hitch on the side of a vehicle is, in and of itself, innovative and leads to many follow-on products. This, however, led to difficult structural issues due to the cantilevered design. Through further refinement, the table was supported by two brackets, each able to withstand a 400 lb. downward force from the table. The table has adjustable height and angle and replaceable cutting surfaces. Combined steel, aluminum, and polyethylene construction enabled a design able to withstand the wear and tear in its use yet light enough to be carried by the contractor.

MasterRack: Reconfigurable Rail Storage[T2]

The second project focused around a young family with kids who rely on their truck for all their transportation needs including hauling tools (a do-it-yourselfer), running errands, and weekend trips. Whenever they use the truck for a different purpose, they have to move their things in and out of the truck bed. Most of the time, they just toss things from the truck into the garage and vice versa. As a result, both the truck bed and their garage have become completely disorganized. The team again sought out and learned the needs and wants of this type of family. They did an interesting ergonomic study, coupled with observation, to realize that only the foot around the rails and tailgate are typically used because that is the only area people can reach. They also found out that most truck owners are quite amenable to after-market truck products. In one of their studies, they found that out of 107 trucks in the parking lots of Home Depot, WalMart, and Dick's Sporting Goods stores (where their target market shopped), only four did not have some kind of after-market product in the bed.

The Value Opportunities focused on independence, security, and confidence within the emotion VO; visual and tactile aesthetics VO; sense of place in the identity VO; ease of use, safety, and comfort from the ergonomics VO; enabling and reliable core technology VOs; and craftsmanship and durability in terms of the quality VO. The alternative was makeshift devices, limited-use devices, or the open truck bed, with each offering limited or no added value.

These insights, along with an understanding of the various uses for an active family that likes to camp, do projects around the home, and run lots of errands, eventually led to an innovative approach to truck storage that targeted a family-oriented segment of the F-150 market. Here a side rail attaches on both sides into the rail posts of the bed (the idea can also be incorporated directly into the bed rails themselves). The simple device (Figure 9.13) has a stationary and sliding rail, with intermittent holes. Containers with specially designed pegs fit into the holes on the rail. The sliding rail is then closed and automatically latched, providing a reliable storage system. The rails can be locked to provide security from theft. Beyond the simplicity of the device, the flexible peg system allows for a wide variety of storage containers and cross-rail configurations. Also, the holes in the rail system can be used for normal rope and bungee tie-downs.

Figure 9.13   MasterRack side rail storage system.

NoFuss: Camping Storage System with Rail Guide Technology [T3]

The last product that we will examine is also a storage system, but a complete one for organizing a family's camping needs. The target market is young families who want to begin camping as a family, much like mom and dad did before they had kids. The family wants the rewards of camping without the stress of planning for and purchasing each individual piece of equipment.

Their competition was Rubbermaid storage containers, makeshift boxes, or just haphazard storage in the pickup box of the truck. Their user research began with 16 in-depth user interviews of target families, especially those that camp (expert users). A nearly universal reason that people camp or wanted to camp with their family was to go back to Nature and get away from other people. Their interview helped them identify the major categories of equipment that are brought to campsites by families. They also recognized the significant difference between backpacking and car camping. Backpackers already had their own equipment and didn't rely on any storage systems in their truck. Finally they found out that the order in which a camper needs his or her equipment matters — objects needed immediately upon arrival at the campsite should not be buried under equipment needed later and the camping family must make sure they have everything they need.

This research lead the team to envision a system where the consumer is provided all the essentials needed for camping in one easy purchase, instead of having to purchase all these items separately. Specific criteria for their target users were:

- *Camping gear for amateur campers*

   Users are not interested in flashy or extreme camping gear. They want reliable, durable equipment that the whole family can use.

- *Organized system for packing*

   Truck owners typically throw their equipment in the truck without much organization and items may be difficult to find or hard to reach.

- *Help to remember what to pack*

   User interviews revealed that preparing for the trip, packing, and loading often takes a full day to complete. Anything to help them remember what to bring would be useful.

- *Easy to load, unload, setup, and disassemble*

   Truck users have to climb into the truck bed to access much of their equipment. Items can be bulky, difficult to carry, and travel unprotected in the truck bed.

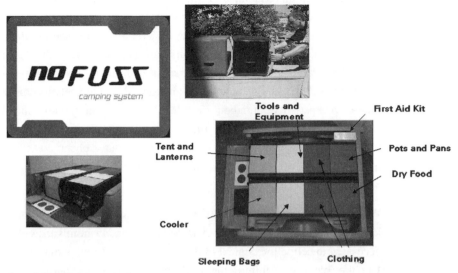

Figure 9.14 NoFuss camping storage system.

The VOs for this product are the sense of adventure, sense of independence, sense of security, and confidence emotion VO attributes, visual and tactile aesthetic VO attributes, sense of place identity VO, social impact VO, ease of use, safety, and comfort ergonomics VO attributes, and quality and core technology VOs.

The NoFuss Camping Storage System (with Rail Guide Technology), Figure 9.14, targeting a family-oriented F-150 segment, comes complete with everything a family needs to begin camping (including two lanterns, four sleeping bags, a tent, stove, and a first aid kit). The only items users will need are their own clothes and food. Each module is color coded to identify what is stored within it and each module is customized for that particular type of item or activity. All modules load and unload on a custom bed liner and fit together securely for transport. The units have a locking mechanism that allows the front handles of one unit to lock into the negative space in the back of another unit, locking them together. A whole train up to four modules can be locked together in the truck bed, which can accommodate two trains. The modules utilize a trigger release to unlock one module from the ones behind it. The basic storage system, though ideal for this use, is also extendable to other applications.

Implications of User-Centered iNPD on the Auto Industry

Through our brief overview of vehicle design at the beginning of this chapter, we can identify how companies can improve their design processes. For starters, the pursuit of identifying POGs and understanding those gaps and the wants and desires from the user are currently limited. Companies often do identify great opportunities through instinct and market research, but at times they fail too. More important, are there opportunities they are missing? Could their vehicles do a better job at meeting the demands of their target markets? Often the engineers and designers who are in the trenches try to design a product for the customer, but each individual has their own interpretation of who that customer is. Often the designers design from their interpretation of the user, based on their own experiences and their lifestyle reference, without really knowing who the user is. Could a better, more uniform focus on the user by the engineers and designers make for a better end product? We believe so. And we have observed the conflicts that arise in the design of vehicles because individuals have a different view of what they should be designing.

We are not suggesting that all 200 members of the development team be involved with identifying the POG for the vehicle or be intimately involved with the user research necessary to define the context of the vehicle. We recognize that marketing will need to take the role in determining the need for a new vehicle, concept studios will generate ideas, and management will make the decision. We hope that those involved in these early decisions and explorations connect with the customer in a deep way as laid out in Chapter 7, though our experience indicates that this is typically done on a more ad-hoc, gut-level basis. Earlier in this chapter, we revisited the product Positioning Map and observed several successful product innovations that moved the product to the Upper Right. That said, once the team is given the program criteria, they can and should practice the techniques described in this book. When decisions need to be made, the view of the customer should provide the answer. This view should be supported with facts from user research. Further, a big part of the program team's responsibility is to determine what features will be found on the vehicle, and here again qualitative research can be a major determinant of these details. The examples of the truck bed after-market designs show how focus on the customer for individual components can significantly improve their success.

Again recall that the car being designed today won't come to market for another three years. The use of qualitative research is the only way to predict with any confidence what people will want to buy in three years. Mary Walton, in her book *Car: A Drama of the American Workplace*,[4] gives a wonderfully detailed account of the redesign of the Ford Taurus, released in 1996. The biggest lesson we take from that study is that, as fantastic as a vehicle may be that is designed trading off cost and features and focusing on style, the car is only going to be successful if it meets the Value Opportunities for the target market. According to Walton, although the process may have at times been painful, the entire design team found the Taurus exceeded expectations in their design criteria. The team did a great job, but they didn't understand their target customer and didn't relate to the value that that customer defined. As a result, the car was very well designed and made but didn't succeed in the marketplace up to expectations. The '96 Taurus was a clear example of designing in our Phase III without understanding the POG or user in Phases I and II.

The number of people involved in the detailed design of a vehicle can be overwhelming. Somehow the team manages to work together and produce a vehicle where everything has a place (real estate allocation), everything works within the style of the vehicle, and everything works well initially and, hopefully, over the life of the vehicle. Yet, as discussed in Chapter 6, conflict is a frequent part of the product development process in vehicles. Most of the findings and methods reported in Chapter 6 stemmed initially from our research in the auto industry. Thus interpersonal and inter-team communications, understanding of perceptual gaps, and appropriate approaches for team negotiation become critical to a successful process. These issues are amplified by the use of full-service suppliers, participants in the design process but dependent on positive relations with the company for future business.

This is further augmented by the number of parts in a vehicle (over 3000, with sub-parts leading to over 20,000), and the complexity in how these parts interact with and relate to each other. Balancing this with the need to add value to the product motivates the Part Differentiation Matrix of Chapter 6, revisited in this chapter. The PDM tells us where team integration is critical in the development of the vehicle.

▌ The ideal product is one that initially targets a specific market but also has appeal to a larger group.

In the design of any product there is a balance between focusing on too limited a target market to make development costs worthwhile, and targeting such a large market that there are no specific characteristics to focus on. The ideal product is one that initially targets a specific but large market and also has appeal to a broader group. As companies look to create platforms that can span the globe, they must balance this with losing the focus of each target (or cultural) market. Pushing one car in all countries will likely fail, especially as other companies realize the potential effects of refining their designs for each market. Again, the most practical approach is the modification of certain parts, based on lifestyle reference and ethnographic research, to meet the desires of each market. A major concern, however, is creating the overall style of the vehicle based only on one (e.g., American) market. Can alternative lifestyles be included upfront? Can style be modified through new outer panels in a cost-effective way to address distinct cultural likes? How can brand be maintained globally, yet address the nuances of different cultures?

Because the vehicle will not come to market for several years, it must be designed to anticipate the evolution of the SET Factors over the time-span. Prediction of lifestyle and cultural needs, wants, and desires are addressed in this book. But the economic health and well-being of society can at best be extrapolated with uncertainty.[5] How will the inevitable increase in gas prices affect the consumer's purchasing practice? Will SUVs and small trucks become passé? Or will companies be able to adapt through new technologies to make such large vehicles fuel efficient? How does a company anticipate what new technologies their customers will want or their competitors will develop? How quickly can a company adapt to new technologies introduced by their competition? Further, although an astute company can anticipate and at times even influence some legislation, societal influences often prod legislators to implement new safety or environmental standards on the industry. Such shocks to the development process are sometimes difficult to anticipate. The teachings in this book, however, can and do help companies prepare for, and even anticipate with a greater certainty, some of the changes to SET Factors. In particular, an effective user-research program, based in the realm of ethnography, cannot only help predict the forthcoming social and lifestyle changes, but also help to understand changes in the financial well-being of the consumer and their interests in emerging technologies.

Although we argue that the auto industry could improve aspects of their approach to product development by incorporation of the user-centered iNPD methodology presented in this book, there are many areas where they do a great job anticipating consumer wants and introducing new products positioned in the Upper Right. We find it exciting and revealing that the methods that help you Move to the Upper Right can help in the design of a product with three components, or over 3,000!

Summary Points

❏ iNPD is critical for the successful design of vehicles.

❏ Both vehicle programs and individual parts require an Upper Right approach.

References

1. Friedman, T.L., *The Lexus and the Olive Tree: Understanding Globalization*, Farrar Straus & Giroux, New York, 2000.

2. Kitman, J., "We Built Disappointment," *Automobile Magazine*, February, 2001.

3. Yamaguchi, J.K., and J. Thompson, *Mazda MX-5 Miata—The Rebirth of the Sports Car in the New Mazda MX-5 Miata with a History of the World's Affordable Sports Cars*, St. Martin's Press, New York, 1989.

4. Walton, M., *Car: A Drama of the American Workplace*, W.W. Norton & Co., New York, 1979.

5. Ormerod, P., *Butterfly Economics*, Pantheon Books, New York, 1998.

Research Acknowledgments

Credit for user research in this chapter to understand opportunities:

T1 Designed by designers Josh Guyot, Mark A. Ehrhardt, and Emily Gustavsen, engineers Scott Froom and Richard Bohman, and market researcher Dan Darnell.

T2 Designed by designers Jeff Beene, Kathryn Cohen, and Lauren Icken, engineers Samuel Ferraro-Pollak and Sreekumar Vijaykumar, and market researcher Linda Bliss.

T3 Designed by designers Elaine Ann and Ignacio Filippini, engineers Steven Goode and Jay McCormack, and market researcher Matthew Gonzales.

Epilogue

Future Trends

The ongoing changes in the SET Factors continue to produce an endless array of new product and service opportunities. In our own analysis of the SET Factors, we are looking at a number of emerging areas for new product development consulting and research opportunities. Carnegie Mellon University is considered one of the foremost research universities in the world. We have leveraged the advantage of being in this context to identify, understand, and develop these opportunities, some of which we highlight below.

First a general comment on the Economic Factor: If the current economic downturn continues, profit margins may shrink. However, the need for value will continue to increase in importance as consumers have come to expect products that are well positioned in the Upper Right. If local and national markets begin to shrink, then companies will need to be even more effective at globally distributing their goods and services. For those products to be positioned in the Upper Right, they must be able to share common platforms but be differentiated based on cultural needs, wants, and desires.

Specific areas that we are exploring and monitoring include:

Aging   During the 20th century, companies developed products and services targeting people between the ages of 0 and 50. In contrast the 21st century will present significant product opportunities for people between the ages of 50 and 100.

289

Bio Medical   The increased lifespan and advances in science and medical technology is creating a vast array of product opportunities to promote well-being throughout the lifespan. As the cost of health care continues to increase and the number of health staff continues to decrease, health centers will be challenged to maintain high standards of health care. This will necessitate the development of new preventive, diagnostic, and non-invasive treatments that minimize patient trauma and the time required to heal.

Personal Health Systems   One particular focus in the area of bio-medical research is the ability to more effectively monitor an individual's health and connect that to a diagnostic system that will provide constant feedback to allow people to continuously maximize their daily routine.

Vehicle Design   The vehicle will continue to be a primary forum for people to make statements about who they are. Mass-customization will continue to grow to meet the demand for niche vehicles. The area of after-market products will continue to grow as people customize their vehicle to meet their own lifestyle needs, wants, and desires. Fuel efficiency will continue to grow as a major factor in the purchase of a vehicle without compromising on style, comfort, and features. Vehicle manufacturers are beginning to integrate a host of new interactive technologies to enhance the driving experience. This will necessitate research in cognitive processing that properly connects features to the driver and passenger experience while eliminating potentially fatal distractions. At CMU, we already see the early prototypes of autonomous vehicles and technology to offset driver fatigue. While these are primarily for professional and military applications, it is only a matter of time before these features Move to the Upper Right in vehicle design.

Energy Efficiency   Energy supply at home and work will cause the need to create more energy-efficient products. This will probably result in a new eco-aesthetic. This will also affect manufacturing and distribution of products, with distributed manufacturing leading to an even greater potential for local customization.

Smart Products   A new level of intelligent and responsive products will emerge as the result of the integration of new materials that push the boundaries on performance; micro- and nano-technologies that integrate electrical, mechanical, and chemical advances; and emerging genetics technologies. How these products interact with the human body will lead to a new understanding of ergonomics and aesthetics of wearability and usability. For example, the Wearable Computing Group at Carnegie Mellon is conducting research on the feasibility of wearable technology. Figure E.1 shows a study by Francine Gemperle, Director of the group, of the ergonomics of such wearable technology.

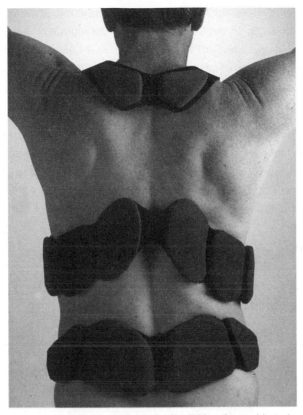

Figure E.1 Ergonomic study on the feasibility of wearable technology. (Reprinted with permission of Francine Gemperle; photo by Rob Long.)

Disaster Management   As population growth overlaps with the incidence of natural disasters, it will require the need to develop a number of services and products to manage the effects.

Addressing the Needs of Emerging Economies   China will become the largest market and manufacturer of goods in the new century. How the Chinese economy evolves will have effects on every other economy in the world. The question will be how quickly they will seek to produce and consume products in the Upper Right. A number of other countries in Africa and South and Central America are seeking to become major players in the global economy. There is still a need and potentially large market to develop products that bridge the gap and serve the needs of people in these countries. By following the lead of the Freeplay radio, discussed in Chapter 8, and creating Upper Right products to serve these markets, companies can often find global growth with the connection to mainstream markets.

Population Distribution Major shifts in population distribution will create new lifestyle preferences for products. In the United States by the middle of the 21st century, the Hispanic population could become the majority and will develop the potential for new products that used to be based primarily on Northern European values. In Europe, the influx of a new wave of immigration from former colonies and former Communist countries will create the need for an array of new products and services.

▋ As technology shrinks and consumers demand more capabilities and faster service, product development will seek to merge complementary attributes into a single product.

An overarching theme across all of these categories is product hybridization, most often seen today in automobiles and portable digital technology. As technology shrinks and consumers demand more capabilities and faster service, product development will seek to merge complementary attributes into a single product. As niche markets continue to develop, solutions through hybrid products will emerge. The challenge of product hybridization is to link functions in a way that does not compromise performance. Very often products made with the claim that they do a number of things fail to do any one thing well. Perhaps one of the most recognized examples of successful product hybridization is the Swiss Army knife. More recent examples include cellular phones that serve as PDAs. In the area of bio-technology, current research is setting the stage for intelligent, adaptive replacement organs and tissue, while in the area of structural design, smart structures will include sensors to sense and react to environmental conditions.

Have Faith in the Leap

At the end of every movie, there is a long list of credits. Only a few people stay to watch them. The credits give you a sense of the number and types of people it takes to produce a movie as well as the location and authorities involved — at times whole towns are acknowledged. Next time you get in your car to drive home, think about how many people it takes to produce the product you are driving. The list of people it takes to develop the products you own is as long as the list of people it takes to make a movie. Every product should come with a list of credits just like movies. Mazda produced a book that chronicled the development of the Miata (and was available as a part from the company).[1] The book highlights roughly 70 different people in the back that were instrumental to the development of the car. It is the only publicly available list we have ever been aware of that conveys the range of people required to develop a product.

A movie and physical product have a lot in common. They both need to make a profit. They both are the result of technical and creative forces working together. The relationship that connects script, actor, camera, director, editor, stunt people, special effects, sound, and music is as complex to manage as any product. Finishing a picture in time and under budget is equally as challenging. Both rely on distribution channels and advertising. Movies are focused on a target audience and timed to release at certain key points during the year.

Dreamworks has become particularly adept at identifying and producing movies that are blockbuster hits. Building on the history of the three principals, Dreamworks, particularly Spielberg, produces movies that are in the Upper Right. They combine elements of technical competence, visual/auditory sophistication, quality acting and directing, and the right level of storytelling to captivate and entertain a broad audience base. There is a shared vision at the top that flows down to the director, actors, and crew. The company supports making movies with a balance of cost and quality. They do not make the cheapest movies, yet they make significant profits.

The best products do not only support our lifestyle, they enhance it and help us create situations where we reach a state of flow. Whether it is as mundane as shaving or as thrilling as mountain climbing, we are looking for experiences that aid in fulfilling our expectations. Watching an entertaining movie for two hours allows us to escape into a fantasy state of flow. We should be able to achieve the same level of satisfaction while driving a car, riding a mountain bike, or preparing a meal.

■ The ultimate win/win for companies is when the people developing the product feel as satisfied with the result and process as the end customer does with the product.

The ultimate win/win for companies is when the people developing the product feel as satisfied with the result and process as the end customer does with the product. The goal of companies should be to not only develop successful new products but to also replicate successful products programs. Methods create clarity and allow for communication and vision produces the emotional element to inspire people to do great things. The best programs combine these attributes to push people to places they never thought possible and to position the result of their labors in the Upper Right.

This book has been a proof of process. It was based on the idea that a book was needed to explain how to navigate the Fuzzy Front End of new product development (our POG). We did our research with a target audience in mind. We developed a network of lead users and expert advisors. We wrote prototypes and put them out for review and feedback. We then reworked the book in several iterations until we felt it was complete. Finishing this book has required the participation and support of a number of people. They are listed in our credits, the book's Acknowledgments.

Developing Upper Right products is exciting and rewarding. Any company can succeed in doing so if it makes a commitment to the process. We hope that you find this book relevant and useful. We now see the world through the eyes of the Upper Right, identifying breakthrough products that are differentiated from the competition through the merging of style, technology, and value. You will too once it becomes a part of your way of thinking about product development. Good luck in the process and remember: have faith in the leap; it's not a leap of faith.

References

1. Yamaguchi, J. K., and J. Thompson, *Mazda MX-5 Miata — The Rebirth of the Sports Car in the New Mazda MX-5 Miata with a History of the World's Affordable Sports Cars*, St. Martin's Press, New York, 1989.

Index

Page numbers in italics refer to illustrations.

A

Aaker, D. A., 86
aesthetics, 64
aging, 289
AM General, 268
AMC Pacer, 11, 257
anthropometric chart, *198*
anthropometrics, 197–201, *199, 200, 201*
Appelbaum, Hylton, 252
Apple Computer, 101–2, 135
Apple G4, 59
Apple iMac, 12
    case study, 248–51
    design of, *249*
    identity building, 92
    product strategy, 85–86, 99
    value of, 59
    VOs, 101–2
Apple Newton, 11
AT&T Dreyfuss phone, 40, 200, *201*
Audi A6, 271–72
Audi TT, 256
auto industry, 12, 254–86
    complexity of, 161, 257–60

design process, 257–60, 290
door systems, 263
future trends, 290
mergers, 260
PDM, *261*
positioning, 266–68
process of, 260–65
product differentiation, 266–68
rear wiper systems, 263–65, *264, 265*
retro craze, 268–83
SET Factors, 255–56
truck market, 275–83
Upper Right, moving to, 266–68
user-centered approach, 283–86
automobile design, 12, *13*, 254–86, 290. *See also* auto
    industry

B

Barbie doll, 12
Barnes & Noble, 50
baseball stadiums, case study, 216–18, *217, 218*
Baylis, Trevor, 252
Beale, Matt, 232, 234
Beatles, 12
Bennett, Tilden, 231, 233–34
Bidwell, Tom, 22, 24, 170

bio medical trends, 290
Bioinformatics, 169
Black & Decker, 5, 51
  case study, 218–28
  identity building, 92, 93
  product design, 191
  VOs, 67
block-level prototypes, *123*
BMW, 100, 267
Bosch, 67
bottom line, 3–9
brand impact, 69
brand strategy, 84–88
Brando, Marlon, 101
brands
  building, 95–96, 99–101
  commitment to, 88–90
  company brands, 93–95
  identity building, 92–93
  maintaining, 95–96, 99–101
  managing, 92–96
  VOs, *80*, 101–2
breakthrough products, 5–6
Bryant, Koby, 166
Buick Bengal, 190
Buick Rendezvous, 257
Busch Stadium, 217

C

Cabbage Patch Dolls, 12
Cadillac, 12, *13*, 256, 258, 267
Cadillac Northstar, 262
Calhoun, Jeff, 81
Camden Yard, 218, 269
Car: A Drama of the American Workplace, 284
Carpal Tunnel Syndrome, 194, 244
case studies, 12–30, 215–53
Casey, Jim, 238
Chadwick, Don, 243, 244
Chevy, 12, *13*, 258
Chevy Blazer, 267
Chrysler
  design of, 274–75
  form and function, 179
  identity building, 92
  product development, 51–52
  team selection, 135
Chrysler Airflow, 257
Cinergy Field, 217
Claritas Corporation, 124

Claxton, Bruce, 165
Coca-Cola, 11, 27, 92, 269
colander study results, *143*
Coldspot Refrigerator, *39*, 39–40
collaboration, 146–48
Comerica Park, 218
company brands, 93–95. *See also* brands
Compaq, 97
complexity, of system, 154–61
concepts, visualizing, 206–10, *208*, *209*
conceptualizing opportunity, 110–11, 126–29
conflict, 146–48, 160–62
connections, 112–13
consumer culture, 36–37
core disciplines, 162–63
core technology, 68
corporate commitment, 88–90, *89*
corporate mission, 89–90, 164
corporate values, 91
cost versus value, 59–62, *60*
Covey, S. R., 152
Crossing the Chasm, 44, 96, 193
Crown Equipment Corporation, 22, 165, 170
Crown Wave
  complexity of, 157
  design of, *23*, 178
  identity building, 92, 94
  PDM, *157*
  Positioning Map, 48–49, *49*
  product development, 22–26, 33
  SET Factors, *24*
  social impact, 66
  VOA, 75–76, *76*
  VOs, *80*
Csikszentmihalyi, Mihaly, 152
customer needs, 8, 174–211
customer research, 171–211
customer satisfaction, 89–90
customer value, 42, 91
customer-zation, 177–78
customers, understanding, 188–90

D

Daedalus Excel, case study, 231–36
Daimler-Benz, 260
Dean, James, 101
Dell Computer, 59, 97
design, 139–46, 161–63
design process, 148–50, *149*, *150*, *151*, 162
desirability, 57, 88

desktop modeling, 209
Dewalt, 93
Dick's Sporting Goods, 281
disaster management, 291
Disney theme parks, 11, 25, 45, 60
Dodge Durango, 52
Dodge Ram, 52
Dream Society, The, 61
Dreamworks, 293
Dreyfuss, Henry, 40, 197
Dreyfuss phone, 40, 200, *201*
DynaMyte, 66, 231–36
DynaVox Systems
    case study, 231–36
    design of, *232, 235*
    PDM, 234, *235*
    prototypes, 209
    social impact, 66
    VOA, *233*

E

E-Lab, 188–89, 275–77
Eames, Charles, 246
Eames, Ray, 246
Earl, Harley, 12, 38
Economic Factors, 2, 9, *9*, 11, 107, 289. *See also* SET
    Factors
economics, 42, 291
emotion, 63
energy efficiency, 290
engineering, 139–46, 161–63
environmental impact, 67
ergonomics, 65–68, 192–201
    analysis, 206
    anthropometrics, 197–201, *198, 199, 200, 201*
    interaction, 192–94
    research and, 178–79
    task analysis, 194–96, *196, 197*
    wearable technology, 290, *291*
ethnography techniques, 108, 183–90
    design and, 204
    E-Lab, 188–89, 275–77
    lifestyle reference and, 205
    model of, *187*
    understanding customers, 188–90
evolutionary product development, 51–52
Excalibre, 269
excellence, 57
experience, 62, 180
extendable impact, 69

F

faith, 292–93
fantasy, 5, 60, 63
Farber, Sam, 14, 16, 17
FedEx, 95
Fenway Park, 216, 217
financing, 134–35
Fitch, 57, 97
Flow, 152
focus, broadening, 203–4
Fonda, Peter, 101
Forbes Field, 217
Ford Excursion, 266
Ford Expedition, 263–65
Ford Explorer, 261
Ford Focus, 59
Ford, Henry, 38
Ford Motor Company
    design of, 278–79
    product development, 182
    team selection, 135
    VOs, 67
Ford Ranger, *276*
Ford Taurus, 257, 284
form and function, 5, 60, 178–79
Freeplay Radio, case study, *251*, 251–53
Frogdesign, 81, *199*, 199
future trends, 289–92
Fuzzy Front End, 3–4, 54, 106–11, *112*, 293

G

Gateway, 97
Gatorade, 12
Gemperle, Francine, 290
genetics, 11
Gifford, Kathy Lee, 91
Gilmore, James, 59
global economy, 42, 291
GM, 12, 38
    design process, 257, 258, 268
    team selection, 135
Golden Strait Jacket, 255
Graves, Michael, 45, 60, 190
Greyhound bus company, 38

H

Harley-Davidson
    identity building, 99–101, *100*, 177
    social impact, 66

HeadBlade, 12, *13*, 191
health systems, 290
Heinz, 87
Herman Miller Aeron Chair
  brand strategy, 86
  case study, 242–48
  design of, 199, *242*
  design references, *245*, *246*
  identity building, 92
  product development, 170
  VOs, 67
Hewlett-Packard, 44–45, 97, 135
Home Depot, 25, 281
Honda, 100
Houston Astrodome, 217
human-computer interaction (HCI), 177
human factors, 45, 175–79, 197, 200, 206
Human Factors Ergonomics Society (HFES), 175–76
Hummer, 256, 266, 268

I

IBM, 41, 97
ideas, visualizing, 206–10, *208*, *209*
identifying opportunities, 8–12, 110–11, 114–20
identity building, 91–94, 99–101, 177
impact, 65, 66, 69, 154–61
industrial products, 79–82
industrial revolution, 36–37, 60
information age, 60
iNPD (integrated New Product Development)
  corporate mission, 89–90, 164
  elements of, 108
  model of, *140*
  phase I, 114–20
  phase II, 120–26
  phase III, 126–29
  phase IV, 130–32
  phases of, 110–14
  process of, 55, 108
  resource allocation, 132–36
    financing, 134–35
    scheduling, 134
    team selection, 135–36
  team integration, *171*, 171–72
  team members, 138
  user-centered approach, 139–42, *140*, *181*
integrated framework, 113
integrated New Product Development (iNPD).
    See iNPD

Intel, 11
interaction, 192–94
interaction design, 204
interests-based negotiation, 148, *149*, *150*, 162
interface design, 204
Iomega Zip Drive, 45, *96*
  details of, *98*
  identity building, 92
  product development, 96–99
  product strategy, 85

J

Jackson, Phil, 166
Jacob's Field, 218
Jaguar, 260
Jeep, 266, 267
Jensen, Rolf, 61
Jobs, Steve, 41
Johnson, Peter, 169
Johnson, Philip, 269
Jordan, Michael, 12, 166
Jordan, Pat, 177

K

K-Mart, 56
Kao, J., 152, 226
Katzenbach, J. R., 150, 226
Kiliany, Gary, 231, 233–34
Knight, Bobby, 166
knockoffs, 50–51
Kodak, case study, 236–37, *238*
Krzyzewski, Mike, 166

L

Land Rover, 267
Leading with the Heart, 166
Letterman, David, 222
Lexus, 256, 267
lifestyle impact, 154–61
lifestyle reference, 35, 190–92, 205
Lincoln Navigator, 256, 263–65, 267
Loewy, Raymond, 39
Lower Left quadrant, 43–44
Lower Right quadrant, 44–45, 55

M

Macintosh, 41, 86, 97, 248–51
Mandela, Nelson, 252
Marathon Carpet Cleaner, 79
   case study, 228–31
   design of, *230, 231*
marketing, 40–42, 139–46, 161–63
Marketing Aesthetics, 132, 176
mass customization, 177–78
mass marketing, 40–42
mass production, 38–40
MasterRack rail storage, 280–81, *281*
Mather, John, 123, 278
matrix, weighted, *118*, 118–19
Mazda Miata, 6, 9
   design of, 178, 207–8, *208, 271*
   design references, *272*
   identity building, 92
   product development, 170, 268–71, 292
   value of, 59
McDonalds, 27
Measure of Man and Woman: Human Factors in Design, 197
medical trends, 290
Mercedes, 70, 88, 256, 267
Model T, 36, 37, 38, 273
Moore, Geoffrey, 44, 96, 193
Moore, Gordon, 11
Moore, Pat, 66
Moore's Law, 11
Motorola, 42, 135, 165
Motorola Talkabout, 6, *19*
   complexity of, 157–58
   identity building, 92, 94
   PDM, *158*
   Positioning Map, 48, *48*
   product details, *22*
   product development, 18–22, 33, 170
   SET Factors, *20*
   social impact, 66
   value of, 61, 88
   VOA, 73–75, *74*
movies, 10, 60, 292–93

N

Nader, Ralph, 41
NASA, 12
negotiation, 148–50, *149, 150, 151*, 162

Nelson, George, 246
new product development, 106–36. *See also* iNPD
Newhouse, Tom, 67
niche marketing, 41
Nike, 91, 135
Nissan Xterra, 178, 256, 267
NoFuss Camping Storage System, 282–83, *283*
Nokia, 42, 70, 95, 200
non-consumer products, 204
non-task conflict, 146–48
Norman, Donald, 37, 177
Noyes, Elliot, 40

O

O'Neal, Shaquille, 12, 166
OEM (Original Equipment Manufacturer), 82, 204
opportunity
   conceptualizing, 110–11, 126–29
   identifying, 8–12, 110–11, 114–20
   realizing, 110, 113–14, 130–32
   understanding, 110–11, 120–26
OXO GoodGrips
   complexity of, 158
   design of, *15, 16, 17*, 178
   identity building, 91, 92, 94
   PDM, *159*
   Positioning Map, 46–47, *47*
   product development, 5, 14–18, 33
   product strategy, 85
   social impact, 66
   task analysis, 194–95
   team selection, 135
   value of, 61
   VOA, 71–72, *72*

P

Part Differentiation Matrix (PDM), 153–63
   core disciplines and, 162–63
   Crown Wave, *157*
   DynaVox Systems, 234, *235*
   model of, *155*
   Motorola Talkabout, *158*
   negotiations and, *162*
   OXO GoodGrips, *159*
   product breakdown and, 260–61
   Starbucks, *159*
   team conflict, 160–62
   team management, 166

Passat, 59
PDAs, 10, 11
perceptual experience, 62
perceptual gaps, 142–46, *144, 150, 151*
Pete, Alfred, 29
Pete's Coffee, 27, 29
Pine, B. Joseph, 59
pipettes, 81, 82, 199, *199*
PNC Park, 216, 218
POGs (Product Opportunity Gaps), 2, 9–12
    case studies, 12–30, 215–53
    changes and, 85
    product development, 107
    SET Factors, 2, 9, *9*
    VOs, 56
Polaroid, 188–90, *190*
Pontiac Aztec, 178, 257
population distribution, 292
Positioning Map, 6, *35*, 43–50
    baseball stadiums, *217, 218*
    Crown Wave, 48–49, *49*
    model of, *6*
    Motorola Talkabout, *48*, 48
    OXO GoodGrips, 46–47, *47*
    SnakeLight, *224*
    Starbucks, 49–50, *50*
    style versus technology, *34, 43*, 43–50
    SUVs, *267*
potato peelers, *14*, 14–18, *16. See also* OXO
        GoodGrips
Pour Your Heart Into It, 29
power-based negotiation, 148, *149, 150*, 162
PRIZM, 124
product brands. *See* brands
product definition, 7, 113, 205–6
product development, 89–90. *See also* iNPD
    case studies, 12–30, 215–53
    cycle of, *89*, 89–90
    ergonomics, 192–201
        anthropometrics, 197–201, *198, 199, 200, 201*
        interaction, 192–94
        task analysis, 194–96, *196, 197*
    ethnography techniques, 108, 183–90, *187*, 204,
        205, 275–77
    evolutionary techniques, 51–52
    human factors, 45, 175–79, 197, 200, 206
    interviews, 185
    lifestyle reference, 190–92
    movies and, 10, 60, 292–93
    observation, 185
    POGs, 107
    process of, 3, 109–10, *110*
    revolutionary versus evolutionary, 51–52, *52*
    scenario development, 181–82, 201–3
    SET Factors, 107, 181–82
    visual stories, 185
product goals, 79
product hybridization, 292
product identity, 64–65
Product Opportunity Gaps (POGs). *See* POGs
product strategy, 84–88
products, 7–9
    attributes of, 180–81
    corporate commitment to, 88–90
    definition of, 7
    expectation of, 180–81
    manifestation of, 180–81
profit impact, 69
program planning, 89–90
prototypes, *123*, 208, *209*
psycheconometrics, 10, 61, 180
PT Cruiser, 6
    design of, 256, 268, *274*, 274–75
    identity building, 92
    product development, 52, 170
    value of, 59

Q

quality, 68

R

Rand, Paul, 40, 238
rapid prototyping, 208
Raskin, James, 226
realizing opportunity, 110, 113–14, 130–32
refrigerators, *39*, 39–40
resource allocation, 132–36
    financing, 134–35
    scheduling, 134
    team selection, 135–36
retro craze, 268–83
revolutionary product development, 51–52, *52*
Richardson, Dean, 170
Right Stuff, The, 98
rights-based negotiation, 148, *149, 150*, 162
rip-offs, 50–51
Rockwell, Norman, 269
Rodman, Dennis, 166

S

Santoprene, 16–17
Saturn, 88, 258
scenario development, 181–82, 201–3
scheduling, 134
Schmitt, B. H., 132, 176
Schultz, Howard, 27, 29–30
Schwartzenegger, Arnold, 268
services, 7–9
SET Factors
    case studies, 12–30, *20*, *24*, *28*, 215–53
    POGs, 2, *9*, 9
    product development, 107, 181–82, 255–56
Sheer Cliff of Value, 6, 55–56
SideWinder side worktable, 279–80, *280*
Simonson, A., 132, 176
Smart Design, 135
smart products, 290, *291*
Smith, D. K., 150, 226
Smith, Dave, 24–26, 82, 165, 170
SnakeLight, 9, 51
    case study, 218–28
    design of, 191, *222*
    details of, *223*
    identity building, 92, 93
    Positioning Map, *224*
    product development, 5
    timeline of, *227*
    value of, 61
    VOA, *225*
Social Factors, 2, *9*, 9–10, 107. *See also* SET Factors
social impact, 66
Social Work, 244, *245*
Socio-Technic Work, 244, *245*
Spielberg, Steven, 293
Staines, Christopher, 252
stakeholders, 7, 203–4
Starbucks, 6
    complexity of, 158–60
    interior, *30*
    logo, *30*
    PDM, *159*
    Positioning Map, 49–50, *50*
    product development, 26–30, 33
    SET Factors, *28*
    social impact, 66
    value of, 61
    VOA, 77–78, *78*
Stark, Philippe, 45
Stear, Rory, 252
Stone, David, 222

Stumpf, Bill, 199, 243, 244
style versus technology, 33–36
    history of, 36–42
    Positioning Map, *34*, *43*, 43–50
Subaru Outback, 256
success factors, 8
Sunrise Medical, 235, 236
Super Dome, 217
SUVs, 10, 11
    design of, 256
    Positioning Map, *267*
    product development, 266–68
    value of, 57, 88
Swatch Watch, 70, 95
SyQuest, 96, *97*
system complexity, 154–61

T

Tang, 11
Target, 25, 45, 60, 190
task analysis, 194–96, *196*, *197*
task conflict, 146–48
team collaboration, 146–48
team conflict, 160–62
team functionality, 8
    collaboration, 146–48
    design process, 148–50
    performance, 150–53, *154*
team integration, *171*, 171–72
team management
    balancing, 164–65
    champions, 169–70
    corporate mission, 164
    discipline, 165–66
    empowerment, 163–71
    rewards of, 170
    support for, 166–67
    visions for, 169–70
team members
    abilities of, 167
    empowering, 163–71
    managing, 138–73
    needs of, 167–68
    personality of, 167–68
    selecting, 135–36
Technological Factors, 2, *9*, 9–10, 107. *See also* SET
        Factors
technology, 11, 33–36, *291*
Tiffany's, 61–62
Tornado Corporation, 92, 228, 230

Town & Country minivan, 274–75, *275*
Toyota RAV4, 266
trains, *38*, 38
trends, of the future, 289–92
truck market, 275–83
    products for, 277–83

U

understanding customers, 188–90
understanding opportunity, 110–11, 120–26
Universal Design, 66
Upper Left quadrant, 45, 55
Upper Right, moving to, 6, 8, 32–53. *See also* Upper
        Right quadrant
    approach for, 139
    auto industry, 266–68
    case studies, 214–53
    model of, *46*
Upper Right quadrant, 6, 34–35. *See also* Upper Right,
        moving to
    position of, 55
    value of, 54–83
UPS
    brand identity, 95
    case study, 238–42
    logo, *239*
    PDM, *240*
usefulness, 87–88
user-centered approach
    of auto industry, 283–86
    of iNPD, 139–42, *140*, *181*
utility, 57

V

VALS (Values and Lifestyles), 123–24
value
    to corporation, 91
    cost and, 59–62, *60*
    definition of, 34, 56–57
    price and, 15, 57–58, *58*
    sheer cliff of, 6, 55–56
Value Opportunities (VOs). *See* VOs
Value Opportunity Analysis (VOA). *See* VOA
Values and Lifestyles (VALs), 123–24
vehicle design, 12, *13*, 254–86, 290. *See also* auto
        industry
VistaLab Technologies, 79, 81, 82, 199, *199*
visualization, of products, 206–10, *208*, *209*

VOA (Value Opportunity Analysis), 54, 71–78, *72*, *74*,
        78, *225*, *233*
Volkswagen Beetle, 6
    design of, 268, 271–73, *273*
    identity building, 92
    product development, 170
    value of, 59, 88
    VOs, 70
Volkswagen Golf, 255–56
Volvo, 260
VOs (Value Opportunities), 56, 62–70
    aesthetics, 64
    brands and, 101–2
    changes and, 85
    charts, *69*, 69–78, *80*
    core technology, 68
    corporate values, 91
    customer values, 42, 91
    emotion, 63
    environmental impact, 67
    ergonomics, 65–67
    impact and, 65
    place for, 78–79
    product development, 107
    product goals, 79
    product identity, 64–65
    quality, 68
    social impact, 66

W

Wal-Mart, 56, 281
Walton, Mary, 284
wearable technology, *291*
weighted matrix, *118*, 118–19
Weingart, Laurie, 148
Whirlpool, 135
Wisdom of Teams, The, 150
Wolfe, Tom, 98
Woods, Tiger, 190, 257
work-related injury, 24–25, 194, 244
Wrigley Field, 216, 217

X

X-generation magazines, 191, *191*
Xerox, 41, 42

Y

Yankee Stadium, 269

The *Financial Times* delivers a world of business news.

Use the Risk-Free Trial Voucher below!

To stay ahead in today's business world you need to be well-informed on a daily basis. And not just on the national level. You need a news source that closely monitors the entire world of business, and then delivers it in a concise, quick-read format.

With the *Financial Times* you get the major stories from every region of the world. Reports found nowhere else. You get business, management, politics, economics, technology and more.

Now you can try the *Financial Times* for 4 weeks, absolutely risk free. And better yet, if you wish to continue receiving the *Financial Times* you'll get great savings off the regular subscription rate. Just use the voucher below.

---

4 Week Risk-Free Trial Voucher

Yes! Please send me the *Financial Times* for 4 weeks (Monday through Saturday) Risk-Free, and details of special subscription rates in my country.

Name _____

Company _____

Address _____ ❏ Business or ❏ Home Address

Apt./Suite/Floor _____ City _____ State/Province _____

Zip/Postal Code_____ Country _____

Phone (optional) _____ E-mail (optional)_____

Limited time offer good for new subscribers in FT delivery areas only.

To order contact Financial Times Customer Service in your area (mention offer SAB01A).

The Americas: Tel 800-628-8088 Fax 845-566-8220 E-mail: uscirculation@ft.com

Europe: Tel 44 20 7873 4200 Fax 44 20 7873 3428 E-mail: fte.subs@ft.com

Japan: Tel 0120 341-468 Fax 0120 593-146 E-mail: circulation.fttokyo@ft.com

Korea: E-mail: sungho.yang@ft.com

S.E. Asia: Tel 852 2905 5555 Fax 852 2905 5590 E-mail: subseasia@ft.com

www.ft.com

FT FINANCIAL TIMES
World business newspaper